ROCKY TRAIL
but
STEADY FEET

A MEMOIR

LOIS SHELTON

Rocky Trail but Steady Feet
A Memoir

Copyright © 2022 Lois Shelton

ISBN Paperback: 978-1-66784-5-487

Printed in the United States of America
BookBaby Publishing

CONTENTS

PREFACE

Many projects get put on the back burner and only come to fruition when there is time, motivation and awareness. In 1978 I was applying to a PhD program which asked for an autobiographical statement which I could not write as it was too painful. I was afraid I would fall into an emotional pit and I had little time. I was working on a better future. My single mother had an uphill start in life being the orphan of new immigrants in the north woods. While she had courage to try to forge a better life I had to figure out many things on my own. Not having much money or support I set out on a long path of establishing my goals and sticking to my path.

After years I had a traditional education in psychology I also sought out other ways of healing. Which in part presented itself in the Humanistic potential movement which emphasized people's strengths as well as their problems. There are creative ways of seeking strength while dealing with life's realities. Previously shy I lead speakers programs and professional training programs with current information in their field. Working with adults but mainly children I did many case studies and this is a study of my life's stumbling blocks and what I found was helpful. I finally had time to reflect on my life and motivation to dig deeper. While my life is more non-traditional in that I never married or had children it had purpose and meaning to me. The goal is for the reader to gain perspective on their own lives as to what their goals are and what has meaning to them in today's ever changing world.

I deeply appreciate those who shared their own stories that gave me energy and others who gave some feedback during this challenging but worthwhile journey

CHAPTER 1

Leaving the Farm Again

My mother was washing the nightly dishes while staring out the farm-house kitchen window at the dark Northern Michigan woods. The kitchen had not been changed for decades, and the wood-burning stove was bigger than the one she grew up with but it took time to burn wood to a cooking or baking temperature. At least she did not have to go outside to pump water and then haul it inside, and there was electricity. But these improvements seemed small compared to living in this farmhouse. I was four years old and I was watching her as with her head hung down and she had a blank expression on her face. I was almost three years old in 1949 when we moved from Pasadena, leaving sunshine and palm trees, for deep snow in the Upper Peninsula of Michigan. She had sworn to herself that she would never get married, have children or live on another Finnish farm. Now she was thirty-six and not only was she married to her third husband, Jack, had two children and was living 60 miles from the family farm that she left in 1934 after and swore she would never return. How did she get herself into this mess?

At age 47, this was also Jack's third marriage, as his second wife had left his farm with their two children for another state and another man. The first one might have died. He was now pleased they had a baby that was his. I was just baggage that came with the third wife. He was nice looking but had a rock-solid routine and was tight with money. At first this impulsive marriage had some hope, but now there was not much talking now between the 100%

Finnish husband and wife. He felt that venison, potatoes and bread was an adequate diet, but my mother wanted some healthier foods and cereal for me and he refused to buy them. He worked hard at the copper mines, came home, read the paper, ate dinner, watched TV and went to bed.

My mother had grown up in a Finnish immigrant family that was struggling to survive and the communication was not easily flowing. Her parents did not speak English and the children had to learn English as long as they were in school. Her frail mother had prayed every morning for her children's well-being but by the end of the 1920s both parents were dead which left eight orphans living in the woods on their own. By the mid 1930s everyone had left the family farm looking for work except Arthur, who was maybe lost in drink, committed suicide. A cousin said he was artistic but it was hard to find work. The older brother, Rudolf, stayed in the Upper Peninsula (UP) to become a lumberjack. The youngest sister, Elna, who had done very well in school and had married a Finnish farmer who had a 120-acre dairy farm that was only forty miles from Jack's farm. Jack's second wife who fled was Elna's sister-in-law, and her husband Urho's sister. Elna could have filled my mother as to why the second wife left. Elna might have raised some doubts or maybe did not want to expose her true feelings. My mother did not tell Elna about the proposal. The October 6, 1949 Courthouse wedding was held in Hancock without any fanfare with just a flower corsage, rings and some smiles for a photo.

While Jack had been working in the copper mine my mother was pregnant, isolated with no phone, car, and church, nearby neighbors or doctors. My mother was nervous, as her 26-year old sister, Ellen, had died after giving birth to her third child near Pasadena. She mourned her death and was frightened. When the delivery date was closer, we took a Greyhound bus down to Detroit to her brother Wilho's small apartment. He worked in the Livonia Ford Motor factory and lived with his wife and two very noisy boys. After the August 1950 birth, the baby added to the noise. I was sitting out on the cement porch by myself and thought I did not want to live. We returned to the farm and most of my mother's time was taken up with the colicky baby. Jack would come home and repeat his routine and sometimes the TV would work but the wires sparked under the TV stand, which was frightening. The silence in the house was stone cold and I was wondering why we were there.

Years later my mother said she was having vivid flashbacks of her grim childhood and was secretly hatching a plan to escape. Jack wanted his new baby daughter as this was his last chance to be a father as the other children left. In an ideal world my mother wanted her too but she felt she could not find work with two children and no family support. I was not his child and my mother and I had been through a lot together.

After World War II mother had lost her Rosie the Riveter position and good paying jobs had dried up for women. She jumped in and out of two marriages and I was a product of the second marriage. Desperation leads to impulsive decisions to survive. The Santa Fe train took us to Detroit where her brother Wilho lived and then to the Upper Peninsula to visit her sisters Elna the youngest child and Ani the oldest child in her family.

Now my mother was busy with a crying baby and seemed to be mostly unavailable to me. Jack was not a playmate or a companion. At four years old I tried to entertain myself. I had walked to the Karhu (Finnish for "bear") farm, as they had reindeer in a large pen. They are gentle animals but they are not used to a toddler using them as a jungle gym. I tried to swing on their antlers, but when Mrs. Karhu saw me she ran out of their farm house saying to walk back to Jack's farm. Another day I found some very old long wooden skis in the shed and dragged them over to a snow bank to try to ski. But this did not work out. Before the baby's birth, the car was parked down on the road and I was put on a toboggan with the groceries for a ride uphill through the snow. Now my mother was house-bound with no phone. One day I tried to walk into the forbidden woods when a soft spot on the snow crust gobbled me up over my head. I screamed and yelled and my mother, finally hearing the noise, wearily donned her winter clothes and boots to pull me out. Indoors I had put a hairpin in a light socket and it burned my fingers. I had seen a deer in the moldy basement hanging upside-down looking sad with the big brown eyes. I felt bad but knew we ate the meat. I was running out of things to do and the adults seemed to ignore me. I remember as I watched my mother do the dishes I was punching a large plastic bag full of white lard-looking stuff that had a few red dots. I was supposed to punch it hard to make the red dots turn the white into yellow that looked more like butter. It saved some money. It wasn't that much fun, but it was something to do and a short relief from my boredom.

My mother was coming to the cold reality that she had made a big mistake and was not going to spend the rest of her life on another isolated Finnish farm raising children. She would kill herself. Jack was not going to let go of the new baby. He had a home, work, and he just needed a housewife then he could continue his rock-solid routine. My mother later said that she met Jack in Detroit and he said he was going to stay there, but that was not his intention or she misunderstood. Now she was secretly looking for another place as nice as Pasadena with work, churches, schools and refined people. It was painful leaving the baby but Jack would not budge. How would a single mother find work with a four-year-old and a baby? Childcare was expensive and there was no supportive family.

It was now the spring of 1951, and the baby was finally sleeping in her crib. My mother bundled me up in a blue snowsuit with white fake fur around the hood. Putting on my boots and then her winter clothes, she grabbed one suitcase and my hand and we walked as swiftly as we could on an icy path going down to the road. We walked carefully as it was very slippery and the snow was still over my head. I raised my right arm toward the house meaning what about the baby? But nothing was going to stop my mother's determination to escape before Jack made it home. The sun was setting and the tall dark pine trees were the only witness to our fast departure. I think we took a bus from Bruce's Crossing to Chicago, which had a women's shelter. She had the bus tickets and $10 in her pocket. I slept all night. All I know is that I woke up in a bare room with a metal frame bed next to my mother. Where were we?

It turned out to be the Pacific Garden Mission's Women and Children's Shelter. They had a radio show called "Unshackled," which offered redemption, salvation and hope to the down and out. My mother was desperate for hope had listened to the radio program *Unshackled*. We walked past men sitting or lying on the streets with red faces, dirty clothes, waiting for the next service and resulting meal. We stayed in the shelter as long as it took for my mother to find work. In 1934 she had escaped from the family farm at age 20 with ten cents in her pocket and worked in Calumet, Detroit and Pasadena as a Rosie the Riveter making bombs. She had worked hard and was reliable. She quickly found a live-in maid position in Evanston, the first suburb north of Chicago. As we left I was deeply frightened by the men on the sidewalk but my mother had a firm grip on my hand. The "L" train was dirty and noisy. When we left the train we went down the steep stairs and walked on tree-lined streets to arrive in front of a large colonial-style home with big white columns.

The family was a couple with two school-aged children. The live-in maid's quarters were at the top of the stairs with a bathroom down the hall. This was not a home but a place of employment, so I was not to be around the house or play with the children. My mother worked and I was bored. Sometimes I found kids in the alley to play with for a short time, and one girl had rag curlers in her hair to make her pretty. I did, however, make mud pies in front of the house one day to sell them to well-heeled suburbanites as they walked by. I knew we needed the money. There were no takers. The couple was not happy with the mess in front on their beautiful home, but tactfully suggested that I attend the National College of Education kindergarten, as there were many student teachers who needed practice. I had lived in three different states and at age four I needed some stability and stimulation, so this was a good idea. However, my mother did not tell me people were coming to take me to the school in a van, and I started kicking and screaming thinking she was getting rid of me as we had left my sister.

Upon arrival at school I hid under a table, as I was badly frightened. I had not played with other children nor had I gone to school. My fearful behaviors lead to a referral to a psychologist for an evaluation. On the appointed day, my mother and I went in a re-purposed Victorian in downtown Evanston. As we climbed the stairs and entered the nice lady's office, I was delighted to see all kinds of toys and she was very comforting. I explained my finger paintings to her and played with a toy family in a doll house. I wanted to stay with the nice lady and play, but I was labeled "normal" and I never saw her again. This was a disappointment, but I will never forget her as she made me feel she was interested in me and I felt safe.

National College turned out to be a good experience for me, as we did interesting things and I was around other children my age. We built a rocket to the moon, which was impressive. Why not go to the moon? I was used to moves. When we completed the rocket, I found out we were not really going and was disappointed. We built things out of wood with a hammer and nails. The student teacher taught me how to angle the nail so it would "toenail" to the lower wood piece to build my boat. We went on nature walks and saw pussy willows, birds and trees. I was happy just being out of the stuffy maid's room and see any kind of nature. Early childhood education is so important for children getting ready for school and I really needed some socialization and education. I felt like someone was taking an interest in me and I enjoyed the attention.

At Christmas time I was sitting at the top of the stairs watching the father play the "Peter and the Wolf" record for his two children and explaining that the different orchestra parts represented characters in the story. I wanted a father or parent who had time to spend with me. Maids worked long hours and we did not have much time together.

In the spring, the couple hosted a party and my mother and I were sitting in the kitchen next to an ashtray with a burning cigarette. My mother suggested I try to smoke, which resulted in my choking. Some people in the kitchen were critical of her encouraging me to smoke. While her intentions were to make me avoid cigarettes, I was only five.

Looking toward first grade next year, my mother appealed to the School Board to let me in as a five-year-old. They gave me a standardized intelligence test, which was easy and I passed. However, I was socially behind and still frightened of change. I don't know what happened, but we left the big white house and were going south of the mansion to a poor white neighborhood. We walked into a rundown Victorian boarding house. Was this our new home?

CHAPTER 2

Two Places on Seward Street

We did not have many belongings, so moving was easy. It was where we moved to that was the problem. The street was named Seward Street, but I thought it was Sewer Street, as I did not know the difference. We moved farther south, which meant poor working people, and a rundown boarding house-with men who seemed to be down on their luck. They were not as bad as the men lying on the street in Downtown Chicago. This was not as bad as the Pacific Garden Mission, but I felt creepy living there. Our room had tired old wallpaper, one bed, a dresser and some straight chairs. The shared bathroom was down the hall. The old man in the dark cold basement collected the rents and it seemed he never came out of his cave. Boarding houses were used by working men but usually not women with children. But it was a cheap place to stay with a dingy kitchen. I never saw anyone cook or eat there. We went for soup at a Chinese restaurant in downtown Evanston.

There was a park across the street, so I went over to use the playground. There were two sisters; one was my age with kinky blond hair and her slightly younger sister had brown ringlets but seemed slow. The punch sisters punched me in the face for no apparent reason. I cried very loudly until my mother came out to scoop me back inside. She then laid me on the bed and looked at my privates. I did not like this. What was she doing? After that, when I was alone, I placed a Popsicle stick near my privates but a splinter broke off. It was painful, but I did not tell my mother so she would not look down there again.

One day my mother and I went down the creaky stairs in the old man's dark basement. The only light came from a large neon clock with rotating ring around the edge that went in a counter-clockwise direction. While they discussed the rent, I watched the clock ring go around and around. When we went upstairs I was playing with the barrel lock on the outside of his door and accidentally locked the old man in the basement for the whole day. When we returned he was understandably angry, but why was lock on the outside of the door? Wouldn't it be better to have the lock on the inside to protect him from the sketchy boarders? He was quite mad and we soon ended up moving to another dark place on the same street.

Our forth move was down the block to an old Queen Anne mansion left over from the time when wealthier families used to live in the neighborhood. It looked like a set for a horror movie. It was a rambling wooden structure with subdivided apartments on the first and second floors. But the entry to our place was under the large wrap-around porch. The lattice under the porch was cut so that it was a hidden door. We had to walk through the dirt in a low clearance, which was fine for me at age five and my mother was only five-feet two inches. Other people would have had to duck. Finally, there was a door with two steps down into to the basement that had two cots, a table and chairs, one small kitchen and a bathroom. It was better than the old man's basement and it was our own place. It was like living in a secret cave.

At age five I was still in the stage that we were on some kind of adventure. This could be fun. There were many other poor people in the small units, and my mother wanted to socialize with them. She told me not to say she was divorced, that I had a sister and not to lie. One day we went to Wiebolt's Department Store, which was less expensive than most shops in Evanston, where she wanted to buy a suit for a dinner. She wanted me to help her make the choice and I was extremely anxious about this responsibility. I did not know we had money for clothes. We went out to dinner but my mother choked on a fish bone and went to the rest room. I was sitting with strangers and thought she might die. I was very upset. Another time we drove somewhere with a man and I was in the back seat with a taffeta skirt that made me slip on the car floor when he stopped. He did not find it amusing. Was I the reason her social life was not taking off? A divorcée with a child, or were there other reasons in the 1950s. I know she did not say she was divorced, but was being an unwed mother better?

My mother found a job working at a diner in downtown Evanston, and had saved up enough money in 1952 to buy a TV that actually worked in our basement. This was a big improvement over the endless days at the mansion with nothing to do after school in someone else's house. My mother was good at finding work. But after a month or so she sat me down and said that she had something important to tell me, as she was getting a new shift from two p.m. to nine p.m. and would not be home until 10 o'clock at night. She said the tips were better but I would have to get my own dinner. I was five years old and not happy with this development, but put on a brave face and said "I can make my own sandwich" as I was too young to use the stove. She cried, and said OK. I don't know if she felt any guilt or was feeling trapped by a job. I felt I was never going to have a mother or some company. I don't remember eating too well and I came down with impetigo, which is a staph infection and I had scabs on my upper lip and face. I was not bathing or getting ready for bed. I would just lay there as I was afraid of the dark under the porch.

My mother had told me that there were bad men on the street and I was not to go near them as they do bad things. It was a good thing she told me, as men in nice cars with white-pressed shirts and ties would pull over to the curb and offers me candy. I knew they were wrong and would walk away, and luckily no one forced me into a car. I had heard about dead girls in the Forest Preserves when I read the Chicago newspaper as I did not have any children's books.

Another event peculiar to basement living was that there were sewer and other pipes on the cement floor between my bed and the outside wall. Early one morning I rolled over in bed and fell into the pipes, jamming my knee. The harder I tried to pull it out, the more it would swell and I was not able to move. The Fire Department came and had to ice my knee to reduce the swelling. I was embarrassed for people to see how poor we were. The firemen finally got my knee out, but it took some time with me lying in an awkward face-down position in my pajamas. We had some nice times at the beach before school started, and I was trying to teach myself how to swim, but it took quite a while. My mother had a long list of supplies she was supposed to buy before school started. We were both surprised how long the list was.

When first grade started, my mother took me to Oakton School so I would know where it was. I liked the teacher, Miss Michaels, as she was pretty and just out of college. But in the afternoon I had to find my way home, entertain myself with TV, read the newspaper as much as I could make out and see if anyone was around to play with. At night I was afraid of the dark under the porch. I don't know how my mother was able to afford a TV but it was my only company. I really enjoyed some of the TV shows such as Liberace, who played classical piano, and his brother George who played the violin. The candelabra looked classy on the large baby grand. There were some good family shows and they gave me an idea of what a family was supposed to be, but it was not close to what I was going through. It was not human companionship, but I was learning some things about middle-class family life. The characters were my companions.

One night I wanted to go downtown and meet my mother at the diner as I wanted to protect her. I picked out the taffeta skirt, white blouse and Sunday school shoes and walked uphill toward the bus stop in the dark. When the bus arrived, I put my nickel in the fare box and climbed up to the seat near the bus driver. I was not sure of which stop in the dark, but I knew it was downtown. I found it as my mother was running out the door responding to a phone call from a couple who was supposed to be watching me saying I was gone. No one told me that there was a couple watching me. Why did I not see them? Why couldn't I watch their TV with them? My mother was very happy to see me, which did not happen often, and we went home. I wasn't going to do that again. I never saw the couple again, but I did have one babysitter in all black and long wavy gray hair who said the Russians were coming and they would bomb our house and kill my black cat. I was afraid to go to school for fear she would be dead. The witchy lady did not last long. I felt like I needed to help my mother. I tried selling magic tricks door to door, but I was really bad at it. People were polite but would shut their door on this awkward little girl.

I was still very shy, anxious and sometimes had a hard time speaking. One night my mother was home and I walked around the table to face her, and her expression was intense with furrowed brows and almost angry. I looked up at her and tried to speak but I could not get the words out. She made mocking animals sounds saying I was an animal that couldn't speak. My existence had been a terrible accident and I felt like she had cut me with a machete and I was bleeding sadness all over the floor. This was not a safe person, and I was being more guarded when around her. The adventure was eroding into despair. My mother bought an old tub washing machine with a wringer on the side. She put me in the tub and told me a story about a woman who got her breasts sucked into the wringers. Why was she saying this? I was frightened to take a bath. Why not use the bathtub? She wanted to use the same water for my bath and the laundry, which was an old habit; but didn't have much but we had running water. While I was withdrawn there were some good times. One night it was pouring rain and we went out to a wooden barrel under the down spout and collected rain water. She said it was better for our hair. That was a fun memory. She said natural things were better and she had grown up without running water. It made me enjoy being out in the rain.

My mother had a large tip jar and put change from her work until it reached the top. She then said that we were going to a hardware store and buy a wagon. We brought the large glass jar full of change, which the clerk patiently counted. We walked miles home from downtown, as we never had a car. I would have rather have had some books, art supplies or a doll but I did not complain. This taught me the lesson about saving up to buy things. I have always been a saver and very careful with my money. We went to Wiebolt's

Department Store at Christmas and I spoke with Santa Claus. He asked where I lived and I said on Sewer. I asked for a doll. They had a stuffed elk and I was perched on its back for a photo. I felt it was a nice gesture on my mother's part and I cherished the photo.

Despite some of her good intentions I was in a state of anxiety most of the time. I was afraid to go to sleep by myself at night, so I would wait up for my mother to come home at ten p.m. This made me very sleepy at school and sometimes I could not keep my eyes open. I remember seeing the teacher write on the chalk board but the figures were moving around in a blur. The teacher wanted me to stay after school one time but I ran away and knew she would never get hold of my mother. Maybe she could have helped, but I was afraid to talk to people about our life. Toward the end of first grade, the drawer under my desk was stuck shut. I pulled hard but could not open it. Miss Michaels helped me get it open. It was jammed with all the homework for the year. Apparently, I did not know what I was supposed to do with it, so I stuck it in the drawer. The teacher was surprised but apparently had not noticed in a year. I was wondering if there was any communication between the teacher and my mother. I don't think I got much out of first grade. The National College of Education, my kindergarten school, introduced the idea of Parent-Teacher Conferences so parents knew what their children did at school years later.

That summer I played with some children and went to a Parks and Recreation program for arts and crafts, but it was just OK. We did make a float for the Fourth of July Parade and we had costumes. It made me feel like there was a bigger community outside of my dark world. I did like Vacation Bible School, as they told stories and we had a treat every day. My Finnish mother also gave me proverbs during my childhood. Her favorite was "life is hard by the yard but it's a cinch by the inch." My favorites were "A stitch in time saves nine" and "an ounce of prevention is worth a pound of cure." However, it was hard to prevent something you did not know about.

The beach was always good. That summer a boy and I convinced a pretty girl to play doctor and take off her clothes. We pretended to be doctors, but I was ashamed that I participated in that game.

Second grade started and Miss Michaels got married, so she had to stay home and become a housewife, which seemed strange to me as my mother always worked outside the home. The new teacher was alright and there were some nice kids in my class. I was invited to lunch with a girl and her mother, but I was so uncomfortable I could barely speak. A boy invited me to his parent's house to see his basement full of a train display that was so large and elaborate. I couldn't believe that his family had that much money. It was great to see it but we never played together. I liked the idea of making miniature models and little imaginary worlds.

One day after the church I ran in a children's race with my dress and legs flying and I won. They gave me a parasol but I did not have any use for it. Another Sunday I said I would only to go church if I could skate there. My mother was upset but let me put on my metal skates on my Sunday shoes. At Easter my mother bought me a live chick and we kept it under the porch until it started crowing and the neighbors complained. I don't know how my mother found a home for it.

The Evanston Public Library had a Friday night program that showed travel movies of places I hoped to go to one day. We put on Sunday clothes and enjoyed the break from routine. Mother tried to make us fit into the community, which was a tall order. They had a large children's library, but one day a man came and sat next to me in a small chair and started feeling my leg. I could not believe his boldness and got up and left but was afraid to tell the librarian. They seemed so unfriendly and official and I was shy. One time this older man tried to spank me and a girl on our behinds, but we ran away. Bad men were everywhere, I had to be very vigilant and check everyone out. I was rarely relaxed or smiling.

It was still warm enough to play outside and one evening Judi and Lynn, the punch sisters, came over and I let them in and soon their 12-year-old brother arrived. He took the $13 rent money in a drawer. I now wonder if his sisters were setting me up. I knew we needed the rent money and ran after him in the dark. I was a determined six-year-old and he was a strong 12 years old, but somehow he relented and gave me the money back. My mother never knew about it. Later, he was put in Juvenile Hall for murder and I was frightened as to what he might have happened to me confronting him in such a bold manner.

Previously, I had spent one overnight at Judi and Lynn's house and it was very bleak, as both parents were alcoholics. The kids did need the money, but so did we. It was a poor neighborhood. But years later I saw Judi pregnant at age 13; she had dropped out of school and her brother was still being held for murder. Lynn was slow and struggled in school. It was a sad scene and one worse than mine. My mother went to church, had morals and did not drink. I was alone but maybe that was better than having a difficult family. I don't know.

A German boy in our class did not speak English. His parents had sent him to school in Lederhosen, which made the kids snicker. I felt bad for him, as I knew it was hard to be an outsider. That Christmas the teacher made me an Elf in the Christmas play and I was so excited to wear a costume. All I had to do was dance and pass things out. I even got out of class, as it was preformed to other grades. But other than that I was more used to staying up late and getting up for school still very tired. I don't remember what we studied, and at home it was just the TV set and me. Again I tried to do magic tricks door to door to bring in some extra money but had no luck.

Second grade was over but I had time on my hands. I noticed some boys playing in a group in the vacant lot near our basement. They might have been slightly older than my seven years but I did not care. I went over to them as they were pouring something in the gas tank of a car. I got closer but they did not acknowledge me. I asked what it was they were putting in the car's gas tank and they said "sugar." I did not ask why I just needed some company. It turns out the boys were planning "outings" of various sorts. One day we went near a garage in the alley and a boy put a match in the steel drum garbage bin and the flames were getting closer to the roof of the building. The boys did not say anything but we all dispersed in case someone called the fire department. The next plan was to break into the school and steal what we could. That Saturday we found an open door and we wandered around the school but there was nothing to steal, so that was a bad plan. The next robbery they planned was the basement lockers in an apartment building. We were able to get in through the small window near the ground. Everyone went their own direction to look for stuff. I was not going to take anything but I saw a shopping bag with bright sparkly Christmas decorations and could not resist. I brought it home and my mother was home early and she asked where I got the goods. I made up a terrible lie as transparent as glass and she cried and said she thought she had raised me better than that. I thought that was funny because I did not think she was raising me at all. I was always trying to figure things out by myself. Then she said, "If you don't have the time, don't do the crime." I understood what she meant, and dropped out of the gang before third grade. I don't know what happened to the boys but they were not much fun. I knew they might get into trouble like the punch sisters' older brother. I and other kids were aware of the crime in Chicago as there were gang or mob stories. Some of the boys thought that lifestyle was exciting. I don't know if my life of crime upset her, but my mother announced that we were moving again. I liked the school but the street was a bit rough. I felt like I was just being dragged around from place to place and school to school.

CHAPTER 3

Two Places on Elmwood Street

This was our fifth move since we came to Chicago but it was still better than the farm. We moved to a lower unit in a duplex in a nicer neighborhood with windows that made it lighter. My mother never told me where we were moving to next, so it was always a surprise. It was still easy to move as we did not have furniture, but yard sales offered many needed items. My black cat made the move and the neighboring houses were more normal with families living in them. At seven I would start third grade at a new school and was old enough to have a latch key and get myself back and forth from school four blocks away. We were across from Nichols Junior High School and they had a large bonfire at Halloween that was exciting as it had very big flames.

I saw a girl with long tangled hair and barefoot like me who lived in a big house a few doors down. We tried a lemonade stand, but I confused sugar with salt and the stand was a bust. I kept trying to find ways to make money. One day I went over to her house as her parents and brother were not home, and I was shocked to see dark crayon scribbles all over the lower half of the walls. However, they owned a house and we rented and had to face a landlord. It turned out her parents were "beatniks" that believed children should not be stifled by rules. I did not have any external rules, but developed internal rules of what I thought was good behavior. But I could see the sadness in her eyes and felt she might be neglected like me. I had the wagon, so we would give rides back and forth on the sidewalk. There were no men stopping by with candy so it was a better place to play. Eventually my cat had kittens and Alice and I would dress them up in doll clothes. However, one day I came home from school and my mother had all the kittens in a filled bathtub and they were frantically meowing as they bobbed up and down in the water. She laughed and said that on the farm they used to drown the kittens in the river. I cried and pleaded with her not to drown the kittens. She said she was trying to get the fleas off them, and when the water was drained there were fleas hopping all over the entire white enamel tub. I didn't know if she was going to kill them, it was supposed to be funny or she was just getting rid of fleas. I was angry and confused. The cat and the kittens disappeared and I have no idea what my mother did with them. I actually did not want to know as knowing might be worse.

The third grade was not very interesting and the teacher looked like she was waiting for retirement. One day our class was running in a big circle around the playground and a black boy pushed me down on the ground and it split my knee open. I did not know him or why he did it, but I had to stay home for quite some time for it to heal. The nurse came by to see how I was doing, but she was not friendly. The principal and assistant called my mother and me to come in to talk about it. But my mother was angry about what they were saying and she stormed out of the meeting. I tried to get her to come back but she kept on walking and the principal did not say anything, so I left. The boy was a bully so I hoped they did something about his attack.

In the fall my mother announced that her older sister Ani, and her husband Erni, were going to visit. This was the first time we would have a visit with a relative. My mother always said our relatives were "evil snakes," and she never wanted to see them, so I was very curious to see what they were like. Aunt Ani was a big woman with eyeglasses wearing a nice dress, shoes and purse. Her husband had a Hawaiian shirt which seemed bright for 1950s men's apparel. The next day we went to the beach, but later Ani got sick to the point that my mother had to call a doctor, who administered a large needle in her behind as she was running a fever. She stayed in the small guest room while her husband stayed on the couch. I was very worried she was going to die, but was able to get to sleep in my small room.

In the middle of the night I got up to go to the bathroom, and Uncle Erni was there and proceeded to rub my privates in an aggressive manner. I don't remember what happened but the next day my aunt and uncle made a hurried exit. Before they left my mother insisted that she take some photos before they left, and one was with me next to the offending uncle Erni. I was very unhappy and tried to pull away and he had a very angry expression on his face aimed at my mother. I kept quiet. A month later I was ironing and had to go to the bathroom but stood there and peed on the linoleum floor. My mother came home and was understandably upset, but I couldn't talk about the incident. I was afraid to go to the bathroom.

Decades later I told her about his molestation, and she retorted, "Big deal, he molested so many girls." If that was true, why was he allowed into our home? Why did she not try to protect me? Was she molested by him when she was a teenager and he was marrying her older sister? I felt I wouldn't get anywhere talking to her about the molestation. She seemed like it was too emotional for her or she did not care. Nothing made much sense to me.

After years of collecting bits and pieces of my mother's terrible child-hood I learned about my mother taking care of the youngest baby girl Elna at age eight, doing all the cooking for the family at age twelve when Ani left to marry Erni, and being the primary caretaker at age fourteen. She did all the cooking, washing, making butter from the cow's milk, sewing clothes for the younger girls until she was twenty and could not take it anymore and announced she was leaving. She missed out on her education while Elna and Ellen went to school with nice clothes. The boys had to quit school to work after fifth or sixth grade but they seemed to have more fun on their off hours. When my mother hitchhiked to Calumet, another mining town, with ten cents she found a good live- in maid job and was able to get eye glasses for the first time. The girls went to Aunt Katherine's and were able to attend Pequaming High School sponsored by the Henry Ford company for workers that made wood supplies for the station wagons or "Woodies." Both girls did well and I know my mother would have done well if she had the opportunity. So this visit was even more of a mystery as she knew Erni was a molester and Ani had abandoned the family for a shot gun marriage. Relatives were evil snakes so why was she so generous in her hospitality and so lax in her protection of her daughter? There were so many things that did not make much sense.

Now my mother worked for an agency that sent her to different jobs. One was being a night janitor in a medical building above the diner where she used to work as a waitress. She would bring me along to clean the ashtrays, empty the small trash cans and straighten up the magazines in the waiting rooms while she did the heavier work. I was eight and could do more work, but I still had school the next day. The ashtrays were always full of cigarette butts and ashes and it seemed really dirty. I enjoyed some of the offices as they had aquariums, mineral collections and some of the magazines were interesting. I studied the fish and minerals carefully and wanted a collection of my own someday. There were medical journals with photos of surgeries, which I looked at but the bloody organs scared me. What did the patients think about it?

Finally, I was exhausted and would fall asleep on a hard Naugahyde couch. My mother would have to find me and we would get home very late, so it was hard to get up for school. One night we were in the elevator and the security guard really stared, so I don't know if he reported having a child along on a job. Another job was at a radio station and she brought me along while she cleaned. I saw the radio tower and started to climb it, as I did not know thousands of watts of power went through it. Finally, an employee noticed and demanded I come down at once. She was not invited back on that job. I was a little embarrassed but I did not know about radio station towers. Another job was at a Catholic school and it seemed dark and dreary but the nuns were interesting in their habits. This was not work I wanted to do when I grew up. Maybe that is why my mother brought me along to discourage me from following in her work. She never talked about what I wanted to be when I grew up. She had left me alone at five years old. Why did she take me along now?

One Sunday night we had dinner in front of the TV and the variety show had dancers performing and I thought they looked so happy, so I said "I want to be a dancer." My mother immediately said that "was sinful, terrible and you would not do well." I never told her my dreams after that, as it was too risky to crush what little hope I had of a bright future. But the truth was I didn't have any dreams just blank darkness.

As winter became very cold, I forgot my key and was locked out after school. It was getting dark and the neighbors sent out a warm bowl of milk! That was nice but I was not a cat! Eventually my mother came home in the dark but I learned my lesson never to forget my key. I had to be more responsible. As Christmas approached, a very unusual thing happened in that my mother took me to see the Nutcracker ballet. Usually, she did not go to secular events like movies. The children sat in the front balcony row and the adults behind. Maybe there was a price break on the tickets for kids. Unfortunately, a child in my row got sick and threw up near me. I was very sensitive to vomiting and was appalled and could not focus on the ballet that much. I did not say anything as I knew my mother made a big effort to take me to the show with dancers.

I don't remember learning much in third grade, but it ended. That summer meant the beach was open and I really enjoyed swimming. I even had a baby-sitter for a while named Sally, who was the daughter of a Swedish woman we knew. Sally had short black hair and was an alcoholic. Her son, Ron, had been taken away as he wandered into the street alone and was hit by a car. He was placed in foster care. She was OK but my mother was totally against alcohol. Evanston was "dry" and the home of the WCTU, or Women's Christian Temperance Union. Prohibition had been a big topic and I thought it was a good idea. Why did I need a sitter now?

Sometimes on Sunday my mother and I would go to the Lincoln Park Zoo, which was free; all we had to do was pay the bus fare. The animals were in cement cages and I would stare into their eyes and wonder what they were thinking. The gorilla seemed thoughtful, chewing his bubble gum and staring into your eyes. The Children's Zoo had a snake which I could pet. Lincoln Park was a nice tree-lined place and it was nice to walk around at a leisurely pace.

Fourth grade was alright, but then we had a started having a hygiene contest. Every morning when we came into the classroom our hair, teeth, and clothes were inspected. We were given check marks next to our name for everyone to see if we passed inspection. I knew I wasn't going to win, but I thought it was unfair for those who did not have a stay-at-home mother or had to dress ourselves. One girl easily won as her hair was always very neat with a barrette, her clothes pressed with a crisp white collar on her dresses and shiny shoes. The inspection taught us what to aim for but it was embarrassing to me. We had spelling bees and I did not always do so well, and my team would be disappointed. I did not have a lot of confidence. I don't remember Christmas or my birthday being celebrated, but we went to church with candles that were inspiring.

In the spring, things were OK, but then something happened that made me question everything. My mother had learned about health food in Los Angeles, and Evanston had a health food store but it was small and did not have juicing machines. So every now and then we would make the journey on Sunday to downtown Chicago on the dirty, noisy "L" train to the big health food stores. We climbed the stairs to the elevated platform and my mother saw a quarter on the tracks and suggested I jump down and get it. Being a Tomboy I thought this would be easy. I did not know about the third rail track that could electrocute you in a second, or that the height of the platform was at my head height. After I picked up the quarter I put my hands on the rough wooden platform but did not have the strength to pull myself up. I heard the distant rumble of the next train coming, which started to get louder, which meant it would be at our stop soon. I was starting to panic. I yelled and was waving my hands for help. People were yelling at my mother to do something, but she had moved to the back of the platform and seemed to be staring into space. I was so anxious and was jumping up in the air for help. Finally, a man in khaki pants and jacket leaned down with his hairy wrists and pulled me up to the platform like I was a feather. When the train pulled into the station, we got on the train, but she continued to stare into space. I tried talking to her but she did not respond. I wanted her to be happy that I was alive or to hug me but that was not going to happen. It was scary and embarrassing to be a public spectacle. I just sat back and watched the city out the window. Was she trying to kill me, or was it just bad judgment? There was no talk as we arrived at the big health food stores but I enjoyed the carrot juice. I had the feeling I had to watch my mother's behavior and be more careful. Decades later when I was visiting my mother the "L" had put a warning sign with a cartoon man leaning near the tracks with a line through it to tell you not to get near the tracks. I had chills remembering that awful day. In high school a boy, in a previous class had been electrocuted by falling on the "L" tracks and his family that was still in grief set up a scholarship fund for him. I don't know if it was suicide or an accident, but it was not for retrieving a quarter.

If I did something she did not like, my mother would say when I was born there was a couple in Southern California who wanted to adopt me and name me "Candy." I knew people don't just go up to the mother of a newborn and say I want your child. So was she telling me she was ambivalent about keeping me, or I was supposed to be grateful to live with her? Sometimes I think about living in a Southern California suburb with parents and what that would be like. But it seemed pointless as I was here now and had to make the best of it.

I did not have many toys or books to read, but one time we were in the Walgreen's Drug Store and I saw a doll on the top shelf and I asked if she would buy it. She said if she spent the six dollars we would not have rent or food. We did not seem to have much anyway, and I was lonely. I persisted and she broke down and bought me Susie, who was my only companion. I promised Susie I would make our life better and I would make or buy her nice clothes. Once in a great while my mother would surprise me with a gift that I actually wanted. That summer my mother came through with a bike! All I had to do was to learn how to ride one. I got the pedals going but did not learn how to brake so I smashed into a tree. But once I got the hang of it the bike gave me the freedom to explore Evanston more and go to the beach by myself. It gave me a sense of more independence and a choice of where to spend my time.

One summer day I went to the beach alone and there was a man and a couple going in the water and I started talking to them. The couple went ashore but for some unknown reason I took a swipe toward the man's penis. The man was understandably shocked and rushed out of the water toward the shore, where he talked to his friends and they left. They probably wanted to get away from the devil girl as soon as possible. I don't know why I did it, but it might have had something to do with my uncle's visit. But I never did it again.

Sometimes people were missing at the beach and the lifeguards would have about 20 of us line up facing the water, hold hands and move toward the deeper water to see if a body was there. I did not want to step on a body, but I did want to help out. We never found a dead body. If you were there all day you could see the arch of the activities from the morning early birds, noon-time lunchers, the Good Humor man would sell frozen treats and the people who came after work. It was interesting to me to see different people showing up at different times of the day. There was the polio scare and we were told not to be in a wet bathing suit, but it was so hot your suit usually dried in the sun. We all got vaccinated as soon as we could, thanks to Jonas Salk.

The punch sisters were friends with a younger teenage mother near our new apartment on Elmwood Street. I went with them one hot day, and the place really smelled of baby poop and I said something. They got really angry with me and asked me to leave. I know the young mother was doing the best she could but it seemed like she was too young to have children. I never saw them again, which was fine as their family was in deep trouble and we had our own problems. I was nine and entering fifth grade and we had moved to a larger apartment across the street from the same school. I even had a room with a bed, and on the third floor we had a view with our own porch with a wooden swing attached to the porch ceiling. It was nice to sit out there and relax. This was the best place we had ever lived in Evanston.

The fifth-grade teacher, Mary Jenkins, was supportive and even was understanding one day when I was emotionally overwhelmed and cried. She had us do a long project concerning the history of Illinois. Instead of reading about it, we did projects such as making rag rugs and candles from scratch, and writing scripts to do a play based on the wining script. But the most fun was when she said we were going to write a book on Illinois, and we all took topics and some of us submitted illustrations. I wrote about Conservation, as I was interested in helping wild animals and natural places. To my surprise my illustration was one of the ten picked for the book. The students doing illustrations were transported by car to a business office to make copies, and we were driven back home. I felt more grown-up. I was pleased to be chosen and learned how to make simple prints. The whole class assembled the book in the classroom and used wallpaper samples on cardboard as the covers to keep the cost down. She was the best teacher to arrange all of this for us. I felt I had finally got some recognition of my abilities and working with a group on a project that meant something to me.

Since our apartment was so big my mother rented out the front living room and bedroom to a German woman and her 14-year-old daughter from Berlin, Germany. The mother was very skinny and did not look well, while her daughter was very robust and healthy. The girl who looked like she was 14 said she had pierced ears, but some boys in Germany ripped them out so she was never having earrings again. This frightened me, and I never had pierced ears. They did not last too long and they moved. An elderly lady was there for a short while. Somehow we had a push-pedal Singer sewing machine, and I started sewing. I took me awhile to learn how to coordinate pushing the petal with your foot while watching the material flow under the presser foot. One day I got too close and the needle went through my finger nail and stopped on my bone! I called my mother for help and she was able to get the needle out of my finger. But it was the start of my sewing, which gave me many clothes to wear when I was older.

There was an empty lot next to the large apartment complex that had tall trees to climb, flowers bloomed and there was enough room to play baseball after school. A few times my mother threw the baseball with me and she threw it hard! She used to play when she was younger. I joined some boys on bikes and we would play "chicken." You would act like you were going to push someone off the road and see if they flinched. I was used to playing with boys, as they were on the street like me. I think playing with boys built my confidence, but we did not talk much.

The oddest thing was some of the older kids decided to start a "sex club" on my porch as they knew my mother was not home. I don't think this was common in the 1957. They also decided that I and another girl were too young to participate, so we had to stay on the porch down below but we could hear them loudly singing the theme song, "Come to the Sex Club Every Day!" This was not exactly the Mickey Mouse Club, which had wholesome-looking Mouseketeers with ears on their heads. I think they were just showing body parts, but it was a bit bold for kids around ten years old. The other girl and I would patiently wait until they adjourned. The boy who had pushed me down on the playground and injured my knee threw eggs on our porch. I have no idea why he was targeting me. I had done nothing to him.

My mother did another one of those private parts exams like she did before first grade. I was very upset and did not want her to do it again. One day I arranged my doll, Susie, and other stuffed toys in a circle on the back porch and ran what I would call a therapy group. I was reassuring them that everything would be alright. I think I was trying to self-soothe myself.

My mother left before I woke up but she would make a breakfast for me with a note on the tray saying good morning. And at night, she was gone and I had to forage for food. One time I opened up a can of cold tamales but could still not use the stove at age nine. It was really awful. There was the "penny bowl," that was white milk glass on the outside and pink on the inside. It was filled with pennies so I could go to the penny candy/convenience store and buy candy. As a result I had a lot of cavities. Sometimes I would open the fridge and there was nothing to eat. However, on Sundays my mother would teach me how to bake and gave me my own recipe book with nice color photos so I could pick out what I wanted to make. I had to measure and plan the sequence to complete the dish. She said I was a quick learner; it was unusual for her to compliment me. The smell of the cake, cookies or main dish baking was very homey. It was my fondest memory of spending time with her. I felt she was trying to be a mother. She also worked for wealthy families that wanted good food, and she was a good cook. My mother had been cooking since she was twelve years old, so she was experienced.

In the winter I had a really high temperature and the doctor who made the house call said that I had scarlet fever and it was serious. My mother actually sat next to my bedside and fed me a steak dinner, as she said it would build up my red blood cells. Unfortunately, I missed 29 days of school, even though I seemed fully recovered. It had to do the quarantine period. It was very lonely all day, and I saw a younger girl and she said her bangs were too long, so I got scissors and cut them. I guess I didn't do a good job, as her mother was angry at me. I finally had a good teacher, but couldn't go to school for what seemed like a very long time.

Later I did make a friend named Gale, and we made up plays, rode our bikes and even did sledding on a nearby hill in the winter. However, one day we were at her house and her mother was giving her a hard time, and I felt the need to protect my friend and told her mother off. This ended the friendship, as her mother was very strict and did not tolerate upstarts like me. I was a little fuzzy about parent and child roles. One day my mother and I were sitting on the swings at the school playground and Gale came and sat on another set of swings. She said her mother wouldn't allow her to play with me and we both were sad. My mother did not say anything to make it better or worse.

I and another friend, Cheryl, were in the Brownies together. We went to the Chicago Forest Preserves, saw the locust invasion and did walks. However, I was playing rough with one girl and she fell into a mud puddle, so that was the end of Brownies. I had played a lot with boys as they were on the street like

I was and playing with girls was different, as was having a parent with rules. Rules were something I had not experienced except for School and Sunday School. In seventh grade, Cheryl died of cancer, and it was a big loss.

The playground was right across the street, so I spent a lot of time on the monkey bars and swings. One day I got too close to the swings and got kicked in the face, which started a long series of nose bleeds. I was at a friend's house and her mother tried to stop a nose bleed. But then it became nine o'clock and my mother wasn't home. The lady sent me home as it was their bedtime. I wanted to stay, but of course I had my own place. But all and all, fifth grade was the best class, teacher, school and place to live so far.

The summer brought a visit from one of my mother's Finnish friends whose husband had died and now she had to move to Florida, as it was cheaper to live there. Her husband had been a jeweler and she had had a nice life style, but now she was poor. It seemed like it was important to make your own money. We went to a fair extolling the wonders of electricity in the future. That came and went with gas, but it is now back again. Two times my mother even took me and a friend to Riverview Amusement Park with scary rides, and it was a lot of fun. But we did not have a lot of money to spend, so we went home earlier than I would have liked. There was always the beach as a fallback for a very nice day. But there were still many lonely days. One day my mother finally came home and I begged her to play one game of checkers with me, but she refused as she wanted to read her books. I had gone through a tornado alone and was scared, but when my mother came home she was just angry that water had been forced under the back door. She yelled at me to clean it up. I wanted her to ask if I was OK.

When I had ear aches, she would threaten to beat me if I complained of the pain. I learned not to complain when I was sick and not ask her for too much. I developed a game called Social Security, as my mother said that was a good thing to have. I designed clothes for my cut-out dolls. I would not use the pre-printed one and make designs and painted them for the dolls. I sewed for Susie, my doll.

My mother, who was nice looking, had lost some weight finally and had a boyfriend. He was an auto mechanic who sold her a 1951 Studebaker with the airplane front. The problem was she couldn't drive, but that did not stop him from having her drive on the street. She was weaving all over and I was hiding in the back seat in case we hit something. I don't know what happened to the man, but the Studebaker sat in the parking lot collecting dust. I wondered why he would sell a car to a person who could not drive, or why my mother would buy it.

I was hoping to have a good teacher like Miss Jenkins in the sixth grade. A woman named Mable came to visit. We had a record player and I was playing an old love song over and over. My mother said I was "in love." I think I was depressed or losing my mind. Mable did not say anything, but I am sure she was wondering what was going on with me or in our household. My mother had inexplicably taken me to a foster home with an overweight woman in a wheelchair with five very-sad-looking children standing behind her. I did not know what this was supposed to mean, but it was a pitiful sight. Was this a threat that she was getting rid of me?

The final straw might have been the day I was followed by an older brother of one of the bike boys. He cornered me in an entry to a basement with chains as though he was going to hit me with them. I was not afraid, as I knew he was bluffing, but my mother came around the comer and saw him and dragged me back to our apartment. She was more upset than I was at the time. My mother rarely shared what she was thinking, feeling or planning but the next incident was beyond anything I could imagine. The adventure had been over for years and I was watchful, but what was I watching for?

CHAPTER 4

The Bombshell of Boone, Iowa

When the colorful leaves started running down the street in the cooler winds, I knew it was time to return to school. I would not have Miss Jenkins as a teacher, but maybe someone as good. It was Sunday and my mother had four women over for an early dinner, as she did not work. These women were middle-aged women who I had never seen before and they did not say why they were there. They had been to the Moody Bible Institute, which was one of my mother's favorite Christian institutions started in the 1800s. I was ignored, but I was used to that. After the dinner was over, my mother announced I was going with them to a place I had never heard of in Iowa. I was so shocked I did not get the details, if there were any. She had packed up one suitcase for me and said they were leaving now. This was such a shock to me that I developed amnesia about three years before the incident but not during the present. I don't remember leaving or her saying anything about where I was going and if or when I was ever coming back. We never had a car, except the lifeless Studebaker in the parking lot, and I was told never to get into a car with strangers as they kill little girls. There were articles in the Chicago Tribune about girls of different ages being found in the Forest Preserves in Chicago. Now my mother had arranged for me to get into a car with total strangers and drive to another state. This was the ultimate betrayal. I had total distrust of her intentions or if she had any concern for my well-being.

The women had a clam-shell-like, dark-colored sedan. There were two women in the front and I was crammed in between two women in the back. I was too upset to think straight and there was little conversation. I remember leaving Evanston and finally seeing the endless cornfields and trucks dutifully going west. The corn fields had given up their fruit and were waiting to die, and I was wondering what they were going to do with me. I was wedged so tightly between the women I could not escape but where would I go anyway?

Nobody talked. It was just silent miles to nowhere. As it started to get dark and the occasional road lamp would light up, the outlines of their bodies that faded into darkness. This went on for hours and I was getting sleepy, which was a welcome relief to the intense anger I felt toward my mother. I felt this was the last stunt she would pull on me. She was getting rid of me for sure and I was on my own. I knew I could not support myself at ten years old, so I had to go along with whatever was happening and then figure things out. I did not care at that point if I ever saw my mother again. I had Susie in my suitcase. Occasionally I could see a farmhouse and I wondered if they were happy on a farm and if they loved each other. I knew we were getting closer to the Mississippi River, and I had read *Huckleberry Finn* and their escape toward Freedom.

Finally, we came to a farmhouse driveway and we were greeted by farm-looking people who were calm, even friendly and acted like this was an ordinary event. Did they steal kids and bring them West? I was really tired of thinking and they gave me a room with bare furnishings. I was grateful to go to sleep and stop my brain from coming up with all the possible bad outcomes. In the morning they made breakfast for seven people, which seemed like a big group to me. They broke an egg for me with a double yoke and they said that was a sign of good luck. Really? Some strangers show up at your home, your mother stages a kidnapping and that's good luck? But I was starting to relax as they did not seem like the gangster or killer types.

They all hugged goodbye and we continued across the Mississippi River, which was very large and exciting for me, as well as seeing the giant silos that held the grain for the cereal manufacturing plants. We eventually came to Amana, Iowa, which was a German colony that was self-sufficient and made many things beside appliances. The women said there were Amish people living there who they associated with, and I was interested as I had never met them in Northern Michigan, California or Chicago.

We then journeyed through more cornfields and finally came to the town of Boone, Iowa, which was named after Nathaniel Boone, the son of Daniel Boone. It had been a coal-mining area, site of the Black Hawk War, and settled by pioneers after the Civil War. It had maintained a population of about 12,000 residents over decades due to industry jobs that keep the people employed and wanting to live there.

The women worked at the Boone Biblical Institute, founded by Lois Crawford's father in the 1800s.He had passed away and Lois Crawford had been in charge for quite some time. They had bought the old courthouse, which had been expanded to a Bible College, dorms, a school house, a nursing home and large basement for dining. The white steepled church across the street also housed a Christian radio station. They had been a hub of activity in their heyday. Now the buildings had seen better days, and the old wooden porch had spindles that needed painting. But the large sprawling structures had a dignity about them. The glory days of educating pastors were long gone, but Lois Crawford kept things going in her elder years. She had wrinkled skin and gray hair that was not combed too much, but she had a kindness about her that was reassuring. I felt like she had a great weight on her shoulders, but I trusted her.

As we entered the building, there was a small living room that led to a one-room classroom with stairs leading up to small bedrooms and down to a very large basement where everyone ate. The other wing had Miss Crawford's living quarters and three stories of a nursing home. The older kids stayed in town to sleep and the younger kids went out to a farm to sleep. The women were plainly dressed in longer cotton skirts, buns and no make-up or jewelry. I was transported back into the 1800s as there was no TV, newspapers, or radio shows that were not religious. I was cut off from the current world happenings and the people in Boone. There was a one-room schoolhouse for the children up to the sixth grade with desks equipped with inkwells. The high school kids had their own sleeping quarters and school. I never saw the teens except for dinner and doing dishes together at night. There were a lot of things that were never explained or spoken about. Like who were these workers and children? Where did they come from, and why were they here? Why was I there?

Life started to have some semblance of routine, but no one explained how long I was going to be there, and I don't remember hearing from my mother. They were largely German and they believed children should work, but this was also because they did not have a lot of funds and we were cheap labor. We were not supposed to speak unless spoken to, and the other kids were not very outgoing. Our younger group was driven to farm at night where we had cots in rows.

The daily routine began with a hearty breakfast, followed by reading the Bible in a group for about a half an hour, starting at Genesis and ending at Revelations. We drove into town in a large station wagon and entered the one-room classroom for all the lower grades. Lydia Smolik, the teacher, was a middle-aged woman with dark hair, glasses and was mildly friendly. She wore a knee-length dress and had her hair cut shoulder length. She looked almost modern compared to the other women. I wondered if she had a family, but I never found out.

The problem with school was that the other children seemed either orphaned or abandoned, and their educational level seemed far behind. I was very bored most of the time. I had been to four schools by that time, but the children had been from educated families and they were on target for their grade. It was a challenge to keep up with them. This was a waste time for me. There was no library to read other books, as the Bible was all we needed. The State of Iowa had rural education packets, and we listened to the radio and we filled out our workbooks. This was a good idea for isolated farm kids, but we lived in a town. Why couldn't we go to the public schools? I liked the teacher, and for her birthday I wrapped a stick of gum for the teacher and she seemed pleased. That is all I had, as I had no money.

The few high school kids had their classes in another building. They ran the Christian Radio station that was in a second-floor wing across the street by making announcements and playing Christian music. One day I climbed the stairs and they were laughing while the music played. It seemed like they were having a good time. Recently, I found one of the girls on Face book. She lived in Orange County and said her parents paid for her to go there. She enjoyed the religious atmosphere and was involved in Bob Jones University. My mother paid $31 a month for my keep, but it was a very different experience for me.

At dinner time we all went down to the basements, which had long picnic tables covered in oil cloth, to eat the food some of which came from their farm. When they sold slaughtered animals, we got the leftover parts to eat such as the tongue and liver. They slaughtered chickens and I was once asked to round them up for the slaughterhouse. I felt like an executioner and did not like it. They were a non-profit and were eligible for government subsidies such as one-gallon cans of peanut butter, honey, canned vegetables and powdered milk. The large cans were stored in a large dark part of the basement. When we went to get supplies and turned on the light a sea of cockroaches began scurrying to their hiding places. I did not like it, but it was a unique visual display of an insect army. I had a feeling that there was plenty of food for us and the cockroaches. We would not starve. There was a large walk-in freezer to freeze meat, government cheese and other food items.

It was a new experience for me to have regular meal times and eating together with people. Dinner was fairly pleasant, but no one carried on an interesting conversation. After the dinner, the children and teens were responsible for doing dishes for 40 people without a dishwasher. We might have 12 to 20 at dinner, but they also had a wing for elderly people who were non- ambulatory and the workers. Sometimes our job was to feed the elders in bed with a tray that we put on the stand across their bed. One woman with cerebral palsy was very friendly but her limbs were very bent and distorted.

I was afraid to go in her room, but she would smile and encourage me to talk to her. The assignment I hated the most was going up to the third floor where a woman was permanently locked into a room and I was to leave the tray in front of the door. I could hear her pacing back and forth in an agitated manner. Why was the woman locked in the room like an animal? Later Miss Reffenstein would come, unlock the door and feed her, as she was strong and could handle whatever transpired in that room. What was wrong with this woman? It frightened me, as I might be locked in a room someday.

After we drove to the country farm I was supposed to collect the chicken eggs. I was a city kid and had no idea how to handle a chicken. The chickens would get upset and fly around, but they did not bite me. I collected the eggs and gently put them in a bucket as I really enjoyed the breakfasts .It was just the long walk to the hen house that frightened me as it was very dark and the corn in the field would rustle.

Back in town I usually got the job of washing silverware in a big tub. The water would get dirty quickly so I had to keep changing it out. The kids got bored and would play tricks on each other. One night I put my hand in the dish tub and it was a dark, bloody, slimy piece of raw liver in my hand. I just got rid of it. Another night they locked me in the walk-in freezer and shut the door. I was afraid I would freeze to death, but they eventually let me out. So doing the dishes was not a fun thing but sometimes we would talk.

After our dinner work was done, Miss Reffenstein would round the younger group up and head out to the farm in a large station wagon. Then we had farm work. My assignment was to walk down a dark dirt path to a chicken coop down that dark path, as it was very dangerous in the city for a girl to walk alone in the dark. But now we had eggs for breakfast and I liked to eat. Once in a while we rounded up the cows to come back to the barn for milking. We did not do the milking. I think the people who leased the barn and fields did it. One time we ran the cows too fast and we were scolded for endangering their health. How would we know? Another time I ran across a fenced-in area with only one cow in it but then someone said to run as it was a bull. I never did that again and learned the difference between a cow and a bull.

We then would have another half hour of reading the Bible. The Old Testament was rather boring and not very inspiring, as people were mean to each other. I was just trudging through the archaic words until it was time for the next child to read. The sleeping room had a long row of cots and I was lucky to have the first one, as the dog would come over to my cot and say hello. This was great, except when he had chased a skunk down. We would go to bed and repeat the cycle over and over again. Eventually, when we were reading the New Testament, the people seemed nicer and there were stories about Jesus that had lessons and morals to them. Psalms was a pleasure to read and brought some comfort to me. However, reading the entire Bible did improve my reading skills, and there was nothing else to read. We had no homework, and the daily class was underwhelming. On Sunday we had to memorize one Bible verse and read it out loud in the service.

My mother had done one nice thing and had sent money for piano lessons that were taught by a lady in the community. It was a private lesson, so I felt special and I was getting better at playing difficult pieces. The piano teacher was all business, but at least I was getting some individual attention and having contact with an "outsider" in town. The money ran out and the workers did not like driving me there, so that was the end of the piano lessons. This was not a middle-class finishing school. It was an unwanted child workplace.

The girls in my group were a mixed bag. Dorothy was close to my ten years and had long blond braids that were in the German style. She was friendly and we spent some time together. She said her sister Peggy was in the teenage group, but Peggy had dark hair in a ponytail and looked Native American. I did not question it but it did not make visual sense. There was an older Native American girl who was nice. There were other girls who were not as friendly, and I never found out where they were from or where they were going. No one asked me questions, so I did not ask them questions. We were just child laborers caught in a time warp. Once a month when the weather was moderate we were given a nickel and allowed to walk to a soft ice cream place down the street. It seemed like low wages and little recognition for our toils. I was tempted to talk to the "outsiders" but it was frowned upon. One day in town, I noticed a young man washing his car not far from the school, and he was listening to his radio. I was very anxious to get some news of the outside world. But I didn't dare to get too close as I did not know how he would react. I was used to watching TV and finding out the latest news. He ignored me and I only heard some of the latest music.

There was a Christian store under the one-room classroom and Mrs. Workman ran the store. She was a short woman with curly hair and wore a suit. I did not see many people going in or coming out. I would go in to look at the merchandise, which was not very interesting. She would watch me like a hawk as though I was tempted to steal something. I had no interest in her stuff. One day I was walking in the empty lot next to the Church and I accidentally stepped on a top of a snake nest. The mother snake was there with leathery-looking eggs. I tried to fix the roof of her home but was not really able to repair the damage. I felt bad but was happy to see her nest. This is one of the more exciting things that happened there.

In the fall we had a picnic out at the farm and it was fun, and Dorothy and I were getting along. I had my old Brownie uniform on, which was getting shorter as I was getting taller. When the fall turned into winter, I made a life-sized snow woman and asked Mrs. Smolik if I could barrow a scarf to put over her chest. I assumed that religious people would not want to look at breasts. She was upset, as it was a good scarf, and I felt bad but my intentions were good. I don't remember Thanksgiving or Christmas being celebrated. Maybe it was too secular for them or they did not want to spend any extra money. At the farm we would hang clothes outside and they would freeze, and when we gathered them up and took them inside they were damp and ready to iron. The sheets were large when they were frozen. I liked the shapes of the clothes.

The male janitor died, and they put his body in a casket in the small living room for visitation. So every time we walked by to school or down to eat we would pass him. I would stand there sometimes, as I liked him and it was a loss. He was nice and one of the few men around the institution. Viewing the body was considered normal before a funeral but for a week?

Sometimes an Amish minister would drive over to our church and preach. He was an outsider in that he drove a car, but some of the Amish had to drive for business or other reasons. We had cars and at times we would go out on "missions," bringing food and other things to poor elderly country people. They were so poor they had newspaper for wallpaper and insulation in the winter. I felt they were on the edge of survival. I had heard about a truck falling on a car on the highway, so when we were driving I cringed when I saw we were passing a truck.

In January I developed a bad case of tonsillitis, and the Iowa doctor said I should have my tonsils out. Since the caretakers were not my parents, I had I had to take the train all the way back to Chicago. This was my birthday month, so I thought maybe my mother would celebrate it. My mother had moved to another boarding house in downtown Evanston that was better than the last one but they did not allow children. So I had to make myself scarce. We went to Evanston hospital through the back door, as they did not want poor clients in the front door for an almost-free clinic. It cost $1 to be seen at the clinic. I had the surgery and was still bleeding quite a bit. My mother went to work, so I would have to sneak into the bathroom down the hall to spit out blood in the bathroom. Later after the lunch hour I would go to a small Greek diner to get some soup. I wanted to talk to someone, but the owner just talked to his friends after the lunch rush hour. My mother did not talk much, and I was too weak to talk to her about my situation. She was dog-sitting for a family out of town and we went over there to walk the dog. The man who had sold her the Studebaker showed up. He had work clothes and a stubble beard. My mother wanted me to kiss him and I gave him a peck on the rough cheek but did not like him.

One night I was taking a bath and my mother threw in dirty clothes as she did not want to waste the water. I was upset and got out of the tub, as I was trying to get clean. I understand she grew up without running water, but this was 1958 with indoor plumbing. Finally, I was well enough to take the train back to Iowa. I felt like I was on an Orphan Train in reverse. The New York children were loaded onto West bound trains from an orphanage to possible homes in the Mid-West. I had a parent, but was being sent on a train back to an orphanage in the Mid-West. Miss Reffenstein was waiting at the train station for me, which was reassuring. When I returned to the school, Miss Smolik read Oliver Twist by Charles Dickens, and I could see some similarities to our situation, even though Oliver Twist's story was in nineteenth-century England. His loneliness, helplessness and being used were apparent. We did have better food. We had custodial care and religious exposure, but not much else. He was required to commit robberies for his keep; I had done it for company. However, he had a happy ending and I had no idea how my story was going to end. I appreciated her reading passages from the Dickens book.

My work was beginning to suffer as I did not care anymore. I threw a bucket of water down an old wooden staircase as I did not want to scrub every worn-out stair by hand. I was not Cinderella or a peasant girl. I talked back to Miss Reffenstein, and she slapped me really hard across the face, causing a bad nose bleed. I did not talk back again as she was a strong woman and my nose bleeds were hard to stop. I was just tired of her authoritarian, cold manner. I never saw her smile. We called her Frankenstein behind her back.

I had two other medical issues I did not know how to deal with. I was always constipated and I had seen a small pig on the farm that was not able to go number two. The farmer who rented the barn and land said they might have to "put the pig down." So was I going to be "put down?" The other problem was a bone in my right foot was sticking out of the arch. It was painful but I started putting cotton into my shoes and eventually the bone went back into place. I didn't trust them enough to talk to them about these issues. My mother in the past had threatened to beat me if I complained of an ear ache and other ailments. I guess I was afraid.

Dorothy and I were supposed to be rehearsing a duet on the piano and I did not feel like practicing the piece over and over and I was making mistakes. Finally the woman overseeing our practice said that was enough and took me upstairs to my "in-town" room and locked the door. Now I knew how you got locked in a room like the lady on the third floor. I lied down and saw all the cracks on the ceiling and thought of them as roads to all the places I would be going to someday. I was content to relax and do nothing for a change. It was peaceful. This went on for quite some time before the door was unlocked. Luckily, I did not have to use the bathroom. I found out what being locked in my room was like and it was not too bad.

But the highlight of me detaching from the place came about when I was fed up with all the work we did for one ice cream cone. I was not expecting money, as I knew they did not have much, but I thought some kind word or maybe a nice desert once in a while would be our due. I organized a letter-writing campaign about all the work we did and some mailed it to their relatives or somewhere. Eventually, word got back to the woman in charge, and there were consequences for speaking up. We were all lined up next to the small front room near the front door and one by one a child would enter the room to be beaten with a large wooden paddle. The line moved slowly so you had plenty of time to figure out what to say and how to handle the paddle. You could hear the scream of pain and the sound of tears coming from the room. I was getting nervous when Lois Crawford, the director, came up to me and told me to come with her. She asked me to pray for forgiveness on my knees. This was a much better alternative. Maybe, it was because I had a parent who was paying $31 per month for my care and could report the paddling as an outsider to the system. I had no idea how my mother would react, as she was not a fiercely protective mother. The government did not seem to have a lot of oversight or safeguards for children in the 1950s. My intentions were good, but they backfired. I was not popular with the girls due to paddling. I was not trying to be popular or be a rebel, I was just trying to stand up for myself and the other girls.

Another incident happened one Sunday when they were badgering Dorothy after the service to give her life to Christ. I had been through this so many times with my mother, including a Billy Graham crusade in Chicago in front of thousands of people. Why was I a sinner? Why did I need to be saved, from what? I went to church, got baptized and tried to follow the Ten Commandments, and that seemed like enough to me. I went down the aisle and asked them to stop but they were really upset and asked me to leave. So I did. There is such a thing as religious abuse. Dorothy was a good kid, and she was crying. I was getting a reputation as a rebel.

Then one night when we were doing the dishes, Peggy, Dorothy's older "sister," was picking on me and I was tired of it. I said I would fight her. This was a ridiculous threat, as she was five years older than me and much taller. She would not stop, so I left and reported her to Miss Reffenstein, the toughest house mistress. She came downstairs to the basement to see what the problem was. No one was making accusations, but somehow Peggy got really angry and ran away. The Iowa State Police were called and Dorothy was really mad at me. I did not expect Peggy to run away. I just wanted her to stop harassing me. I knew it was dangerous to run away unless you had a place to go. I never found out what happened to her but I lost Dorothy as a friend.

So things were not working out for me, but I was not sorry for my actions. They had their rules and I followed them, but I had to stand up for myself. I think growing up without any rules or much discipline I had developed my own sense of right and wrong. I made up my own mind about things and how I felt. Just because someone was an adult did not make them right, but they had more social power, money and physical strength.

I don't know if they contacted my mother or if she contacted them saying she wanted me to come "home" in April. I was happy to leave and see what the next change would bring. Some good things had happened here, but I was ready to move on to some place in the twentieth century and with more contact with the outside world. This was a very isolating time warp.

This time the train ride back from Chicago was more eventful than the other two trips. The orphanage had packed up my suitcase with the old Brownie uniform, Susie and my few belongings and gave me a cotton handkerchief with some coins in it. I had no pockets so I held on very tightly to the change. I was sitting in the front row next to a room with a table and chairs filled with five gangsters. They sat around the table, smoking, drinking and playing poker. They were a loud bunch and I was getting nervous as I was not used to men, let alone ones that were smoking or drinking. Evanston was a dry town, and the Christians surely did not approve of this behavior. It was an all-night train ride and the conductor would walk by every now and then, but did not say anything. I had dozed off and in the middle of the night the train came to an abrupt stop and the conductors kicked the men off the train in the middle of a cornfield that still had snow. I was relieved, but what do you do in the dark empty corn field in the snowy cold? It was not near a town or any lights. It was a drama and with an unknown ending

My mother was waiting at the downtown train station and we walked to the dirty, noisy "L" to see where she had moved to this time. I was happy to be back but was wondering what was going to happen next in my life with my mother. I would be living in another new place and attending another new school. But I had gained confidence since I left. The strict routine at Boone had made my life predictable and the rules made it clear what was expected of me. The endless Bible reading had helped me read difficult words. I had expressed my true feelings and acted on them; that did not work out well, but that was OK. I had gained something from the strange experience. I wondered how long the place was going to be able to survive, as it was an organization from the past. But I liked Miss Crawford and Miss Smolik and being in the country for a change. It got me away from a negative situation at home, and I had learned to live with people but not in a very social manner. It was a learning experience.

CHAPTER 5

Return to Chicago

It was awkward being back in the city after a cloistered rural life. I felt like I had been in the 1800s and now a train ride later I was back in the 1900s. I was not sure about seeing my mother, but again where else could I go? She had lost some weight and seemed upbeat so it was an easy reentry. My mother was OK despite the broken arm with a cast from wrist to elbow. She fell off a chair in the kitchen trying to reach a top shelf. She was still doing "day work," where you might go a different place to work most days. The dingy apartment had the same old furniture in it. The apartment buildings had about twelve units in each and were placed one right after another to house as many working people as possible. The fixtures were old and they had not been updated for 20 years, but it was a place to sleep.

The local school was in walking distance, and as it turned out was in a predominately Jewish area. Almost all the sixth-graders were Jewish except for one Catholic girl and me. I quickly found out they were interested in studying and were good students. This was a welcome relief from the children in Iowa who were behind and not trying too hard. One problem we had was that the teachers seemed to be in turmoil. Our main teacher was an older lady who said she was being fired for being a communist, and would talk about this quite a bit. She seemed sad and alone in her defense. In 1959 it was the end of the McCarthy "Red Scare" era. While I was sympathetic, I did not know what students could do about her problem. From strict Christianity, and Bible reading, Judaism to Communism was quite a shift in my mind. The boys and girls were enrolled in shop together and we would make things sometimes out of plastic. The teacher had quite a temper and he would get angry at us and throw things at us. We would duck, just look at each other, and stay calm. But I do remember feeling like I was back on track in school and liked the students.

The back porches were for fire escapes and not a place of relaxation. The sun light barely made it through the narrow spaces between buildings. I missed the open land of the farm but not much else. In the alley was a cement wall that was the Evanston boundary and a Catholic cemetery, and I and other kids would play there sometimes as it was the only green space around. One time a white rabbit sprang out of the side of a tombstone, and we were alarmed but it was peaceful and better than the street. The living room had the mohair sofa that we had before I went to Boone. It was deep burgundy and had seen better days, but was warm and familiar.

I did not want to sleep in the one room in front with my mother who was home nights. I found that if I squeezed myself under the clothes in the walk-in closet, I could put a blanket down and sleep on the floor. My mother would walk by to use the bathroom, but I wanted a safe place to myself. My little hiding place in the closet was threatened. One day my mother brought home an acquaintance named Josephine, and said she could sleep in my closet space under the clothes. I was so mad. It was my safe spot! The next day Josephine told me that she had heard that my father had died in southern Illinois. My mother had said he was from southern Illinois, but I had never asked about my father. Later I did want one photo to see what he looked like but that was the limit to my curiosity. Now, I was trying to adjust to yet another move. I stayed quiet as I did not believe her. I think my mother put her up to it, but why did she do that? It did not make any sense, but I can't solve all the mysteries in my life as there were too many.

Juneway Terrace was the last street in Chicago. Sometimes I would walk towards the "L" station to just see what was there. It was a crowded, dirty area with many bars, as Chicago was "wet" and Evanston was "dry." The signs said "no minors allowed" and my spelling was so bad I thought it meant my family that had been miners up north. Why were we excluded from these dark, smelly, smoky drinking places? This was a big a contrast to the isolated farm in Iowa. The small stores and quick eating places were crammed in together. There was a lot of street traffic to keep them busy. I hated this area and did not want to live here. I wanted to move back to Evanston.

My mother had found a new Baptist church that was a few "L" stops south in the Rodgers Park area of Chicago. I must say she was resourceful in finding new places to live and work, and churches to attend. At Easter we got up before dawn for the Sunrise Service, and I was surprised that the minister wore a tuxedo with tails and the people had very nice clothes. We saw the sun come up, which represented Jesus rising from the dead. It was a long morning. I was enrolled in the confirmation class so I could be baptized. My mother was determined to make me religious. I went along with it, but it meant taking the "L" south and walking to the church on Saturdays and returning on Sunday. Finally, the day came when I was to be baptized on a stage that held the baptismal tank with steps going down into the water. I wore a black robe and walked across the stage to the minister, who also wore a black robe, and stepped down into the tank where I was quickly pushed under cool water and was up again in seconds. I was supposed to be changed, but I was still confused and disoriented from all the changes in my life.

The one event I really enjoyed was going to the Villa of Sweden after church for a really good smorgasbord. This was a sunny place with real Scandinavian food, tablecloths and a wide variety of little breads with fish, cheese, cucumber, salads, meats and vegetables spread out down a long buffet table. There was a small amount of sweets, usually berries with cream or small cakes. There were no Finnish places, so Swedish and German places had to do. Much later I found out that Sweden had controlled Finland from the 1200s to the 1800s, taking wealth and not allowing the Finns to get an education, speak their own language and determine their own lives. But for the moment I was very happy with the smorgasbord and spending time with my mother in a nice place. I felt like we were a mother and daughter doing something enjoyable.

While I did not see my classmates after school, I met a Jewish girl named Sherry who lived with her mother and older sister in an apartment across the courtyard. We had talked about having a sock hop in a local recreation hall without any money or contacts. We both wanted better lives and to have some fun. I looked into this, but had no idea how to make it happen. Her mother and sister were thin and seemed anxious, while Sherry had a Mona Lisa smile and was calm. Her mother had a breakdown and they had to move so I lost another friend.

I was depressed as I hated this place and was still angry at my mother for putting me through the Boone Iowa experience. I knew I could not confront her about it, but I was at the end of my rope. Why did she send for me? Much later in life she said she was lonely and to meet her needs I was uprooted again. My mother made arrangements for me to talk to a Christian counselor at the church. I was even angrier. Why didn't she go to counseling about her poor decisions? I went to the meeting but refused to talk to the man. There was too much and I didn't trust him.

Boone Iowa had been good for me in the sense that is gave me a strict routine—something I had never had before. The routine was simple and repetitive, which turns out to be a good remedy for traumatic chaotic, demoralizing and disorganizing experiences. It gave a sense of order in my life and gave me some confidence. I wasn't peeing on the floor or watching the "L" train coming at me. It was boring but predictable and comforting. But I wanted more in life.

My mother worked and I understood she did not think things through very well, protect me or have consideration for my feelings. I think she was impulsive, as she wanted to control the situation and did not want any input, discussion or reflection. The abrupt "kidnapping" had further damaged my trust in her and resulted in amnesia about events leading up to that event. It took decades to recall things and put them into place. The only way I knew where I had been was due to a chance event. In my forties my mother was cleaning out old papers and mailed me my elementary schools report cards. I did not even know she knew I went to school. Using the dates on the cards, I was able to figure out where I had been. The amnesia did not affect my life that much, but it was like an eraser wiped out part of my brain. Now the hole was filled.

One day there appeared a four-foot-high and six-foot-wide pile of clothes in the middle of the living room. I guess my mother had saved them up from previous moves. I invited a friend over, but when she saw the very large pile of clothes she backed out and said "see you later." I did not even think it was weird and did not even look at the clothes. Now I lost another friend who could not take the weirdness of my life and sometimes the weirdness of my behavior. After thinking about all that had happened in the last few years, I decided I had had enough of this chaotic lifestyle and wanted some stability to finish my education. I confronted my mother and told her I had had it with instability and wanted to move back to Evanston and attend Evanston schools until I graduated from high school. I was hoping to go to college, but that seemed like such a big mountain to bring it up. I was calm but firm in my tone of voice.

To my surprise she agreed! I still had to finish the sixth grade in Chicago, my second school in one year, but this gave her time to look for a new place to live and to apply to Evanston Junior High School. I was not sure it was really going to happen, but I was feeling more hopeful. The sixth-grade class was an improvement and we had a fun sock hop at the end of the year. I danced with the Jewish boys, and I think we were all happy the year was over. I don't know where they were going to High School, but I thought they would do fairly well in life as they liked to study.

Sometimes I took a tennis racket and hit a ball on the downstairs wall. The only sound was the ball hitting the dark brick wall and the concrete. I would have liked to play tennis, but you need two people. Sometimes the kids climbed the cement wall into the large cemetery, but they also liked to play with the dead rats in the alley. That was not for me.

The beach was not too far to walk and then swim. The sand was pebbles, which was harder to lie on. I was at the beach with Sherry and a fly was bothering us, so I threw a stone into the air, hit it and it fell to its death! Maybe this was an omen that things were on target! There were piles of broken tomb, stones on the waterfront, as Lake Michigan can have high waves in the winter months. I ran as fast as I could on the tombstones, which meant quick footwork. It was fun to run, as I liked sports. I don't know why they had broken tombstones. One swimming day I was floating in the water staring at the sky and wondering if my life would ever make sense and would I fit in. I did get laryngitis and the doctor had to make a house call and gave me some penicillin. I think my body and mind were tired. Finally my mother said she got permission to return to the Evanston school system, and we would be moving toward the end of summer to another unknown place. We continued to go to the fancy Baptist church and enjoyed the Villa of Sweden smorgasbord, which made life bearable. Our moving date did not coincide with the school starting date, so I had to take the bus into Evanston for a while. My period came, which I was not expecting, and I had an embarrassing accident. Now I was older and ready for a new life with more positive possibilities.

We finally moved to the one-room apartment on Chicago Avenue, which was on the third floor. It had a similar layout with a big room, bathroom, small kitchen and a fairly large walk-in closet. It was on the third floor and it faced west, which meant it was hot during the summer sunset. In the winter the radiator would start banging about five a.m. when the furnace was stoked. It was noisy, but I was able to sleep on a day bed in the comer. On the ground level there were stores such as a Chinese laundry, a diner, an Oriental rug company with excellent rugs and across the street was a big car dealership that had a loudspeaker to call salesmen into the office. There were no bars, as Evanston was "dry," which meant no smelly, smoky bars with problems.

Chicago Avenue was a four-lane road that had trucks, buses, cars and traffic most of the time day or night. We all had a common porch off the kitchen for hand laundry. There were two sets of train tracks for the "L" train and the Chicago and Northwestern commuter and long-distance trains. This was noisy and not a desirable location, but I knew I was going to be in one place for six years, which was heaven after eleven years of moving.

When I entered Nichols Junior High School, I felt more grown up, but I had to work very hard to get caught up to the kids who had been in good schools and in a stable home life for all these years. The school gave us achievement tests, and to my surprise I was put into algebra classes, science and Spanish classes. Now I had to work even harder to catch up.

One day my mother and I were turning into the front door of our apartment building and she stopped and said that I cost too much money and she would only buy me a winter coat, boots and essentials. I was not that surprised, as she rarely bought me things. I took her at her word and decided to look for work as an eleven-year-old. Maybe my father had been paying child support and stopped for some reason. I doubt if my mother or father had any contact. The story about my father dying did not make sense, but many things never made any sense. The $31 a month for the Boone orphanage was a bargain. I was most worried about getting good grades to compete with the other students, and I thought I could handle babysitting on the weekends.

The kids at school had just come from various elementary schools, and this was a new school to them. So I was not at a disadvantage as I usually was as the "new" student. I liked the teachers, especially the art teacher, who dressed all in black with a black beret as he was a "beatnik." I knew about beatniks from meeting Alice who scribbled on her parent's walls. This made me curious and I wanted to do more art work. Most of the male teachers wore suits and ties and the female teachers wore dresses and heels. The kids were fairly friendly and talked openly not like the orphanage kids. But I still had to be secretive about my mother being divorced, my sister living in another state, living in a one-room place over stores and being poor.

I did get some babysitting jobs including one that had a three-year-old and a new baby. I was surprised they would trust me with a new baby, as I knew nothing about caring for a young infant. But it worked out. Then I had money to go to Vogue Fabrics and pick out the pattern and fabric. This took a long time, as I had to calculate the yardage and expense of the fabric. Woolworth's had some fabrics and one I bought for fifty cents a yard in a nice batik design; but when I wore it, the die rubbed off onto my skin. There was a dingy thrift store that did not have much.

My mother continued to do "day work" from an agency that would call for different jobs; but some were ongoing jobs. My mother worked for a woman who had "spoken down" to her was calling, and asked me to tell the woman she was not home. I did not like lying, but did it. She said she was not going to put up with this type of treatment. I thought this was a good idea, but what about the rent and food? The truth is she always paid the bills. One day she turned to me and said we were "white niggers," which meant we were at the bottom of the white social structure. I understood what she meant, as we were poor but we had a clean life style, good values and were law-abiding. It turns out this was the term used for anyone doing menial work, which she was doing. My relatives were miners, which did not require English but it cost my grandfather's life. This term was also used for immigrants such as the Irish, French Canadians, Italians or anyone doing menial work. There was an unusual story about a wealthy British man who went to India and was fascinated by the Indian traditions, food and culture and was not interested in his British upper-class life style and this was unacceptable. He was out of step with his class, and although he was wealthy he was labeled a "white nigger." Now mixing of ethnic groups, cultures and races is more accepted. But there are still many class and racial tensions around the world.

Evanston was an above-average income area, with a middle class and poorer people, which included the black community. Evanston was founded by Methodist ministers who wanted educational institutions like Northwestern University, Garrett Seminary and the National College of Education; and businesses; and this brought up the standard of living. They were also abolitionists who brought slaves and free blacks to town in the 1850s. I walked around the black area around the school and noticed they had ranch houses and two cars parked in the driveway. They seemed to be fairly well off, which to me meant middle class. But there was segregation. Generally people still looked up to English customs even though they were not English. I think it had to do more with class and trying to compete socially but in a subtle and gentle manner.

My mother was getting tired of her menial work and traveling to different homes. If she had been able to finish high school she would have done much better in the work world. But her life as an orphan was hard and limiting. In World War II, she had taken a Red Cross Nursing class and had worked as a physician's assistant in California, when there were many strict requirements. She helped deliver babies and had other skills. She was a hard worker and could be friendly. Eventually, she joined an agency that sent women out to work as private duty nurses, which led to steady all-night work in people's homes. This meant she was in a nice home to spend the night in and I was alone all night, which created some problems. This latest move back to Evanston was an improvement for her and for me. The stability was good for both of us, but it was not ideal.

Because I was happier, I smiled more, and it was easier to get along with the kids. I liked changing classes every hour, as it gave me exposure to different kids. I was actually making some friends, and was interested in student government but too shy to run for office. My grades in seventh grade were above average and I was happy about that. That summer I babysat, went to the beach and actually got invited to two parties. I could take my bike around town, to the lake and back or to the store. I just had to lock it downstairs as it was a busy area. I went to some movies on Saturday when kids would go and matinees were still twenty-five cents. Life was making a serious up-turn. However, I still lacked confidence and was home alone, and my only activity was going to the drugstore a few blocks away. I put on one outfit and then another and was afraid to walk to the comer store. I had to improve my self-esteem. Things were better on the outside but not on the inside. I would watch the car salesmen work, or stand around looking for customers as I did not have regular friends to talk to. I did meet a woman who worked at the Oriental rug store and she was friendly, but of course she was working.

One day my mother got angry as I tried to talk to her, and came rushing out of the kitchen with the table meat grinder and I was really scared and put my hands up to protect myself and she hit my hands pretty hard. She retreated but I had this egg-sized red lump on the side bone of my hand. It felt broken, so I went downstairs to the see the woman and she said she would go with me to the hospital after work. I waited outside and we took the bus to the poor people's clinic in back of the hospital. They X-rayed the hand and said it was OK. They did not ask for a parent or how the injury happened. The woman and I left, and I thanked her for going with me. My mother never asked how I was, where I went or explained why she attacked me. I knew not to ask her as I never knew what response I was going to get. I know her brothers had been pretty rough.

My mother paid for a summer class for girls at the YWCA and we did some ceramics and some other things that I enjoyed. The YMCA had a large pool, so I took some swimming classes, which I enjoyed but the high diving board was my nemesis. I did it once, but never again. I had met a black girl at school and invited her to come to the free swim, as it said you could invite a guest. We arrived and were shuffled into the office while the receptionist disappeared for a few minutes. She came back and said we could not swim. I mentioned I was allowed to bring a guest, as it was on my membership card, and I insisted we swim. She went back to another office, and returned red-faced but she said we could not swim. We went to school together so it never occurred to me that we couldn't swim together. We gave up and walked back to my place. We talked for a while and she went home. This visit resulted in angry notes under the door saying they were going to have us evicted. I was not sure if they could do this, but I was really upset as we had moved so many times and this was our first stable place. When my mother was home, I talked to her about it, and she said that she did not know who did it or what we could do, but it was safer to not bring my friend home. We were poor and not exactly up on our rights, so we gave in. I did go to my friend's house for an overnight sleepover. She had a bedroom with a bunk bed and her older siblings had left the home. Her parents were nice. Her mother was a seamstress and her father worked somewhere. But then we drifted apart but she graduated from college.

Eighth grade started and we knew we had to take the U.S. Government test at the end of the year which was important. I had a science class, and before we got our exams back the teacher asked who they thought had the highest grade. Kids mentioned all the boys. I thought it was one boy but, finally it came to me and he said "yes." I was so amazed and pleased that he would do that for me. Maybe he sensed I was not very self-confident. In Spanish the teacher asked a question and I was too shy to raise my hand and everyone had spoken except me and I gave the right answer. That was amazing, as there were 28 other kids in the class. I felt a bit more confident that I was learning things and could do well. We had classical concerts with Dr. Zipper in the auditorium and I really enjoyed the classical music, and it was not that expensive as we were middle-school students. It was a great program.

Sometimes I would stand out on the wider porch to get fresh air and talked to the boy next door, who was a first-year engineering student at Northwestern University and lived with his mother. He was making a flight stimulator in a church basement he rented and we went to see the tables full of labeled parts. I was amazed at how complicated it was. He was 19 and I was 13, but we could carry on a conversation for quite some time. This was fine, except I took it as company and he took it as something else. My mother was working all night at this point and I didn't see her much, even on weekends. One day he put his hand on my breast and I said "no" and I "could not see him again." He was upset but did not say anything. But after that in the middle of the night he would go to the kitchen window off the porch and try to look in the window. The back door and window were locked, but I could see his shadow like Alfred Hitchcock's introduction to his scary TV show. The front door had 12 small window panes and the small pane near the locking side was cracked, and he would use a nail file to try to push the curtain back to see me sleeping on the old mohair sofa. I never knew when he was coming and I lost a lot of sleep at night and did not know who to talk to. I finally told my mother, but she did not respond, like it was not important. I was afraid to call the police, as then they would know I was home alone and she might get into trouble. I did not feel very powerful. About a month later we were both home during the day time and the Peeping Tom put the nail file into the broken window pane and she was lying on the sofa. He tried to open the front door curtain during daylight hours! She screamed and called the police. The police came and talked to my mother, and his mother but not me. They took him down to the police station and the mother and son moved very quickly. Peeping Toms were not taken very seriously at that time, as "boys will be boys," but now it is seen as a stepping stone to other serious deviant behaviors against girls and women.

My mother was not concerned with my safety and I was really disappointed in her self-centered view of the world. If it impacts her, do something. If it impacts me, it was no problem, like my uncle's visit. The problem was physically solved, but I was still nervous and could not sleep well. I kept waking up to check on the doors. I still do this to this day. I am never relaxed or feel truly safe. After that there was a young adult man at the end of the porch who drove a Mercedes-Benz, which was odd as no one could afford a car. I spoke with him one day and he invited me in his apartment, but I saw liquor on the kitchen table and said "no" and never saw him again. Then there was an article in the newspaper about him committing suicide and being the heir to a rich Eastern family fortune. What a waste of potential. After that I did not talk to older boys, as it was way too risky. I did not see anyone else on the porch to talk to during the daytime.

I took art class with the "beatnik" teacher and enjoyed painting as it was something I could do at home besides homework. I did not want to take Home Economics again, as I knew how to cook and sew. In eighth grade I asked to be put into woodworking shop as in Chicago the boys and girls took the class together. In Evanston it was just for boys, but I insisted and they let me in the class. There was one girl in there that was considered slow. But we all did our own projects and we asked for help when we needed it. I made a plaque for the English teacher, who was exceptional and I wanted to acknowledge him. He was very funny but he had an assistant who stood by him in class and did not seem to do anything. He made English fun, and I presented the plaque to him at the end of the year in front of the class.

There was a negative event in that a friend had left her wallet on her desk. I knew we would see each other at lunch, so I put it on top of my books to return to her. I was confronted by a teacher so I gave the wallet to him. This led to the principle and a teacher opening up my locker and emptying it in front of everyone to see if I had stolen anything else. It seemed punitive to me, as I was not hiding anything. A boy walked by and said "Now what are you up to, Shelton?" We laughed but it was not all that funny to be falsely accused and embarrassed in front of everyone.

Somehow I was becoming more popular and became friends with three girls and I became the fourth one in the clique. It was nice to know who I was doing things with. We would do things on weekends like go to the library to study, go to the soda shop or shop for clothes, but I did not have much money. They also babysat, so we could talk on the phone when the kids were asleep to break up the boredom. Two of them lived in apartment buildings and one in a townhouse. They were not rich like many of the kids. I mentioned the meat grinder incident with my mother, but one girl said her father threw her down the stairs so it was not a big deal. I felt it was important but kept quiet about my feelings. I wanted to talk to the art teacher about what was going on at home, but I could never bring it up. Probably in 1958 there was no procedure for students talking to teachers or I would get my mother into trouble. There were no counselors, but otherwise it was a good school.

I did enter the yearbook cover contest and took second place. I put a lot of work into to it but was happy with some recognition as they posted our artwork in the hall wall with our names. We took the government tests, which required a lot of studying and I did fairly well. When we were close to the final grading period, I got mostly A's, which surprised me, but I had been working hard. I went home and told my mother, and she went into a very negative tirade about she did not have a chance to get an education and did not say one encouraging word about my grades. I was not totally surprised, but I was disappointed that she was not happy for me. I thought she was a bigger person than that. This started a pattern that went on for the rest of my life. She seemed jealous and could not be happy for me. But I was going to continue doing the best I could, as I did not want to be poor all my life, and it was my life.

One day I walked down the back wooden stairs in our building to a narrow sidewalk, and the dirt on the side of the cement was black. The one-foot strip of soil was black with oil as it was next to an auto repair place. Imbedded in the soil were small pieces of broken glass that were sparking in the light. I realized you could find beauty anywhere. While this was pretty, it was not plants, flowers and trees that you could sit near. Natural beauty was important to me. This image stuck with me the rest of my life and directed choices about where to live and how to make things beautiful.

Toward the end of eighth grade, a nerdy boy had a party as his parents were out of town. I liked him but he was thin with glasses and wore adult-type clothes. I was not looking for a boyfriend, but a boy at the party was nice to me and wanted me to sit on the couch and make out. He put the boy who was the host in the closet, so we would have privacy. This was wrong, but I did not object and feel bad about that. But our kissing took two minutes and the boy was released. I usually stood up for the underdog like me and didn't want to be with people who were mean to other people.

At graduation dance a boy walked me from my place to the dance, where the boys and girls spent the evening separated, and he walked me home. But it was a nice gesture on his part. The graduation was a in our auditorium, and afterward I could not find my mother and families were talking in groups and I felt isolated and awkward and just walked home. She claims she was there but I never saw her. The two years in Junior High were very important in shaping me as a serious student, a worker, an amateur artist, and as someone who could have friends and some recognition as a solid person. My mother was gone most of the time and I had activities on weekends. We did not see each other that much except on Sunday, when we went to church and had Sunday dinner together. I feel practical nursing was more rewarding, paid fairly well and she was "taking care of her dying mother." She had her days free until the afternoon. Dealing with thinking, feeling child was too much for her and it was safer for her to avoid the situation. I would have liked a mother, but our place was so small it would have been hard to study and feel at peace. We had a small TV and it would break down, and sometimes she wanted it fixed and I did not, and other times the reverse was true. We both liked to read and I needed to study, so in this sense our lives were similar. But our lives were like passing ships in the night life-style, which had its advantages. Maybe it was the best arrangement for both of us. However, it did not teach me how to be with a family, to communicate with an intimate family member or feel loved. There was so much I needed to learn about life the hard way.

CHAPTER 6

ETHS

The summer was good, as I had some fun and was able to save some money from my 50-cents-an-hour babysitting work. I would go to fancy stores and see what was in style, and then go to Vogue Fabrics. Lucky for me the A-line skirt was easy to sew and I could buy a matching cardigan and a white blouse at the less expensive department store or from the Montgomery Ward's catalog. My friends dressed simply and there was not a big concern about fashion in those days. However, there was a sense of conformity and competition, which is typical in most high schools.

I was surprised at how much the required books were at Chandler's Bookstore store. They were old and marked up but still pricey, and they were only used for one semester or maybe a year. When you returned them you got very little back. This seemed like a racket. My mother helped me buy them. There was a library only two blocks away and I used it a great deal.

Evanston Township High School was started in 1857 as a preparatory school for Northwestern University. In 1883 it was established as a high school for Evanston and a small part of Skokie. Now due to the dramatic increase in the Baby Boomer generation there were 4,000 students and the school was divided into four separate high schools easily named South, North, East, and West Halls, with each having a separate principle and Homeroom directors. The Head Principle usually had a PhD in Education. Many of the teachers had Masters Degrees. There were many facilities there, such as a TV and Radio stations, training shops, sports arenas, and a theater with high-quality sound and seating. One play from our class was put on national TV. The whole campus occupied 65 acres and the football. There were academic, social, accommodation for special conditions, and athletic clubs. The athletic teams were competitive and usually won some state championships.

The buildings were big, with castle-type spires which gave it a college feel and it was big. There was the central building and four connected high schools. It was not college, but it was leading up to college if you wanted and could afford to attend. There were vocational courses, and I did take store management and typing, but did not want to pursue that work. I wanted to be in an academic field, but it was too early to decide.

I was excited about going, but my mother had never gone to high school as she had to drop out after eighth grade to raise her younger siblings. But she sought out a community with good schools, and this school was highly rated in the United States. Being part of the Baby Boomer generation created optimism that things were possible. I did not have a close family, but I was a part of something that was going to make a difference. Of course, my mother's generation went through the hardships of immigration, two wars and the Great Depression, which was very challenging. The advantage of having parents who were strong, determined and had wisdom about life was very influential to the Baby Boomers. I admired my mother's determination to have a better life and overcome some obstacles, but she still had scars.

At age 13 I got off to a good start and enjoyed the usual basic courses. In European History the instructor dwelled on the Russian Revolution and the struggles of the Proletariat class. This fit in with Finland's 500- to 600-year struggle with Sweden's control and domination. The Bolshevik Revolution was the reason the Finns could become a country in 1917, as Russia was struggling. I was disappointed that the monarchy was replaced by bureaucracy and military control. I felt I was forming some of my ideas and identity. I wrote a paper on Mozart and how his operas were a statement of support for the underclass, not the upper class that paid for them. He was surprised but approved it. This school was becoming interesting to me; however, it was a challenge, as it was much bigger and more competitive than anything I had encountered before.

On the other hand, I was a part of the four-girl clique which wanted to join the Young Republican Club, and I wanted to be accepted so I joined, too. I was elected Secretary and had a sense of belonging to some group. One day we had a joint meeting with the New Trier High School group and their President Jay was at this meeting. I don't know how we connected. He said there was a Christmas party, but I would be young for that, but we did connect. Since I was home alone, this filled a big gap in my social life. At first we did they were typical teenage things that were fun. My mother was very unhappy about this, but she was not there and was not involved in my life. Jay had good manners, was soft-spoken and comforting. I trusted him. We were both somewhat shy but wanting to get good grades and go somewhere in life. His parents lived in a north farther suburb. His parents had already bought him a new convertible when he was 16 and probably had an idea about where he was going to college. I remember Jay's parents took us to their small country club and I thought the appetizer buffet was the whole dinner and piled food high on my plate; they stared a bit but then announced that dinner was served! I was so surprised that people had so much food, and I was embarrassed, but I was learning. So this was a huge change in my life to see how these people lived.

On weekends I would get babysitting jobs, saving up money and making clothes and studying. The presidential election in November 1960 was with Richard Nixon running against John F. Kennedy, and I was supposed to be passing out literature for Nixon. As I walked around neighborhoods, I noticed how Kennedy looked and started listening to his platform. I liked it better, but did not want to tell my friends or Jay. I was not voting for eight years so it did not make much difference. Jay took me to downtown Chicago to the Republican convention. I wore a dress and low heels and he wore a suit and tie so we blended in the crowd. I noticed how the grow-ups were acting as though it was a big party and drinking, which I did not like. After the election my friends and I were not very active, but Jay and I still saw each other occasionally. I went to his high school senior prom as he was graduating in 1961. During the summer he would go on a big vacation while I worked or went to the beach. My freshman year was a success in many ways, as I was introduced to a whole new world of academic challenge and socially things were working out. I made a model Cadillac like Jay's parents and my mother was angry and said we were Democrats. I did not want to be rich, as that seemed out of the question, but I did enjoy making the model. Later, however, she became more conservative and I became more left-leaning. I was sad to me that we could not share a party for the working person, as she worked so hard for a living. She became even more religious and I was not.

My sophomore year I was 14 and Jay went off to a big private men's university in Indiana, which was not far, but our worlds were very far apart. I did go down for a homecoming dance and wore a dress I had bought at the thrift store which I made more modest. I borrowed my mother's pantyhose that were the wrong color, and tried to act like I fit in with a college crowd. This was a big stretch for me. Jay did not seem to notice, and I stayed with his buddies' girlfriends and returned home. This was very exciting to me, as it was a big event on campus. I had a secret life, as I did not share my activities with kids at high school. I was naturally quiet, had to keep secrets and only talked about the high school classes and activities.

The clique had been fun, but we ran into a big problem that had a big impact on me. I had befriended a girl named Rebecca, and her father was a guest professor at Northwestern University. The clique noticed this and said that I had to give her up because she was Jewish. I thought she was intelligent and very worldly-wise as her family traveled and her grandfather had been on the Supreme Court. I thought they were kidding, but they were not. I said I was not giving up her friendship. They said I could not be friends with them. I know two of them had parents from Austria and maybe they were conservative Republicans. The third one was half Jewish and half something else. Decades later I found out I was part Jewish on my father's side. I guess I did not realize how much anti-Semitism there was in some parts of the community. The friends I had depended on abandoned me. Of course, I could have dropped Rebecca as a friend but that was not like me. I was adrift and depressed about the loss. Rebecca and I continued to be friends, but her father announced that he was going to teach at Cornell in New York, so they had to move. I was insecure, but I visited them in Ithaca New York that summer. Jay drove me to Ohio and then I took the train to New York. Traveling made my mother and my life more separate, as I was getting more independent in a larger world.

In English class I met Marty, who was very sensitive, artistic tall boy and we became friends. Marty's world was almost totally about his family, and he did not do typical teenage thing except sports. His situation was an extreme opposite as I hardly saw my mother except on Sunday when we went to church and had dinner together. I went to Marty's house for dinner, and it was nice to be with a family. His mother was artistic and very interesting. His father taught at Northwestern University, and I was a bit intimidated as he was well-known. Marty, his parents and I went downtown to a big movie theater and saw "To Kill a Mockingbird" with Gregory Peck as a southern lawyer who was defending a black man falsely accused of raping a white girl. It was moving, but it was hard for me to summarize what it meant. Roger Ebert gave it two and a half stars and called it a wishful rewrite of 1932 Alabama by 1960s liberals. I know Marty's parents really liked it. History gets rewritten all the time depending on the politics of the time. People change their minds and the media changes what they cover. But this was a nice evening out with a family that knew their way around in the world.

That Christmas Jay always did something nice when we were dating and made it special. In Junior High my mother said she did not want to celebrate Christmas as she worked on holidays for extra money and the tree was a hassle. I can understand as we did not have a car to transport the tree, but what I wanted was for her to spend some time with me.

I enjoyed skating on the pond near Lake Michigan, but the problem was the wind would come off the lake and make ripples on the ice which were hard

E T H S

to skate on. There was a warming stove in the change house which could warm you up. I loved the whole winter scene.

In 1962 I turned 15 and went down to Jay's college at different time for dances, and at Christmas he gave me a very nice present his father helped him pick out. I was moved, as my mother only had an orange when she was a child, so she was not used to thinking of presents. We did go to Christmas Eve service, which I liked because they had candles on the end of the pews, which was lovely. I went over to Jay's family as my mother worked on Christmas, and I know one year they had pheasant that his father had killed by hunting. The only problem was that there was buckshot in the meat. It was a very nice dinner and family. Jay had a sister in California from the father's first marriage, but they rarely saw her.

Jay let me drive his convertible with the top up, but the stick shift was hard on the ice- and snow-covered roads. I turned a comer and the car slid into a couple's front yard. The man sitting in front of the picture window was reading the Sunday paper, which he dropped on the floor as a car was coming towards him. But Jay quickly said put it in reverse, which I did, and I drove away. The only damage to the yard was tire tracks on their front lawn. I appreciated Jay taking a risk with me. A year and a half later, I was 16 and could take the high school driver education class, but by then I was an experienced driver.

In the spring there was a dance at Jay's university that was very special and I felt very close to him. That summer Jay took my mother and me on two trips, which was amazing as we never, had a car, so this was expanding our world quite a bit. One time we went to Wisconsin near the Dells, which had Indian huts with elderly native women weaving baskets. We rented cabins and there was a large stuffed bear. The other trip was to the Indiana Sand Dunes, which are very large dunes across the lake from Chicago. I think my mother enjoyed the trips despite the fact that she was afraid of travel for leisure, but she was not afraid of moving to other places to live. I didn't mind going out with a chaperone and I appreciated Jay taking us to nature places.

In 1964 after high school graduation, my mother did take me to a Youth for Christ summer rally, in Indiana, as we could take a bus. I have a memory of Jay loaning me a machete to bring along. Instead of going to a meeting under a tent I decided to walk around a lake and cut vegetation with the machete. I had seen people on television going through jungle vegetation, and I thought it would be an adventure. The Youth for Christ wanted young ladies to wear a dress, so I looked a bit weird with a machete. However, I came to a swamp and there was a gap to the other side of the lake. I was standing there pondering my options and whether to swim across when a man showed up with a canoe. The man in a canoe offered to take me across. He did not flinch at my big knife and dropped me off on the other side. I made it safely back to our cabin without any incident or being arrested. I did go to some meetings so my mother would not be disappointed, but her efforts to convert were again dashed. She felt that being a Christian was the only happy solution to life, but it didn't seem to make her happy. She still mourned her mother's death, which she blamed on her father. She never got over it or tried other solutions. When she lived in Detroit as young woman, she went to big-tent revivals, which were a big breakthrough from the drudgery of the farm. She was reliving her past and saying it was for me. This was part of the Billy Graham organization and it was for her, however it was a trip together.

My junior year, I was getting more serious about my life and tried to get better-paying jobs such as being a waitress in a soda shop. When I placed an order I was expected to yell the order to the cook. I was too shy to yell. It seemed undignified, so I was fired. My cousin Carole, Aunt Etna's daughter, came down for the summer to work as an au pair in the wealthier suburbs. She and I had some time together walking on the beach and talking. She said coming to the Chicago area and working was a big step for her. She said the experience and money was a big help for her. She and her younger brother eventually went to Northern Technical University in the Upper Peninsula, where they graduated and moved down toward Detroit. Many Finnish people found work and got their start in Detroit. I was glad to see her.

Aunt Ani, who had been married to Erni, came to stay with us. She had been released from a mental hospital and she had stayed in our one-room apartment. She slept on the kitchen floor and played solitaire all day. On my 16th birthday I came home from school and my mother and Ani had already eaten. I asked for dinner and my mother threw a dollar bill in my face and said, "If you are so damn hungry go to the store and buy a TV dinner." I had been to a fancy Sweet Sixteen luncheon for a classmate and thought 16 was a special birthday. But my mother started harassing me about her childhood, which she did for the rest of my life. I was crying and Aunt Ani said, "Why are you doing this to Lois?" It slowed my mother down just a bit and I went to the store to get a TV dinner. My mother never answered that question, but it was good for once to have one witness to my home life. Eventually, Aunt Ani found a live-in maid's job, which lasted almost a year before she had another breakdown. I stayed there one night and their dog was happy to have company and my aunt kept the busy family running smoothly.

I had not seen my sister since she was a baby in the crib the day we left. But Jay drove me to Northern Michigan to Aunt Elna's house to meet her when I was 16 and she was 13. It was a bit awkward in that we had been raised in very different places. I think her father said negative things about her birth mother. Jack had married my mother's first cousin for his fourth wife. My mother and cousin got along, but it was awkward with Jack. My mother never said anything negative about her father or my father. Jay also took me up to Aunt Elna's in the winter to ski with my sister and cousins. I was very grateful to him for making this possible for us. When my sister was 15, she came down to work as an au pair as our cousin Carole.

My mother was a starting point for people getting started or restarted in their lives. She even sponsored a Finnish woman for citizenship and introduced her to her husband. She was helpful to people and offered housing, food, and some guidance in finding work. I guess our mother–daughter relationship was more estranged and entangled or I was able to find my own way.

Junior year I also went to college representative meetings, although I felt like an imposter as we had little money. I wanted to hear what they had to offer. The idea of a small college really appealed to me, but they were more expensive. If my classmates could do this I wanted to do it. I had a built-in competitive spirit that I could be as good as they were. I took classes that I thought would help me get into college but was not brave enough to apply for Advanced Placement classes. I took three years of Latin, as I did not want to speak. One Latin teacher, Miss McNally, was very funny and made Latin a joy. We also learned a lot about the history of a ruling society that lost its power for many reasons. This was a big lesson in how and why powers change. Latin helped me understand the roots of English words and politics.

The high school had a full range of art classes, and I took most of them. One of the art teachers divided us into two groups: those who could make it as an artist and those who could not be professional artists. I was in the "could not" group, but I thought that was realistic. However, in the 1962 yearbook there was a full-page photograph of me making a ceramic piece. I also liked design and painting. The Chicago Art Institute is an excellent art museum and I was able to go there once and see the paintings we covered in Art History. I really was awed by the impressionists and surrealists.

The school had the Girls Club, which many girls belonged to, but I took a big risk and ran for a board position. I was terrified and there would be a lot of competition in South Hall. The day of the winner's announcement we were lined up in Homeroom and I was one of those who were elected. I was so shocked I called my mother to tell her. I cried I was so happy. I was on the board for two years and we planned dances and other events, but it was just good to be on a committee of girls who were organizing things. I was the Vice President of Advertising, and I don't think I did a good job, but it gave me more experience in being a leader.

My friend Ali and I were in a YMCA teen group for girls that provided an opportunity to socialize and activities I would not be able to do otherwise, such as skiing. We had a pizza party to raise money for charity. The senior year

I made a yearbook with a group photo and had them do a self-sketch and sign their name. The leader was a positive role model for us.

Jay was still at college and I was in class when I was called out of class to get a phone call, which was strange. I went into the Assistant Principal's office and it was Jay, and he just wanted to talk! I tried to act calm, but after I hung up the Assistant Principal said "This was not an emergency!" I was embarrassed and told the truth, that it was my boyfriend just wanting to say hello. I was not sure why Jay would lie, as he could have called me at home in the evening. My mother had said she felt he was dishonest and I took her advice into consideration, but I was in love with him. One weekend he told me that he was part of the FBI junior program and we were going to go to a John Birch Society meeting. I agreed, as I will try many things once. They showed a film about the "Free Speech" movement in Berkeley, California. The police were dragging protestors downstairs to remove them from university buildings. I was neutral in my opinion as I did not know much about the reason for the demonstrations. The meeting was something to do with Jay and I was always interested in the things we did together.

When he came home for Christmas break, we went ice skating with a couple of his friend and they had drinks. I was just turning sixteen, so I did not. He gave me very nice Christmas presents, which his father again helped him buy, and I really appreciated the thoughtfulness. We had gone out to dinner in nice places including the opening of O'Hare Airport's new restaurant. One time we went to the Kungsholm Restaurant that had a large curved staircase, and I felt like royalty with my prince. It was fun to get dressed up with Jay and do something that was very new to me. We even went to a nightclub and ordered soda while watching a famous performer. We looked and acted older than the average teenager. He was older, and I had been through a lot in my young years.

In the spring Jay took me to the Department of Motor Vehicles to take the driver's test. I passed on my second try. His parent's large Cadillac was hard to park between the cones. It was these very important mile stones that made me confuse Jay with a father. He was my boyfriend, but he was so helpful to me and acted more mature than the average teenage boy. Never having had a father, I think I was confused about father, boyfriend or husband roles. I had seen women get shabby treatment while I was babysitting and I was not sure that marriage was a good option.

That summer as a 16-year-old I was able to get a job with my Social Security Card at a nylon stocking shop downtown. I dressed up to be respectable and tried to be professional. There was a middle-aged woman that worked as an acting boss and we got along well. A Navy man from Great Lakes Naval Base came in and ordered nylons for himself. I was not used to this, and went in the back to laugh and the older woman joined me. We regrouped and went back to serve him. One of our teachers was gay but I did not know they wore nylons. There is so much to learn about people in the world. Some women were very picky about which nylons they wanted, so it was an education in how to deal with the public. I made $1.35 an hour, and our pay was in cash in a very small envelope, which was appropriate for our pay. But the average hourly wage was $1.25 in 1963, so I was actually making more than adults who had to pay for housing and supporting families. I was working part-time and trying to get to college.

There was time for beach lounging, and the transistor radio was a big item. Jay gave me a squirrel hide that was big enough to put the radio on to keep the sand out. Again, we had some nice times and he was going into his sophomore year at college while was I going into my senior year in high school. So junior year I had gained more confidence but was still frightened to be around a crowd and had never really regained a steady group of friends at school. Just a few individuals I would talk to once in a while. I was still somewhat insecure and lonely.

I was on the Honor Roll and I qualified for the Honors Study Hall, which meant you could decide how to spend your time. Marty had been on the basketball team, as he was six feet four inches and liked the game. Somehow he had mononucleosis and missed quite a bit of time recovering. I saw some of his games but also liked to see gymnastics and football games. Our football team was always winning, which I knew was not the norm in life. The Homecoming dance was good and I admired the homecoming queens as they seemed so lovely and poised. The advanced placement students seemed so confident, and were deciding where they were going to college, or their parents had already made that decision for them. It was becoming clear that I had to make some decisions, but I was not very optimistic. I took typing and that was the only "D" I ever got, and I decided I did not want to be a secretary or a file clerk. I wanted more out of life.

Swimming the last class period, my hair did not dry and I liked to walk home after school as it was a break from school and homework. Sometimes Ali would walk with me, as she and her parents lived in an apartment building downtown, and then I would continue to Chicago Avenue. However, I got pneumonia and was very ill. I was coughing and it was hard to get my breath. One day I fell down on the carpet at home as I was having trouble breathing, and my mother said "Get up or I will kick you in the ribs!" So I quickly got up and called a friend, whose mother took me to the emergency room. I was admitted and put in the isolation ward. This was OK, except being on the "poor folks" program, a doctor and interns would come to look at my chest. I was embarrassed but felt I had to consent to this exam. Finally, I was stable enough that I could be discharged and Jay came with my mother and drove us home. I coughed for six months afterward and was embarrassed to leave class to cough. In the morning when I walked in the winter to the school bus, my nose would freeze shut as a scarf over my face did not protect my air intake. Pneumonia and scarlet fever were my biggest illnesses, as I was usually healthy.

That fall Jay had me over as his parents were out of town and we had our first sexual encounter. I was totally inexperienced, as we had just made out before. This was a good experience as I loved him, but I did not know about birth control and neither did he. When my period was late I was very upset, as I wanted to go to college. Abortion was illegal. He was Catholic and I did not know what to do. I took some quinine. I read my mother's books on the subject. Jay and I looked at rings and I took a class on becoming Catholic. This was devastating to me, and I was determined we were not going to have sex again unless something really changed. Disappearing to have a baby for adoption was not something I would do. I did not want a back-alley abortion. Abortion was legal in England, China and other countries but not the United States. In China they were 35 cents and took 15 minutes. The crisis resolved, but this was the turning point in our relationship. I wanted to be with him, but we did not seem to be able to have a good conversation about this problem. In the past I had not been able to tell him about what was going on at home. Or if I tried, it did not seem to go anywhere. I only told one girlfriend and she was supportive but did not know what to do about it.

Another girl who lived with her wealthy family had a drinking problem. Her parents would go away to Europe and leave her alone with a stocked liquor cabinet. She confided in me but I knew very little about drinking and did not know what to say to her. I felt bad. Another girl had been raped by some football players, but it was never talked about openly as she did not want it revealed, as the victims were often blamed for the assault.

Later, I had football players come to my door as there was the Chinese laundry down the street and their house had a red light, which was part of their religion. I opened the door and they said they saw the red light. I said I was busy and was able to lock the door. I felt because we were poor, they thought it was OK to try to take advantage of me. Another boy was drinking and driving and a passenger was killed when he struck an "L" cement piling.

There were some important things happening to teenagers, but no real place to find information or to get help without parental involvement. Parental involvement is good if it is helpful. In my mother's case, it would be sketchy. At the end of senior year the homeroom instructor told us all to stand up and then told 20 to 50 kids to sit down, and that this is how many die in traffic accidents, heart attacks, cancer and so on. It was a good lesson in the fragility of life. The summer of senior year, Jay had taken my mother and me to a college in southern Wisconsin, which was a nice gesture, but the small college was not affordable and I don't think he understood how poor we were. I was beginning to worry about getting into college.

Then an event happened that changed the direction of my life. I took a chemistry class and during an exam I got a bloody nose that was going to drip onto the test, so I went to the girl's room. I was finally able to get the blood to stop and reentered the classroom to finish the exam. Later I was referred to a counselor, as the teacher thought I might be cheating. This was upsetting, but I was happy to talk to the counselor as I needed help. He understood about the nose bleed, and since my grades were good he suggested applying to the very large University of Illinois in Champagne-Urbana. The tuition was only $435 a semester, but it did not include living expenses or books. They wanted us to get a birth certificate, my parents' divorce papers, and transcripts and take the ACT test. I had lived in Illinois for 13 years and I never met my father. My mother had to write to California for papers and I had to study for the ACT test. This seemed like a lot to ask, but my mother came through for me and she was willing to pay the tuition. I did well on the ACT, with a lower score in English, which was always my hardest subject, I think because I was isolated and did not have people to talk to growing up, had gone to seven schools before entering high school, and had a lot of emotional trauma that impacted my brain development and thought processes. But nonetheless I was accepted at the University and was so happy to have some avenue of hope for my life. I was also frightened by the fact that my entrance happened because of a nose bleed. I felt like I had little control over my life and I was hanging by a thread. I think the counselor referred me for a scholarship because I was one of only eight kids on the stage on awards day. Mine was probably based on poverty, but it was some badly needed encouragement. I was grateful to be with kids who had many advantages in life, but I had l to put in the time and effort to be prepared for life. There was a small article in the newspaper and I was very happy and grateful to the counselor who helped me.

We had a small senior class demonstration and some dressed like their interpretation of a "beatnik/hippie" dress. I wore a bright-flowered A-line dress and sprayed my hair gray. We pounded on lockers and just made a lot of noise. It was fun to release tension after four years and final exams. The high school experience was challenging but one of the highlights of my life so far. The Senior Prom's theme was San Francisco, and was done very well with Alcatraz mug shots, the Golden Gate Bridge, China Town and the Henry Mancini band for dancing. I was still upset at Jay for the pregnancy scare and wanted to be with my classmates for the Prom, so I invited Marty to go with me. I felt bad, but Jay was older and not part of this world. I made a light blue linen-lined floor-length dress that only cost me $5 but many hours of work. We had a good time and I wanted to go to some parties, but Marty and his parents were flying to Africa the next morning, so we had to leave early. I was disappointed, but parties where not the most important thing. Getting an education was my number one goal.

My years at ETHS were over, and it was sad as I had so many good experiences there and worked hard. That summer I got a job at Wiebolt's Department Store selling clothes and did some modeling when they had fashion shows. It was fun except I would go swimming before without doing my hair and make-up. They gave me the least attractive clothes, but that was OK with me. I was not into a lot of fuss over my appearance. I knew two girls who were professional models and my mother and I went downtown to a modeling agency. They said I was too short, had not put on much make-up and I had a hard time modeling expressions. It was not to be.

One time Jay came to visit work dressed as a woman with a large scarf over his short hair, dress, low heels and did not fool anyone. The security guard was onto him and he said "hello" and had to run. My supervisor asked if I knew him, which I denied. Another time was after work and it was nice to see him in a relaxed way. He was with a high school friend of his, and she said I had lost weight and looked better. I thought I looked OK and was an average weight. He was starting his senior year at university and I was just starting the 33,000-student University of Illinois. The 1964 election was Vice President Johnson, as President Kennedy was tragically assassinated It was such a horrible event in 1963. It was a big loss for our generation, as we had high hopes for the future. Things had seemed easier before but now we knew tragedy can strike.

Before I left, my mother and I got into an argument and I said, "When I leave I won't come back," and she said "Good, don't come back." Of course I was still dependent on her helping me get through college. I don't think she ever knew how to repair a relationship or make it loving. I was fed up and looking forward to my future. I was used to her hurting remarks but this really cut me in the heart and I felt totally unsupported going off to a strange new experience.

CHAPTER 7

U of I Champaign-Urbana

While I was relieved to have made it to the University of Illinois by a nose bleed, it was not a great experience. Knowing I needed a smaller college and Champagne-Urbana had 33,000 students, which was the opposite extreme, I felt lost. It did not help that my mother had said to leave and don't come back! But she had abandoned me, so it might not be a bluff and I was very hurt as I approached one of the biggest challenges of my life. My mother had an eighth-grade education, so I was the first to graduate from high school and there was no model for going to college. Due to the Civil Rights Movement there were some black students who got tuition if their grades continued to be good. I talked to some and they said they did not want to be "patronized." I said I would love to be patronized, I was glad they got some help, but poverty comes in all colors.

The eleven-story dorm was full of girls who had never been away from home and were excited about socializing and experiencing too much freedom. To make matters worse, I was in a three-person room and I was used to being alone all the time. One girl from New York was brash and the other a timid girl who followed her around like a young child. Had she no back bone? But it was two against one, so I had to play my cards right. It was miserable.

Registration was in the Quad, and there were tables with long lines of Baby Boomers and overworked counselors. Since I had taken three years of Latin, they suggested I take a proficiency test. That worked because I was required to take only one semester of fourth-year Latin to meet my two-year language requirement. However, my English proficiency test put me into the remedial class with football players and foreign students. English was my hardest subject, and this was embarrassing. My grandparents never learned to speak English, and my mother had to learn English when she went to first grade. She had a strong Finnish accent, and people constantly asked her "What country are you from?" The angry reply was "Michigan." Many immigrants do not learn English and rely on their adult children or younger relatives to negotiate the outside world. I managed to finally figure out the other required classes but it was stressful. The roommates were so noisy that I had to walk to the library to study, which took time. It was handy, as I took books from the library or the bookstore for the semester as I could not afford to buy them. I returned them at the end of the semester.

The dorm included food and I had a job taking in trays as they came back with disgusting slop on them. We sorted the sticky smelly food into the trash and all over my uniform. Then I had to dress and rush to classes, which were spread out all over a very large campus. Some of the girls were going to rush sororities, but this was never in my cards and I objected to the blatant separation of classes. My mom or dad was a Zappy, Delta Tippy. I was part of the underclass and we couldn't afford it or have Greek letters. I was miserable the first semester.

Jay hitchhiked all the way from his Indiana private University and my friend Marty came one time, but I was so depressed that their visits did not cheer me up. I signed up for counseling, which was with an older lady from the education department. It someone to talk to, but I was seeing gray, not even colors, in my mind. I endured and passed the remedial English class. The fourth-year Latin class was not that hard, but the teacher was archaic. He wanted me to wear a skirt with Arctic air blasting the prairie. I wore pants and as the only woman in the class the instructor singled me out to stand up and admonished me for not wearing a skirt! The boys were silent and I just took it and sat down. But I passed and that freed me to take other classes that

I really wanted to take. My psychology major was considered science, and it was a Behaviorist school. Meaning rats ran mazes, there were stimulus-response studies and hypotheses that had to be proved. It turned out later I loved demographics, philosophy and geology, too. Basically I loved learning anything new to me.

At Thanksgiving break I went home with Ali but my mother called and said I needed to come home. I left, as Ali's parents had plans. My mother just said "don't be silly" about my efforts to avoid her. It was true I still was not independent, but that does not mean my feelings were not important. It was a bad feeling to be disregarded and not taking seriously as a person most of my life. It was hard enough being a young woman and judged on your looks.

At Christmas break I was happy to see Jay and his family, but had to study as we had final exams when we returned to campus. Toward the end of the first semester there was an increase in tension with my threesome dorm room. I found a woman who had a double room and needed a roommate. I was really looking forward to having a better living situation. Life was better with Mary and we had some fun. She had grown up in Wheaton, which was my mother's second choice, but I was so glad she chose Evanston. Mary had an embarrassing experience with a date. I had avoided beer in high school and did not intend to drink any in college. Besides, I was still with Jay even though those ties were weakened with the pregnancy scare my senior year. I just wanted to avoid sex all together. I did meet a German-American farmer who wanted to go to church. He showed up in a suit and tie and I had a dress and low heels on and we went to the local Methodist church. I decided since I did not live with my mother, I did not have to go to church. I found out that Eugene's farming family did not mean they were poor like my relatives. They had large quantities of land and were quite well off. He had a very confident air about him like most boys, but he was not in a hurry to date anyone or decide his future. I had Jay, which was familiar and I still loved him, but did not know what to do with our relationship. It was just hard. The year went on and I did pass all my classes with a great deal of stress. It was almost impossible to find a Teaching Assistant, let alone an instructor. I was shocked to find out that 25 percent of the freshman class flunked out. I did not flunk out, but the administration thought my GPA wasn't strong enough and I should go to another college for my sophomore year and bring my grades, up. In high school I was an Honor Roll student in a competitive school, so this was a big disappointment to me. I wanted to succeed, so whatever they said I should do, I would do.

Jay graduated from college and I went down with his parents and older sister from California to attend his graduation. He was making an easy transition to law school and I bought him a Law Dictionary to help him get started. He could afford books but I wanted to help him.

Evanston had a two-year college that I could walk to, which meant living with my mother again and attending Kendall College. She paid for the tuition. I was very happy to be in a smaller school as the students were serious and there was no dorm. Kendall College had been set up in the 1890s to educate working students like me. The founding fathers had a vision to help lower-income students. Students worked hard and could talk to the instructors. I took many classes, as my interests were diverse and I needed to get the basic courses out of the way. My grades were good and I was a much happier person.

I had worked over the summer and Jay was home part of the time as he traveled to Europe or fishing trips up north with buddies. I wanted to be with him and I was afraid to be with him. He started law school and kept sending me special-delivery letters. The special delivery man was happy to see an attractive co-ed on his route and we started talking. I ended up not only going out with him but we had a brief torrid affair. He had friends who were making racing cars, which I found refreshing. At Christmas I told Jay about this, and he was understandably very hurt and broke off the five-year relationship and I did not see him for years. I don't know why I did such an impulsive thing, as it was not like me, and my priority was school. I was very hurt and lost, as Jay had been my focus for so many years when I was young. Since I never had a father and he was older, I think I was rebelling against my father figure. I just wish I had the skills to talk to him or he had the skills to talk to me. He was one of the best things that had ever happened to me in my life. I was so confused about the role of men in my life. I wish things had turned out differently, but I was not getting married young or having children until my education was completed. Jay had Law School, and that was the most important thing to him. We had been serious students and we had chosen similar but separate paths in life.

When I broke up with the mail man, he was very angry and threatened to kill me. He had a limousine business on the side and was threatening to run me over when I least expected it. I lived on a busy street so this was a possibility. Things blew over and I was able to complete my studies with much-improved grades. To my surprise I met all the requirements for an AA degree. Jay, my aunt Ani, my sister and mother came to my graduation so it was like having a family, which had never before happened to me. I think Jay was just being nice as I went to his graduation. We actually took some photos of the event and it was a very upbeat day.

After reapplying I was very nervous about the University of Illinois taking me back to complete my Bachelor's degree. They have a huge bureaucracy and a man agreed to drive me down to talk to the registrar's office in person. The registrar's office said it was just a "joy ride." I was embarrassed, as I was very nervous that I was lost in the shuffle of thousands of students, but I was accepted back. I never expected things to work out for me. I thought the cards were stacked against my mother and me and we were the underclass. We were ants in a world of anteaters.

Mary, my roommate, had found a situation that was a big improvement over the dorms. Europa House was a new place with two-bedroom apartments for four girls. You could pay extra for a bus trip to Europe upon graduation. The kitchen allowed girls to pay for their own food, which saved a lot of money. Mary and the other two girls were nice, but I was trying to keep up my school work and was again going into another depression and made a suicide gesture. I took a dull knife which left a skin burn on my neck. I wore a turtleneck sweater to cover up the burn, but the weather turned warm and people asked me why I wearing a sweater. I avoided their questions and did not feel comfortable talking to my roommates. I missed Jay but I knew it was time for us to part.

I had dated a Jewish man who was a genius. He could go to two classes and he would get an A. He needed to be in an advanced learning situation while I was trying to keep my grades up. During a school spring break we went to visit his parents, who lived in a high-rise apartment on the Gold Coast in Chicago near the Lake. His parents were Holocaust survivors and they were so depressed they barely spoke. The apartment was in a nice area, but it had no hint of joy inside. I was shocked by the bleakness and this made my mother look lively. We did not date long, but I later learned he committed suicide and I understood what he must have been going through. He needed to be in a challenging situation, have some therapy and have some input from his parents. It was a sad lesson in intergenerational trauma and Holocaust survivors. He was isolated.

The other problem was getting steady work and buying food. I would collect glass "pop" bottles and exchange for some money at the liquor store. My budget was five dollars a week for food, but I was not eating well. Finally, I went to the Dean of Women and said I was pregnant and needed money for nourishment. I am a terrible liar and she gave me fifty dollars, which helped me eat for almost two months. I felt my mother was living up to her end of the bargain to pay my tuition and I should keep mine to buy books and food. She probably would have helped me out, but I was not used to turning to her for help. More currently there are food banks for college students and other aid to keep them in college.

I was withdrawn and barely social, so the girls in my apartment did not relate to me. I understood this, but there was not much understanding of depression nor did I not ask for help. Mary had met an engineering student and I dated his roommate mainly to be near people. This was sort of pathetic but I was pretty passive. I did not have many clothes, so I borrowed Mary's, which was upsetting to her and I don't blame her. The current roommates were getting their MRS degree while I was trying to survive and graduate. They said get married now or never.

The next semester I moved into an apartment with three other girls including a German girl who was angry. I had not done the dishes and she put them all in my bed. She had been abused by her parents when she was a child and was upset. It was OK and I tried to study and keep up the housework to calm her down.

That summer I was able to get a job at AAA near my mother's, planning trips for members. I had not been too many places, so I had to look them up before I mapped them out. One person called and wanted to drive the Pan-American Highway, and I said "sure" but it had not been completed yet, so I had to tell them about my mistake. One elderly woman had lost much of her nose from sun damage, which was a good lesson in being more careful of sun exposure. I had spent years at the beach. I enjoyed the job and the people as it gave me a sense of what it might be like to drive in a car and see the United States.

I ran into a high school classmate who lived near the lake and had a small sailboat. It was a diversion for me, and he was a writer, which was interesting. Later I went to his college campus and found out in front of people he had many women he was going "steady" with, and they laughed at me. My self-esteem was pretty low at that point and this was driving it lower.

My senior year I had an apartment with more strangers, which was alright as I just wanted to study. I had taken many of the required courses and was adding a teaching certificate to increase my employability. I had really enjoyed philosophy courses, but they would not help me find work. Toward the end of my senior year I was dating a man who was getting a PhD in psychology, and we went to some faculty parties. I could see that it was a male group. I was intimidated but it was an eye opener as to whether or not I wanted a PhD. I think the man I was dating had questions himself in academia as he was a very sensitive man.

Returning to counseling, I met with a jolly older man who thought I was very funny He was nice but not deep. I had to hide my feelings, as my mother would trample all over them and I did not have good role models for openness. I enjoyed seeing him but it just cheered me up a bit. Meanwhile my Aunt Ani died in a mental institution of pneumonia as she seemed vulnerable to getting sick. I was home on Spring break and my mother took the call and put the phone down and we sat in silence. Aunt Ani had lived with us before she found a live-in job. Her standing up for me meant a great deal to me, as I was always alone. Aunt Ani just said "Lillian, why are you doing this to Lois?" My mother never answered that question. I hid in the bathroom and cried. She never would answer most questions the rest of my life.

I thought I could handle the loss of my aunt, but all my feelings were stuffed in some deep, dark place that came out in the most dramatic way. I had been invited to a weekend lake party at school in Indiana. It was just a way for me to have a much-needed break. We went to a lake and the girls had blankets out and were drinking Southern Comfort, which was made popular by Janis Joplin. I was not used to drinking and the sticky sweet liquor blew the lid off my grief and somehow I ran into the lake supposedly to drown myself. I don't think I was trying to kill myself and I am an excellent swimmer, but it was a gesture of despair. The next thing I knew I was in the sorority house with a powder blue carpet, got sick and went to sleep. I was then transported back to Europe House with much disdain. When I got back to my apartment, my roommate Nancy from New Jersey was playing her guitar. I told her what had happened, and not being a fan of sorority life she broke out into laughter. I was surprised but pleased that she was not trashing me for despicable behavior. I didn't dwell on my Aunt's death and I knuckled down to finish my last full semester and the teaching certificate, which required quite a few classes.

In June, I could not graduate with my class, but my mother had come down. Her second visit in four years. The first visit on Mother's Weekend my mother had to deal with Aunt Ani breaking out some windows in the apartment and calling the police to remove her. The next morning she was able to take the train down to my school. I admired her strength and calm like nothing had happened. This was the second visit, and we sat up on a hill overlooking the flying-saucer-shaped auditorium where commencement was held, and she said "so what was the point?" I thought she meant of getting a bachelor's degree, but years later I thought maybe she meant coming down without a ceremony. Visiting me was not enough of a reason. That is how bad our communication was, and I was so heavy-hearted I could not clarify any meaning.

That summer I rented a room in an apartment with a delightful Jewish couple. The man had thick black hair and beard and had a habit of wearing his partner's feminine pink bathrobe around the house. I thought it was charming. I managed to get through the teaching classes and finish a presentation. I had to go to the office to register for the certificate and I ran into the freshman-year counselor who said "I didn't think you were going to make it." I was offended at her lack of confidence in me, but that was the sad truth, which was that there not much support and it was a miracle I was graduating. I really disliked the large university. There were no work placement programs except in business. One had to leave campus and figure it out on your own. I knew I needed a PhD if was going to climb the academic ladder. After getting my BS degree, a PhD seemed like a huge ladder to climb.

My undergraduate career ended on a positive note in that I finally had time to take a drawing class. The instructor said I had my own "style." For the final exam he said we could go anywhere. I had borrowed a motorcycle and went out to a small water mill that caught my eye. When I motored back to class, they were all inside doing a still life. I missed the message as usual. I got an A and felt it was a very upbeat ending to a dark experience at a big University. My rented room went to the end of the month, so my sister came down and we and another student went to a dance place and had some fun. She had graduated from high school and was living with our mother until she found a job. She had been in a party crowd that had some scrapes with the law and her father contacted my mother and asked if she could come down and my mother agreed. So they had some time living together and my sister said it was fine. My sister later said she left home on her own free will. I did pick her up from jail one time and was never going do that again but she changed her ways. She acted out as a teen I acted out later as I was on a school track.

Europa House was going on the chaperoned European bus trip with the nice house mistress. This did not appeal to me, but I did want to go, but had very little money. I met a woman who was a free spirit from an upper-middle-class home and spoke French and Spanish. I "spoke" Latin. We hit it off and decided to go together. Not knowing how I was going to pull this off, I was in the cafeteria and a man was sitting across from me and was telling me about his divorce and how depressed he was. Then he asked me what I was concerned about, and I explained I really wanted to travel but had no funds for the round-trip airplane ticket. To my shock he wrote a check and gave me an address to pay him back. This was a small miracle. Jonna and I agreed to meet in New York and set a date in September at the airport. I was really excited about seeing the world.

CHAPTER 8

Trip to Europe

In September I was able to fly to New York for $20, as the airlines were enticing Baby Boomers to fly. Running down the closing jetway I took a big seat in front not realizing it was first class. No one said anything so I just stayed there until New York. My friend Tony picked me up, as I could stay at his place for a few days before the Lufthansa Airlines flight. He had just graduated from the U of I and was trying to decide whether to establish himself in New York or London. His family was from Bethlehem until the Israelis took over that area and their property. His siblings went to London to study, and his parents to Dearborn, Michigan, where there is a large Arab community. He was able to sublet a rent-controlled apartment near Central Park. So we spent a few days going to museums and taking photos. We visited one of his fellow countrymen, and the apartment had carpeted boxes over room-size carpeting, so you chose which level you wanted to sit upon. They had an intense conversation. They were very involved in the Palestinian movement and conflict with Israel, which is still going on today.

Finally, the day came to meet Jonna at the airport, and I was very excited and nervous about the upcoming adventure with someone I did not know too well. I knew Jonna was from an upper-middle-class family, seemed easy going and was multilingual, which would come in handy for part of the trip. She was much more outgoing and seemed self-confident and was not busy snagging a man. I found her at La Guardia airport and the Lufthansa Airlines area. This was the cheapest possible flight and had an open itinerary, but you had to return in one year. We had no itinerary, but we had a general idea where we wanted to travel. I had moved around a lot, taken trains but I was totally inexperienced when it came to negotiating foreign countries. The passport was fairly easily and I was so excited about seeing the world. Luckily Jonna had more experienced and was flexible. I would find out how flexible later on. I did scrape together $530 in American Express Travelers checks and $65 in cash plus my round-trip air ticket. I don't remember my mother having a reaction to my plans, but I was doing this trip. We were going to use American Express to send and receive mail. This was a valuable service, as you could also make phone calls in case of emergency.

I saw Jonna just had one suitcase. She was a little shorter than my five feet five inches and did not wear make-up but had long blonde hair in a loose pony tail. She was friendly and would smile easily. So we boarded a Lufthansa propeller plane, probably one of the last ones they used. It was a night flight and the little boy behind me kept kicking the seat, so I got little sleep. I think his mother was tired of telling him to stop as he might tantrum. We landed in Luxemburg, which is why it was cheap, and had to find our way to the English Channel ferry as we wanted to start in an English-speaking country. The ferry crossing in the Channel was cold and rough. People were seeking shelter in passageways so we huddled with the masses. This included some Scottish men who were friendly and we exchanged information. We were able to get cheap bed and breakfast in London and explore the old established sights as well as the exuberance of the 1960s youth culture. We shopped at the Marks and Spencer store, where I bought my first bikini bathing suit, as Evanston had not allowed them nor men without shirts. I was getting bold.

There were pubs but they had beer and Scotch, which I did not drink, and no music. They had a ladies entrance so ladies would not be subjected to vulgarities in the Victorian era. We tried it once as an English peculiarity. Jonna knew a boat captain and we stayed there one night. He seemed to drink a lot. England wanted tourists to spend three months and leave and come back, so we plotted a rough itinerary, and after two-and-a-half weeks headed back to the boat to France and Paris. The Left Bank was the place to be, and we found a really run-down place. If you went down a flight of dicey stairs there was a toilet that didn't always work. The Metro workers and the electricity company were on strike, and it was raining so we had no Metro, lights or dryness. We walked in the rain and saw candles in the shop windows, which added a historical feel to the street. We managed to get a boat ride down the Seine River. The French women were nicely dressed women compared to the "hippie" garb in the United States. We saw the Eiffel Tower in passing, but did not go to it, but we did go to the Louvre Museum.

We had planned on eating street food, as the restaurants were pricey, which usually meant eating at crepe stands on the street. We met some Algerian men who said that they could get us a ride through France to Spain. We went to the Arab section farmer's market and were approached by French undercover police who said not to hang out with these men. It turns out they did not have a ride and just wanted attention. After seeing Notre Dame Cathedral, we left Paris and started hitchhiking with a middle-aged man who took us south to the countryside. He then said he would pay for sex. We declined and he promptly put us out on the road. This was our first attempt and only proposition for the rest of the trip together. But we were determined to make it to Spain and we only had 680 more miles to go. The problem was that there was not much vehicle traffic, so we ended up walking quite a bit with no wheels on our suitcases. One young man was quite nice and put our luggage on his bicycle and walked with us for a long time. A woman picked us up and drove us a long distance and she was nicely saying be careful. We were able to take a local bus for part of the journey south. There was no street food in the country, so we mainly survived on sandwiches. As we got further south there was a sea of vineyards and it was grape harvesting season. Some town had long lines or trucks, horse or hand carts or anything that would hold grapes to sell to the crushers. The fields had terra cotta tiles to help keep the moisture in the soil. It was a very rustic and beautiful scene. We did not drink wine so I guess we missed some of the "best" wine at that time. Our travel style was below economy. The farming scenery was good, but walking so far made it harder to enjoy the journey.

We finally found a train that would go south to the Spanish border. We had not eaten, so we bought some ham, bread and cheese to eat on the train and the people were staring at us as though we had a feast. Maybe they were Spanish workers picking the grape harvest. There were some chickens and goats and this was a rural crowd. We decided to be more careful about eating in public places. At the border we had to change trains, as France and Spain had different-sized tracks. Spain was still controlled by the dictator Francisco Franco, which added a note of caution to our travels. The military police were very aggressive and wanted to give us rides on their motorcycles. Their patent leather triangular hats gave them an austere air. Even the bus drivers would make a pass at you if you were alone on the bus. There was a feeling of war in the air and I noticed women would walk with their grandmothers on the street as chaperones. It was nice but maybe a safety necessity.

In Barcelona we were able to see some of the sites and get a cheaper hotel and food. One night we were walking home from dinner when an older man was following us. As he got closer, we would speed up; and if he lagged behind, we would go slower. He was out of breath so we finally ran home. The Antonio Gaudi cathedral was only in the beginning stages, with men carrying stone bricks by hand, and it would take decades to finish. I loved the apartment buildings he designed with the wavy balconies. This was a stark contrast to the rectangular skyscrapers in New York. The afternoon siestas were a big change to U.S, hustle and bustle.

We went down to Valencia and had a room over a bar for 50 cents, but we only stayed one night as it was dirty and the bar was noisy. We then went to Madrid, which was a very somber place without much merriment on the outside. We had to get used to the businesses closing for "siesta." We saw Pablo Picasso's Guernica mural commemorating the Civil War and the bombing of the citizens of a small town. In the subway there were billboards plastered on the wall with the backside of jeans that said "Lois" on the butt. I had never seen anything with my name on it or a symbol of modern times. Jonna's Spanish was good despite the Castilian accent. On Sundays they made donuts in large vats of oil that were very good. We had been traveling for some time and decided to take a break from traveling and go to the island of Majorca. We decided every three months we would take a vacation from our trip.

Before we left from Barcelona we went to a bullfight which was hard to watch, but it was amazing how much the Spanish idolized the matadors. They were pop stars. We noticed an old man and young man sitting behind us and they started talking to us. It turned out the old man was an American, long retired, who traveled, as his wife had died some time ago. The young man was a Canadian who was avoiding the draft by traveling in Europe. He might be there a long time, as the war in Viet Nam was still raging. After dinner we made plans to meet in Genoa, Italy on a certain date after our Majorca trip.

Getting to Majorca was a bit scary in that our plane had an old wooden ladder leaning on the side of an old plane to reach the seating area. We decided to get a rum and Coke drink before we climbed the ladder so we could die happy. We made it and found a small hotel in an olive grove a far walk from the tourist beach area. It was a relaxing time to swim, talk to people and eat some local seafood. However, at night it was a bit scary to walk in the dark in the olive groves to our small hotel. There was a gruff night watchman with a German Sheppard on a chain. We had been together for over a month when Jonna did not come home. I thought this was a one-night stand, but she did not come home for days. I was mortified and frightened that she had been murdered and what would I do? The Spanish police seemed dangerous. We had never discussed men as I never considered this possibility. One night I had dinner with some Scottish tourists and a young man said he would walk me home. We passed the rough-looking night watchman and his chained-up German Sheppard, and I showed him my room with two beds and asked if he could stay as I was afraid. He said his family would be very upset, so we said good night. I had heard something outside the window which reminded me of the peeping Tom in junior high. I turned off the lights and looked out the window and it was the night watchman trying to peer into the window. Now I was really upset with Jonna not telling me where she was.

She did show up, but was unapologetic and seemed to think I was too "square." This was probably true for the times, but we were in a foreign country and I thought we were on this trip together. I felt a loyalty to protect the one I was with; also being a woman in a foreign country, I thought it was risky. The honeymoon was over but we enjoyed the rest of our break from traveling, although I more vigilant now. I was not sure I could trust her.

Finally, we were totally relaxed and on October 30, 1968 we took a boat to Genoa, where Paul and Brian were waiting for us with a rented Mercedes-Benz. Paul was a man in his 80s, a widower who had a career in radio transmission and communications. He had worked with Marconi and Edison, which was living history. Brian was easy-going and amicable and seemed to get along with Paul very well.

I was happy to have other company as I was still a bit angry with Jonna. Paul drove and we took a tour of Florence, La Spuga and then climbed the Leaning Tower in Pisa. At the top were American Mormon missionaries from Utah doing their two-year work assignment. We took a walk up a big hill and we were surprised that Paul could keep up with us 20-year-olds. We spent one night and then proceeded down the scenic coast to Rome. I was not expecting such a nice ride through part of Italy compared to walking through France.

We finally made it to Rome, which is a very big sprawling city with the history I had read about for years in Latin class. We tried to park the car near the St. Regis Hotel where Paul was staying. Jonna and I got out to help squeeze the car into a tight space, which attracted some Italian military who saw blond hair. But we got it parked and went to dinner and our entertainment was watching Italian traffic in a round-about. They had a lot of guts and not too much concern.

Then Paul went to the St. Regis, and I never knew if Paul was taking care of Brian or he had money himself. We needed to find a *pensioni* and it was getting dark. We finally found one and went to sleep. In the morning it was full of tall Somali men in long, brightly printed skirts. They were attending the University there. It was one of the surprises of traveling. We had breakfast with Paul and Brian did some sightseeing for a few days, and then we took a bus down the coast to Naples, which was much rougher. The street boys hanging on the back of trolley cars harassed us. But we found a good pizza and enjoyed what we saw. We encountered two Italian taxi drivers and they wanted us to go to the beach and dance. We went and they had a portable record player and wanted to do the tango. This was not the smartest thing we did, but it was delightful dancing on the beach, and they took us back. The next day we took a bus going east and ended up in a small mountain town. There was nothing to do, so we attempted to play pool after dinner, but this caused a large male gathering so the police said we had to go back to our room. I was wondering what the women were doing at night or in life.

We made it to the port city of Brindisi, which I had studied in Latin as the sailing point for Roman soldiers conquering the Mediterranean. I felt like I was reliving history. When we landed in Greece we mixed up our passports but the authorities didn't bother us. We encountered poverty and people were trying to get us to stay with them for a small fee. We were interested in meeting some Greeks at home, but we did not know how safe it was. We saw men on donkeys and the women walking behind carrying the load. This seemed really unfair. At least put the load on the donkey! We spent the night in Corinth, which was a historic city that had horse-drawn carriages. It had been bombed in the war but parts had been rebuilt.

We took another bus to Athens and reached the American Express office in the dark. American Express was our connection to the United States. I got a letter from my mother with $20 in it, which I greatly appreciated, and some letters from a friend back home. I was sitting on my suitcase reading a letter when I realized that Jonna was gone! She did it again and I did not know why she could not at least tell me she was leaving. A Greek man came by and saw my forlorn look and asked if I would want to go to a party. I said OK but I needed a place to stay. He knew of one that was 50 cents a night but only had a cold-water pipe for a shower down the hall and a bedroom with a cot. I said that was fine, so I put my suitcase there and met some of his friends, who seemed to be up on the politics of the world. He dropped me off and agreed to meet the next day. The next day we went to the Parthenon, which was being restored, and wandered around Athens, which was his home town. The street food was good and cheap. I was frightened by the idea of being on my own but I was done with Jonna. Her behavior was too erratic and inconsiderate of me. We made it three months together but at least I was more confident.

One day I went alone to the outskirts of Athens and wanted to climb a small mountain. When I reached a plateau to my great surprise it was a village. I proceeded into the village and they were surprised to see an American woman and got the doctor, as he spoke English. They were so happy that Nixon, a Greek, had been elected President of the United States. I understood that pride. I had a skin infection on my hand, and the doctor gave me medicine, which cured it. I think I had picked it up at a cheap hotel in Spain. I also had severe water poisoning from drinking tap water. Low-budget travel has its risks. But this was my lucky day to get help after climbing and seeing a local village and how they lived.

I met a Rhodesian man who was on vacation from being a Captain of mercenary soldiers in Africa. He had wanted to become a lawyer, but the revolution nixed his plans so he chose this well-paying job. He said the men were rough and he did not have much of a social life. He let me use his hot water facilities, as the cold-water pipe was getting old and cold. He was delightful and I felt bad for him and his family living in the wrong place at the wrong time. He wrote to me for a long time about life in the Sahara Desert, but I did not have his address as they were on the move.

I told George that I wanted to go to Crete since I had studied Minoan history. He said that he would help me get a ticket to that side of the island and meet me there in a few days. He spoke Greek but somehow he managed to get me a ticket to the wrong end of Crete. I was on an all-night boat that included a French acting group and they, like most Greeks, thought I was French. Even when they found out I was American they said they wanted me to join their acting group. I was not an actress and was suspicious of their socializing, which might be too loose for me. So we parted ways at the dock and I took a bus to the right side of the island and found an inexpensive room. The next day I set out for the Palace of Knossos and met a man who was educated, spoke English and told me more the history than I had known. It was a fun day. I saw some other sights. Eventually George showed up and was very tired and rented a room in the middle of the day. An old man asked me why I was not with him, and I did not like the implications. George and I had a good meal and spent some time wandering, and he returned to Athens. I had a few days of enjoying the sunny climate and laid-back culture, and then took a boat back to Athens. A man proposed marriage to me after giving me some chocolate and liquor. The sugar made me sick and he got the idea that we would not wed. I felt badly for him as he was desperate to get out of Greece, which did not have much work.

George met me at the boat and said he had a woman friend and I could stay with her for a little while. She lived up in the hills overlooking the city and worked. There was not much transportation, so I did not do much. Somehow I found out where Joana was and she was having a birthday party, so I went. I had a lovely evening with Greeks who know how to party. She was dubbing movies into English and could do different accents. She usually feigned a British accent to be more sophisticated. She thought being an American was too ordinary. She was going to stay in Greece. I had been a to a movie theater and saw Jane Fonda's Barbarella movie, which was considered "porn" in Greece, so the theater was filled with "dirty old men." I would not want to have much to do with the movie scene there. That settled it, I was making plans to leave on my own but before I made plans I got an unexpected invitation.

The Secret Police requested my company at the Police station for interrogation, as the woman I was staying with and George were "radicals." There had been some bombings and they were trying to find out more about the group. I was left-leaning but did not discuss their politics in detail. I acted dumb and they finally got tired and let me go. I felt now was the time to leave Athens and I wanted to take a boat to Brindisi again. Somehow I managed to work this out, and met a Norwegian Canadian named Alex, who was traveling to Norway via Italy, Austria and Germany. We agreed to travel together as I did not want to face Italy alone. Alex was in his twenties, easy-going and smart. We took a bus through the southern part or Italy and started hitchhiking north of Naples after taking a quick look at Pompeii ruins where Mount Vesuvius had smothered the inhabitants. We were able to get a big semi-truck with two bunk beds in the back of the cab. The driver was playing opera and it seemed like a fun ride. Alex got in the back and I was sitting in front when the driver held out a wad of Italian lira. There was great inflation so it took a lot of bills to make a decent sum of money. I said something in English to Alex that we might have a problem. The driver just held it out and I declined, and that was the end of it, but I was getting nervous. Finally, Alex was able to sit in front and I was able to get some sleep in the back. When we reached Milan, the ride ended, and we found a *pensioni* to begin our journey the next day. I like stopping at coffee bars as I could say "latte" and would get steamed milk as I did not drink coffee. It was warm and comforting to me.

There were great mountains and the color of the Italians was getting lighter in complexion, hair and eye color. There was mixing from the middle to the north of Italy. But the tension was very serious. There were men on the Austrian side with signs and Italian men on the south side of the border. We did not understand what was happening but were aware it was not a good situation. We were able to get to Innsbruck and get a nice room in a Tyrolean Inn painted with flowers. We also had a good hearty dinner. The next day I wanted to ski, as it was the site of the Olympics but it was too expensive. We settled on ice skating in the very large Olympic ice rink. Alex and I had spent a lot of our childhoods ice skating. For him it was probably hockey, and for me bumpy ice, but it was a fun day skating together and being off the road.

We were able to get a variety of rides on the fast Autobahn to the slow bakery truck and the driver sipped schnapps liqueur while driving. We made it to Munich and had a night of beer drinking. I did take a tankard home with me. The south of Germany was scenic and seemed peaceful. We finally made it to Frankfurt where they were having an outdoor Christmas fair with food, arts and crafts. It was very colorful and the food was good. This was, however, the end of the road for Alex as he was going to take a boat from Hamburg to Norway. I felt very secure with him and he was a good traveling companion. I was feeling very insecure going on the open road by myself for the first time but I had to make it back to England, which was 285 miles on the open road to the Dover ferry. I don't remember how I got started on the road as I was deeply frightened. I did get rides fairly easily and dropped off in the direction I was going from Frankfurt toward Amsterdam. One man asked how far along I was. What was that? I finally realized that the $3 Greek Fisherman sweater was too big on me and it bulged out in front of my coat so they thought I was pregnant! This came up another time, and I just smiled and did not explain my sweater baby. I had accidentally got the perfect cover to get rides and min-imize unwanted attention. I made it through Ostend and Antwerp, Belgium and was trying to get through the Rotterdam tunnel to the ships. It was rush hour and the traffic was very heavy. There was no way cars could stop for me. Then a man stopped and said he was a Swedish missionary and would take me back to his home to wait for the traffic to die down. I was reluctant, but he had a Swedish accent. The home was decorated with the traditional Swedish Christmas ornaments on a tree with red candle holders and white candles. It seemed like a fire hazard to me, but it was attractive. He served me a small dinner and took me to a place to catch the Dover Ferry. It was an all-night ferry and reminded me of the first time Jonna and I took our first hopeful ferry to England. Now we had been through many things together and separately.

I was tired but I was looking forward to meeting Ian for Christmas in Scotland. I took the train from Dover to London. When I arrived, Ian's father was visiting and insisted we go to a steak house which was expensive to me. Maybe this father wanted to check me out before we came to visit. On the 24th we had Christmas dinner and took the all-night train to Aberdeen. The

Scottish passengers were very excited about being home for the holidays and were drinking all the Scotch in sight. It was a party train. On Christmas Day we met the Baird family, which included his mother, father and younger sister, and they were very nice. I was slightly hippy with a navy broad-brim hat with a ribbon tied under my chin, but tried to be very polite. Their son had moved to London to work in an office and was a good lad. His sister was taking an academic track and was more serious. I don't know if his parents knew he frequently did the numbers. He had a bookie problem and I was afraid he was a gambling addict. He made average money. It was his money, his life and he did not want to talk about it. Scotland was a picturesque place, but it was hard to make a living and the money was in London. On the 30th we went to a party at a friend's house. New Year's Eve is a big deal in Scotland and it seemed like the whole city of Aberdeen participated, as they go from house to house all night. I was staying at a women's house as not to disturb his parents. We would go to smaller houses and some had pianos with people singing old familiar tunes. I made it to two a.m. and had to go to sleep, but Ian and his friends went all night. I arrived at the women's house and had to pee really badly, but the zipper on my pants was stuck. I found a razor blade to cut it loose. The woman came in and thought I was trying to kill myself! I reassured her and went to sleep and later found out someone in her family had just died. On New Year's Day I got some flowers for her to thank her for her hospitality, but she said I got it all wrong with my flower choices and their meanings. This was news to me, but I had made an effort.

New Year's Day, after drinking all night, means serving Haggis, which is sheep stomach filled with meats, spice and some veggies. I liked it and was not hung over. January third, Ian and I went to his uncle's house, which was very cold and typical of Scottish houses. I was given a small hot-water bottle to sleep with for some warmth. Finally on January fourth we took the all-night train back to London, which was much quieter, as the party was finally over.

Ian had to move, so he decided to get a place in Earls Court, which had many night spots but now is a very posh area. I got a room in North

Tottingham in a flat with community college students, as my money was running low. I found a job in an Indian Restaurant as a hostess, which required me to wear a pink sari made of six yards of material wrapped around my waist and shoulder. I was an illegal worker. I was allowed to eat with the family and employees before the restaurant opened. They were well dressed but ate with their fingers, but had silverware for the patrons. The food was pretty spicy, so the cook would add cream for me to soften the blow.

I was the hostess and people were surprised to hear an American accent, but it was an easy job. On my 22nd birthday, Les, the renter of the flat, said he could take me to a dance at school in a plain recreation room but it was free. We were dancing when some black Caribbean men broke into the room and started stabbing some of the white students. There was blood on the floor. I don't know how long it took the police to get there but we ran out the back door. It was shocking turn of events and it was another spoiled birthday. I did not know about race relations and violence in England but this was a really bad situation.

I had made friends with an American named Dean, who worked in a youth group home. He had a beard and was a little overweight but looked strong to handle teenagers. I had applied for a job in the Hospital doing research on depression, but I lacked confidence and I might want to travel. I liked Dean as he was very sensitive and had a soothing voice. I think he liked talking to me as someone who knew what he was dealing with at work. I did not ask him why he was in England. Ian and I went to Hyde Park where people would stand on soap boxes and speak their minds as long as they were not hurting anyone. Another woman and I went to see the play "Hair," which was popular then and the theater was very reasonable. English theater has always impressed me, but the most memorable performance was Janis Joplin at Royal Albert Hall. I went with Ian, Fly and some of their other Scottish friends. They were passing a hashish joint around in public. It was a good performance but she was a tragic figure and did not live too much longer. At the end of January, Paul, the man from Spain and Italy, came to visit me and suggested a trip to the

Canary Islands with Jonna. He was there to meet her as I later found out, she was having a legal abortion in London, and it was illegal in the United States. One night Paul, Ian, Dean, another man and I went out to dinner. Maybe Paul was checking out who I hung out with. It was an odd collection of diners but people who travel are more flexible. I did not tell Paul that Jonna and I were not traveling together, but accepted his invitation to the Canary Islands. This was a great opportunity.

On February 5th Jonna and I flew to Barcelona to meet Paul and catch a plane to the Canary Islands the next day. I think Paul found Jonna more interesting but I had more in common with him. Once we arrived in Las Palmas, Paul rented a very nice apartment for us. There were lush palm trees and English, German and Swedish tourists escaping the winter cold. We went to the dog race tracks that night. Jonna and I went horseback riding the next day. She had a wealthier upbringing and was used to handling horses, while I just hung on. The Spanish did not give rules or instruction and we just rode off by ourselves. While crossing a small river, her horse decided to buck her off, but she got it under control like she did many people. Luckily my horse was tame and merely walked through the water. We made it back in one piece. That night after dinner we went to a disco around a pool and there were German boxers who thought it was fun to throw me in the pool with my clothes on. The Swedes were animated, the English reserved but the Germans were rowdy. People stayed in their groups and did not mix that much.

We left Las Palmas and went to the volcanic island of Tenerife to a very special black sand resort. I thought I had died and gone to heaven. If you were on the beach, the waiters would come out and serve food and drinks. Paul took photos of us in bathing suits that were in good taste. One night we went to a restaurant that was down a deep spiral staircase into a cave that had a polished stone floor, guitar music and good food. That was so unique. After dinner we went toward a cave and saw albino fish and arthropods that had never seen the light of day. I really liked this place. The next day we went on camel rides and a volcano tour, as the island was clearly volcanic with black sand and rocks.

After that we went back to Las Palmas and had dinner at an elegant French restaurant, which was a big change from street food. Paul was very well off and was sharing this with us. He gave us a big opportunity and we gave him some company after his wife's death. Sometimes Jonna and I would go off for hours and Paul rested. Paul found out that Jonna was seeing a man and blew up. I felt this was a long time for her not to disappear. But Paul was being more of a father guardian and didn't know her habits like I did. After her operation maybe he thought she would calm down. She did eventually show up.

Paul suggested we take a cruise to Africa and of course we agreed as we could never afford this trip. We boarded a small ship under a Yugoslavian flag that was older but was nicely maintained. At night after dinner they had music and dancing. I slow danced with a Yugoslavian man. Jonna found someone. I think Paul was playing it cool and not being the grandfather. He was a tactful person and knew we were just out of college.

We finally made it to Dakar, Senegal, and visited a mosque. Senegal was a French colony, and in the market they had beautiful fabric with African designs. Women would wrap themselves up and put a snug baby loop their back. The country was peaceful and fairly prosperous. On the sidewalk was a barber with hand-painted men's hair styles wanted. Everything seemed casual.

The next stop was Gambia, which was a British colony. We met a Gambian man who was sitting on a metal drum and said he had graduated from Oxford and had just returned. What was his life going to be like here? He could make so much more in London, but his family was here. Jonna and I walked around and saw grass huts sharing one electric cord. How do they turn the lights off at night? I was not used to a group culture, as America was more individualistic. We walked through the countryside and saw women making boutique material. I bought some material and later made a top out of it. There was a nearby pond and the women said not to go near it as there was a crocodile that might get us, and we listened. Later these countries became independent and had economic and political problems but had their own identity.

The food on the ship was excellent, but I was seasick and could only lay in a deck chair and try not to throw up all day. I got a bad sunburn that went down to my nose cartilage. When I was at the table there were little guard rails to keep the plates from sliding off onto the floor, as the sea was so rough. When people danced they would go to whatever side the ship was tilting toward. It was a smaller ship and more social. The next day we went to Spanish Sahara, which had been taken over by Algerians in 1976. An oasis tour was offered, but Jonna and I thought that was too traditional and set out on the Sahara Desert on our own. We quickly understood why they wore cloth over their faces, as the flies wanted to get up your nose or anywhere with moisture. We finally came to an abandoned cement building that I think soldiers used as an outpost. It was vacant but had graffiti all over it that was sexist and violent. Had women been dragged out here and raped? It looked that way. I was afraid and said we should walk back. When we got back into town, somehow Jonna found a hashish joint, and we got stoned and lost track of time. The ship sent out men to look for us and dragged up back. I wished I had gone with Paul on the Oasis trip and learned more about the Saharan culture. I was just happy we were safe and regretted the joint. The trip with Paul was wonderful and we had a few more relaxing days before we left for Madrid and then to San Sebastian. We then went to Paris, and Jonna took off on some adventure, leaving Paul and I to go to the American Embassy, Sacre Coeur, and I had my first real French dinner in a restaurant with violin music. He took some photos of me near the Seine River that were very good. He had a good camera and a lot of experience. We went to American Express and my mother sent 26 dollars, which I really needed. I had 176 dollars left after six months in Europe. Paul had helped us out tremendously and I think he enjoyed our company. He was very alert, intelligent and active for his age. He had an interesting life.

Paul flew back to New Jersey and I left to go to Amsterdam to meet Dean, the American worker. We took a bus to Marken, the Dutch village with big windmills. It was interesting but very cold near the ocean. We did a little more sightseeing but Dean had to get back to work. After the Dover ferry we saw

Swan Cottage and Canterbury Cathedral, and I had no idea where Jonna had gone. I had a birthday party for Ian at his place in Earls Court.

Les, who rented out the rooms, suggested we go to Brighton to see his parents on Sunday afternoon, which sounded like a nice trip. His parents seemed like a pleasant middle-class couple who had this wild son. He suggested seeing his childhood bedroom and I thought that might be interesting. He pulled out a joint and I took one puff. I don't remember anything after that but apparently we had sex. I never consented and I don't remember going down the stairs, talking to his parents or getting to a road where we hitchhiked 82 miles home. He was knowledgeable about drugs and I think he drugged me. He had never made any moves toward me in the flat and I was never interested in him. He was so different from his parents that I think he was adopted or maybe something more sinister was going on with them. Ian and I saw *The Prime of Miss Jean Brodie*, about a schoolmarm who ended up alone. Would that be me? At 22 I was feeling old and tired, as too much had happened. From 1968 to 1969, London was drug- and sex-oriented. I was sinking into something I had not bargained for when I left Illinois. I bought my mother a tea set, as she had sent me twenty-five dollars every now and then. She did not like it, but she never liked my gifts. Then my life took a serious turn for the worse. I found out that in the brief encounter with Les that I was pregnant. How could that happen? I talked to him and he wanted to get married, and I said "no" and I was getting an abortion. He was really angry and said the last women he went with did the same thing! Maybe he should find a wife the old-fashioned way instead of drugging and getting women pregnant. Now, I was pregnant, afraid of Les and I had to move as I could not live near him anymore. He frightened me. I had to quit my job. I asked if I could stay with Ian for a while, and he was agreeable. I had to apply for the National Medical Plan. There were no questions asked. The situation was upsetting but I had no money, did not want to be forced to live with my mother and wasn't ready to raise a baby. I did not want to ask my mother to raise a baby; we had a lot of unfinished business. Abortion was still illegal in the United States, and in

England it was not only legal but they had health care coverage. I made an appointment with a doctor in a very fancy office who would do the procedure. This was a horrible incident and a bad ending to my trip.

In the meantime I went with a woman to Swansea, Wales to get my mind off things. It was springtime and the lambs were jumping up and down without a care in the world. My life was sort of a mess but it was good to get away as Wales was beautiful in the spring. I had moved in with Ian, but when I showed up he was sound asleep and would not answer the door. I heard a party next door and it was gay women from New Zealand who were enjoying some freedom from the strict anti-gay rules in their country. They let me stay there until the next morning when I could get in. I went to American Express and called Paul and explained my problem. He was more of a father figure to me, as he was fatherly without being overbearing.

I did not know that Jonna had had the same situation. This was his second time with the two of us. When he met Jonna and I, we were fresh out of college and he enjoyed our youthful excitement about being in Europe, where he had been so many times with work, his wife and friends. I did not expect him to come back and there was time before the procedure, but he did. Now he was a friend and had come to our rescue a few times. We walked around London and he suggested that I go with him to Scandinavia in the summer. Later he suggested a trip around the world where I would take notes for his book and he would pay for the travel. He had had an interesting life and wanted to get the notes down. I declined, as I wanted to get my life going. We had been there almost eight months! Jonna agreed to go around the world but I never heard anything about their trip except that they went to an Officers Hotel in Saigon during the war.

Ian's friend Fly had asked him to move to Wimbledon in a shared flat, and I moved with Ian as I did not have much more time left in Europe. The day of the abortion I took the Tube all the way into London, had the procedure with 15 other women in one room, and took the Tube back to Ian's. I lay down and he sat there and did not say a word. I had not told him but I think he knew. I was so embarrassed about the "incident "and it had nothing to do with him.

Paul was still in town and he wanted me, Jonna and Brian to have lunch at the St. Regis. I was in bad shape with anesthesia and a medical procedure. I needed to rest, but I felt I owed it to Paul to accommodate his wish. I took the Tube back to London and we talked about old times that were really good times. This was our good-bye party as we had started our foursome in September 1968. Eight months and so much had happened to each of us and I wondered how long Brian was going to be wandering Europe, Joanna doing whatever it was she was doing, Paul trying to get his memoir done and me trying to find my way in life.

Jonna and I went shopping, as my old raincoat I had slept in so many times that it was worn and smelly. I bought a new one to wear going home. Paul had flown back already. I really liked Ian but was not sure how his life was going to be with gambling. I wished him well and I thought Fly would be a good friend. Scotts are level-headed people with a few quirks

Luckily, I did not have to go to Luxembourg to on the return flight as I could leave from London. I had been there eight months and two weeks and a lot had happened. I had seen many countries and experienced what life was like in other countries with all their challenges and history. This was a very different trip than the Europa House bus tour with co-ed women. They probably had a lot of photos. I had a lot of memories and education about life's good and bad experiences. I was glad I took the time after college graduation for a long trip, as I never had that much time again until I retired. When I landed in New York I almost kissed the ground, I was so happy to be back in the United States with all its problems, failures, greatness and successes.

My Lebanese friend Tony picked me up from the airport and we went out to dinner. He was going to try to make it in New York City as an architect but he eventually set up a business in London. His family lives on two continents but they are successful and can visit. There are more displaced people today and Lebanon is now in a very unfortunate situation. I called my mother to tell her when I was coming home to O'Hare airport. She was ecstatic to see me, which was always a surprise. She had been a role model in the sense that she had taken many chances and trips to change her life and this was definitely a trip of a lifetime for me. It was also an excellent antidote to the depression I felt at the University. I had expanded my world immensely and experienced some rough areas but had gained more self-confidence and determination about what I wanted to do with my life.

CHAPTER 9

Getting My Life Going

It was no surprise that my mother had moved again, but she had lived up to the bargain to stay in one place until I had graduated from high school and even college. She picked another one-room apartment with a bathroom and small kitchen. There was a locker downstairs and she had moved some of my things. I never had any input into what was moved, so it was always a surprise, like the place. There were only a few things I cared about keeping. This was an older building, but it was in a large U-shape with landscaping in the courtyard, was near downtown and on a quieter street. This was a big contrast to the busy four-lane street. This was a step up for her. When I got off the plane she was happy to see me and even took a photo. I think the eight-month separation was good for us both. Her life was about taking care of elderly women in their homes, and some of them were long term, which added stability to her life. I needed to get on my feet and start moving in a new direction. Paul had offered the trip around the world taking notes for his book, and I knew he had an interesting life. The instability of my younger years was still with me and I needed to set a path to somewhere. I wanted to get a PhD in Clinical Psychology, as I liked research, but it seemed like such a big goal and I was broke. My mother had been generous to pay my undergraduate tuition, so now I needed to pay for my graduate work. I need to take one step at a time.

I applied at temporary agency and got a position at Evanston Hospital, where my mother and I had gone to the low-income clinic in the back entrance.

This time I was working in the business office doing uninteresting work, but it was a start that was short lived. I had always been political since the first grade when Eisenhower ran for office. In the spring of 1969 the Vietnam War was still going on and there were protestors and rallies. One day I had fliers on my desk for a rally that I was going to pass out at the "L" station after work. I did not talk to anyone about it, I just did not hide them. The office manager went ballistic and said I was "fired" and escorted me out the front door and down the steps. I finally made it to the front door in the most unexpected way. I was appalled he did not talk to me about it, as I could have put them in a drawer. I contacted the ACLU and asked if this was legal. They said they were working on Black Civil Rights so they were just taking cases for African Americans. I needed to move on.

The employment agency said they had a position in downtown Chicago at a big insurance company. This required taking the "L" downtown and worked there for a month or more. It was doing paperwork, and I learned how much financial influence insurance companies had on the American economy. What was good was the location had many demonstrations, and I found out about a position at Cook County Social Services that paid well and was taking applications. There was also information about Roosevelt University, which was started by Eleanor Roosevelt and others to help working students get college educations. They had a master's program in Clinical Psychology and the tuition, while double that of the University of Illinois was possible. I was working with a young black woman and we were talking about our childhoods. When I was ten and in the Boone, Iowa orphanage, she was ten and looking for her parents in New Orleans. While I was working too hard she was on the street and found some relatives sitting on the steps in front of a building. We both hated the insurance company but needed the money. We could openly talk about race relations, which does not always happen today.

I applied for a Social Work position at the Cook County Welfare Department, and it took a while to process the applications. We had to sign a loyalty oath to the United States. I had no idea what I was getting into, but it paid well. Chicago was a big place with all kinds of ethnic, racial and social groups spread out over a very large area of about twelve million people. Evanston had some urban issues, but was a cocoon compared to Chicago. Chicago had a lot more going on, which I liked. I also applied to Roosevelt University and had to get my paperwork together for admissions.

So while I was waiting, my mother worked nights and I worked days, so we did not see each other except on Sunday. I did not go to church and she did not push it, so we were getting along. My mother's new place was peaceful, but because it was an older building it had some quirks such as cockroaches or water bugs. We were sitting in the kitchen having dinner and a very large water bug came out of the kitchen sink. My eyes were wide as I had not seen a bug that big in Evanston. My mother calmly took the hammer and nail that were sitting right near the sink and drove a stake through its heart; it died. She tossed it into the trash and we continued eating. This must have not been her first time dealing with this issue. She was a not shy about finding solutions to a problem and solving them herself. She was not used to getting help from other people or complaining.

Meanwhile, Paul came to visit at my mother's place but of course he would be staying in a nice hotel. He had told my mother about my abortion without my consent and I was 22 years old. She never let on that she knew, except one day she said, "I could have taken care of the baby." This was what I did not want and was glad it just happened to be in England. We had a pleasant dinner. Paul talked about hopping rails, which my uncles had done, working with Morse code and well-known men in the communications field. He had a full life. My mother did not talk about the "hell hole" and was fairly quiet. I thought it was good for her to spend some time with Paul instead of wondering what this man was like.

Afterward, Paul asked me if wanted to go to Scandinavia with him, and since I had time before I found out about the job and school, I said yes. My mother's family was from Finland and I could take some time off of the temporary job in a few months. I had time to save up for a new place and school.

It was a time crunch but it all seemed to fall into place. I wanted things to happen, so I took what was in front of me to move toward my goals. Trying to get a scholarship for another school might not work out. A bird in the hand is worth two in the bush.

During the rest of the visit Paul and I talked about our political positions. I was steeped in the antiwar movement while he had been involved in international communications in Europe during World War II. So we had the typical inter-generational discussion that did not go anywhere. I wish we had spent our time talking about something else. He was an important person in my trip and life during my time in Europe. But it was a brief experience of what a father or grandfather might be like.

Time passed quickly and I rarely saw my mother, and I think she was relieved I would be leaving soon. I was too, but it was good we had this time together that was not full of problems. Meanwhile, I finally found a room for rent in Chicago, as it was closer to what I would be doing. For some reason Les from London came to visit with a new girlfriend, and I only had a room with a mattress on the floor. I had not been in contact with him, so I think my mother must have given him my address. He was pretty pleased that he had caught me in a moment of seeming poverty. Which just pointed out to me his weak character? Maybe his new girlfriend would have a baby. She looked suspicious and I hope she examined him more closely. But it was not my problem. Meeting him was a terrible part of my life and I just wanted him to leave, which he did.

Then there was the trip to Scandinavia and I flew to New York, as Paul lived in New Jersey. We went to Norway first, to Oslo, and then took a train to Bergen to see the fjords by boat. It was incredible to see who people lived in steep crevasses between rocky mountains. These were tough people. We saw some of the older churches that survived the extreme weather. Lepers had a window in the back as they were not allowed to sit in the church. I did drawings of things we saw. Vigeland Park was amazing in that Gustav Vigeland had made over 200 sculptures of human beings in all stages of life and emotion. This was his life's work and it was very impressive. Sweden was next, and I could see the big difference in their wealth as the jewelry stores had gold jewelry. We saw the sights and an art museum with modern art I liked. We drove up to Upsala, which is a university town surrounded by wheat fields. Lastly, we went to Finland, which I was very curious about due to other family connections. I did not know where they were and my mother had never told me she had been corresponding with them by letters. We were in Helsinki, which was darker stone buildings and I could see their jewelry was made out of well-designed wood instead of gold. Later I would understand the history between Sweden and Finland, and it all made sense. People spoke Finnish to me, so I felt like I looked Finnish even if I did not know what they were saying. The language does not have linguistic roots and is very difficult to learn.

We found some merriment in the hotel with music and dancing but the city was somewhat somber and we did not know the language. Paul rented a car and we went to the Punkaharhu district or Lake District and saw a castle on an island. I decided to swim to the island, as we did not have a boat. As I arrived in a bathing suit people were dressed for a tour of Savolinna, where they had opera performances. I later found out the Swedes, when they occupied Finland, built castles for soldiers to defend and keep control of the peasants. It was a good trip and we did spend two days in New Jersey and saw Paul's house, which was on a cliff overlooking his lake. This was beautiful but I could see why he would be lonely without his wife and his children who were grown and had their own families. I was grateful to Paul for this opportunity, but I needed to get back to my life.

Without much of a transition, I started training for my new job at Cook County. They were trying to meet the needs of people who had migrated from the South, mainly from Alabama, Mississippi and Louisiana, looking for work and a new start. It was a part of the Great Migration for African Americans. Cook County had built high-rise buildings to replace the old buildings. Maybe Cook County had Federal mandates to meet some standards or someone was running for office. While I think the intentions were good, this created a cluster of poverty with rural people who did not know how to live in a big city. Part of our job training was how to roll under gunfire. This should have told me something, but I was so happy to have a job that would pay for my tuition that I did not question it too much. The Baby Boomers were influenced by John F. Kennedy, who emphasized helping people in need yet people helping them to solve their own problems. I was in a group assigned to the Oakland Bank Building at the Chicago Stockyards. I had read The Jungle by Upton Sinclair, about the horrible working conditions processing meat let alone what the cattle went through. The building was old but designed after the Philadelphia Independence Hall and is now a Historic Building. The problem was getting to it from the North Side meant taking the "L" train to a poor neighborhood and then taking a bus to the Halsted Street location. This was a long, dicey process to get to work, especially when it was cold and windy.

The Welfare Department downtown was largely run by blacks who had been promoted to higher positions. The local supervisors were black and had been there a long time. The new social workers were white and recent college graduates. The clerks who process the massive amount of paper work without a computer were black and overwhelmed. It was an interesting sandwich of humanity dealing with big social problems. When you came upstairs there was a large open space with a few private offices but mainly supervisors on the side and long rows of Social Workers. My supervisor was an older black woman who was very kind and understanding that this was my first full-time job and would be working under very difficult conditions "out in the field." When I had the basics down, I was able to take a bus to the 16-story high-rise buildings and had to walk a few blocks and I was vulnerable. The Police and Fire departments did not go into the area, as it was too dangerous. My clients knew when I was coming so they would look out for me, but what could they do? I was assigned the Ida B. Wells Building, which like the others was 16 stories high with 10 two-bedroom apartments on each floor. They had a long balcony on the outside, an elevator that did not always work and two stair-cases on either end of building. When the elevator was broken, I did climb 16 stories to get to a client's apartment. The staircases were dark as the light bulb had been taken or broken so someone could sleep there or maybe commit crimes. It smelled of urine and was a scary place. I was debating climbing the dark staircase when three little girls came by carrying a loaf of bread. They smiled and said "Hi." So I decided if they could do it, I could do it. Maybe it was more dangerous at night then during the morning or early afternoon, as people are sleeping things off.

The apartments were plain but women usually decorated them so they were homey in the living room and kitchen area. There was evidence of Southern cooking, most notably to me making corn bread in a cast-iron skillet, but I am sure they made many other dishes. They would tell some of their story and explain what they needed which was mostly money and food stamps. But sometimes they would talk about health or child problems. The elementary school was not too far away but the walk could be treacherous. There were gangs that would try to recruit boys from eight years on by terrorizing the community or offering rewards for doing certain tasks. Usually shooting started at 3 p.m. when the kids got out of school. I tried to get there early and leave before three p.m. One time I was late and I crawled on my hands and knees to walk down the 16-story staircase. Once you were downstairs, the area was open with bare dirt, so you were totally visible and I walked fast to the bus stop. I did not have money for a car and Cook County did not provide cars. Since I was there from 9 a.m. to 3 p.m. I needed lunch but there were only bars. Sometimes I would go in and buy a candy bar but sometimes the rats ate part of them. Rats seemed to be everywhere. There was still a policy banning Man in House with single mothers, as the men might be taking advantage of the women or creating more children on welfare. Some women were on birth control pills, but the pills were very strong so some women had side effects like high blood pressure. It took years to get more effective birth control. I participated in a demonstration to legalize abortion outside a meeting of the AMA where doctors were attending a conference. So there were raids and men would hide in closets if they were not tipped off. I was not involved in this, so I am not sure how much it happened. I know some of the women were in abusive relationships or using substances but there was not much help for these problems and it was their choice to associate with whom they wanted. Poverty does limit your choices, and one does the best they can.

As I got to know the families I would understand more what their problems were. Such basic things like medical care were hard to get, as one had to take a long bus ride to the hospital. One woman had her sick baby on the bus but it died before she made it there. I got to know the children, and some of them were murdered by the gangs and part of my job was to make burial arrangements. It was painful for everyone. Sometimes the mothers would send their young men back down South for the "Southern cure," hoping they would regain some of the values of a stable community, going to church and not being influenced by the gangs. The South had a stable society as people knew their place and how to get around in their place. In the city, everything was up for grabs and very unstable. It might have worked in some instances, but the lure of money and power was very appealing to boys until they died.

If one wanted to work a legal job you had to take transportation out of the area and there was no child care, unless you could get another mother to watch your kids. Some did find work. Years later I heard about the Ida B. Wells building in the news, as a seven-year-old boy refused to give up his candy so the other boys threw him over the balcony to his death. This was still shocking to me. Recently I met a black pilot on a plane and he said his parents lived in that building! His parents did not have problems, so I would not have met them. He and his brother were given scholarships to Northwestern University in Evanston as part of helping equality with the Civil Rights Movement. Both had good jobs. This was good to hear, as I only heard the worst stories and he understood what I was talking about. Most people could not imagine what was going on in the South Side and parts of the West Side. He was the only one I could talk to in depth.

When there was an election, the Democratic Party would offer jobs, but usually they were short term. The other party would not show up. After a while, I was transferred to low buildings in a neighborhood. It was nicer in that there was not a high concentration of poverty. One of the people in that area was Muddy Waters, the famous Blues musician from Louisiana. He rented an upstairs unit out to a woman with seven children. He had to sign a statement as to the rent amount. He and his wife would go to Europe to perform and he was very popular. They chose to stay in their old neighborhood. He would play on his porch and I could listen to his music from the South that had been combined with other styles. There were many talented musicians.

One time I visited an old man who had a severe cut on his right arm and I asked what had happened as he was not going to volunteer information. He said he got his Social Security check but some young men wanted his check. They cut his arm to encourage him to give him the check or they said they would cut off his arm. There was no way to get a replacement check as there was no police report or evidence. I felt bad. If you reported the criminals, they might kill you.

Another thing I found out is that TB patients wanted to leave the sanitarium as they could not drink or do drugs, so I was exposed to TB. I tested positive but then tested negative. They talked about rolling under gunfire, but they had not talked about emotional job stress, danger or health risks we might encounter. At least two workers were victims of assault.

Back at the office there was a union, which I joined, and they would try to help the workers and clerks to get a reasonable workload, but it was an uphill battle. We had meetings after work at a soul food restaurant on the Near South Side after work. Chicago has very windy cold winters and women were still expected to wear skirts or dresses. This put women at risk of cold but also assault. One social worker was raped and one man was beaten rather badly. We were nervous about just wearing pants, so we wore a skirt with pants underneath. We made a statement and eventually they did let us wear pants to work. Because it was the late 1960s, there was marijuana around and some made brownies and brought them to work. Some went down in the abandoned vault and smoke a joint. But the work was so hard most people were not trying it. You could do what you wanted on your own time.

The Chicago stockyards were still running and they had an annual rodeo in the amphitheater. Then we would see cowboys who would eat at the same diner next door. It was a bit of cowboy culture you did not see in the big city. When the weather was warm and the windows were open, the stench from the stockyards was so bad they would let us go home as there was no air conditioning.

One of my co-workers was into riding bicycles, and I did do the ten-mile ride all the way from the North side to the office a few times, but the traffic was very dangerous, let alone a stray bullet. When I was leaving for the West Coast he wanted me to ride to California on a bicycle, but that was way too far and vulnerable for me to consider. I was getting more cautious.

The office environment was pretty congenial but stressful. Filling out forms was not of big interest to me, but if the client was going to get any benefits you had to fill them out correctly. Then they might sit on a clerk's desk as they worked through the huge pile. This was unfair to her and the clients. Some of my co-workers were in a communist group and I joined, but did not have a lot of time. They were very intellectual but concerned with workers on the bottom, like my mother. This meant that the Red Squad of the Chicago Police was assigned to follow us around when we had a peaceful demonstration, and later they even put a man with a tri-pod in front of my new apartment. I knew they had to do their job and was not too concerned about their presence. I think it was easy detail for them compared to many difficult ones in Chicago.

My photo was in *Jet Magazine* for a civil rights demonstration. I was not trying to get known, I was just active. Thousands of young idealistic people were thinking of the possible answers to big problems. Chicago was a political town and things were happening all over and were ignited in part by the 1968 Democratic convention, civil rights movement, feminism, Native American AIM, anti-Viet-Nam-war rallies and the beginning of Gay Rights. There were hippies who advocated for health foods, tune in and drop out and vegetarian restaurants with good food. The music scene was lively and with a lot of talent in Chicago and Motown from Detroit. There was Chess Records and all types of musicians from the South. My mother had liked Black Gospel music as it was upbeat and not somber as some church services.

Eventually I was notified that I could start Roosevelt University when I was 23 years old. I had saved up enough money to pay the tuition, but had to keep going as I paid semester by semester. This meant working all day on the South Side, grabbing something to eat and taking classes till nine o'clock. I came home and tried to relax or do some more work.

I did find a group of male students which wanted a fourth roommate at a reasonable rent. The three men were in a three-bedroom flat, but the Pakistani man, a business student, took the living room, as he was the organizer of the group. A Scottish man took the second bedroom and I took the third. This left David, who took the room off the kitchen and then used the dining room to store piles of snakeskins; he made snakeskin belts on an industrial machine for Saks Fifth Avenue. That was his income. I had been used to playing with boys when I grew up, so this was not an unusual situation for me. We got along well and we were so busy working, and going to school, we hardly ever saw each other. I did notice that there was a pile of dishes in the kitchen sink and there were all kinds of different-colored molds on it. I thought it was beautiful, but did not do the dishes and I had no idea how they got done or if they ever got done. It was not a high priority as every minute of the day and night was occupied.

In my new location in the field, I had some eccentric families such as a mother and daughter who lived on the second floor of an old home that had been a very nice residence. I think the properties closer to the lake front had been a prosperous area at one time. When I entered the lobby, there were rats running back and forth on the stairs and I had to stamp my feet to get them to clear a bit for my passage. The mother and daughter had on lovely flowered dresses and when they were outside they had floral parasols. I think they were recreating living in the South in some sort of fantasy world. They functioned alright. I was not sure the daughter was into the fantasy as much as the mother, but she went along with it. At some point I knew they needed to get better housing as it was clearly substandard, but they were in no hurry. I knew if one unraveled the mother's fantasy there might be a breakdown. People cope with adversity in many different ways. So I helped them with other issues and let them be.

But toward the end of my employment I had a case that I still have trouble forgetting. An elderly woman was living in the ground floor of a duplex, and one night gang members showed up on the porch with a teenage girl. They proceeded to harass the girl, which lead to them sawing her in half. The elderly woman had to listen to her screams in the last moments of her life. She could not call and maybe the police would not come anyway. The next morning she found the girl's body was in the trashcan. I came out and she wanted to move, so I began making all the contacts I could to find a fast replacement. Sometimes the Mayor's office could cut through red tape. I was able to get a senior apartment, but it took a month. The gang had randomly chosen her porch, so she was not in immediate danger, but there was shock. I know some people are high on drugs to dull their brains and they are trying to send rival gangs a message or scare women into doing their biding. What was the mindset of the gang members? What did the girl do or not do? How can people be that inhumane? How can you dump a body like trash? The cruelty was way beyond anything I had ever imagined.

I had a few Black Muslim families that did not want to talk to me as I was part of the "white devil," but I did what I needed as efficiently as possible and let them be. Jesse Jackson had programs for the community and his church. Fred Hampton and others founded the Rainbow Coalition in 1969 and emphasized races working together for a better society. There were many student movements at the time, which I was not involved with. At one point there was a suggestion to give money to the gangs, specifically the Blackstone Rangers, and they would become good citizens. I think they did get some money and spent it. So there was a multitude of groups including churches working on urban, racial and social problems. It would have been good if there was more inter-group communication. While I was interested in all this happening, I needed to study, work and maintain my sanity. Roosevelt University was located on Michigan Avenue downtown near Grant Park. It was easy to get to on the "L" and the students were good, classes a smaller size and the professors were involved. This was a big improvement over the huge Illinois. The Clinical Psychology department was Freudian-based, so this was a departure from Behaviorism. While not analyzing rat mazes, we did some social experiments, such as dividing up into couples with mixtures of race, age, bearded, clean shaven and asking for directions, as though we were tourists. We recorded the responses. It turned out the beard got the most negative responses. The combination of interracial couples was not that different.

I found reading the older thinkers was helpful, as it filled out the history of psychology. We were trained to be psychologists, as the law in Illinois at the time was a Master's degree as the standard. While I was there, it changed to PhD to conform to national standards. I had to study every spare minute I was not working but had some time for fun. Once I got into the routine, I was not as exhausted, but I had to back off a bit on my political work. One time some students met for a picnic out in Grant Park before night school, but the police were doing something with a demonstration and they were tear gassing, so we had to move to finish our dinner. It was an active time period.

The students were from different countries such as Africa, Israel and a mixture of American ethnic groups. We were graded on a curve and we could count on the Israelis to be competitive. I did not care if I got straight A's, but I wanted to do a good job. Some Sundays we would have a study group, which was a morale booster. That November I was going toward the end of my first semester at night school and was pretty exhausted. It was Thanksgiving and I waited to see if my mother was going to invite me to dinner, but I never heard from her. So I spent the holiday with Wobblies or Industrial Workers of the World, who were older radicals from the Great Depression. They had made a paella dish that was really good. Fred Hampton was shot in a massive police attack, but the bullets were only going one way. This was a big upheaval in the political community, as he was the leader of Rainbow Coalition. He was trying to get different racial groups to work together. Someone decided he was getting too powerful.

As the holidays approached, one of the professors asked me out to dinner. This felt strange but it was just dinner. However, he liked to drink wine and when we got back to my shared apartment he was too drunk to drive to his fancy apartment on the lake. My roommates talked about what to do, but we felt we would just let him sleep it off. They took a photo of him snoring. I slept on the sofa near where the snake skins were stored. The professor was looking for a wife and eventually did marry one of the students. Things were not as regulated as they are now.

A co-worker at Cook County asked me to go to New Orleans around the winter break. I said yes, and we drove in his van on smaller roads in a winter storm. This lead to sliding into a ditch, and we slept and in the morning a farmer was there to pull us out. I then found out he had been fired for using heroin in the work bathroom. He said he was going to go through withdrawals as he wanted to stop taking the pure heroin he got from his family pediatrician. His father owned a huge men's clothing company, but I think his son was lost. I knew him well enough to know he was a smart, thoughtful person and was telling me the truth. He seemed to be OK. We made it to New Orleans and did a few things, but I was anxious to get back home and work. I flew back to Chicago and he took off to whatever his life was going to bring. I was too willing to experience things and had to be more careful about accepting invitations. But I knew he trusted me to help him through to a possible sobriety.

In the spring I had a phone call from my sister, who had worked near Evanston for a while, moved to Milwaukee but ended up in Boston. Things had turned sour as her roommate had some lower mob association. I suggested she move to Chicago, and she accepted. This was a really bad idea in that I was almost at the breaking point with stress, but we had never lived together since I was four years old and she was eight months old when I left the farm.

This also meant I had to give up my affordable "student housing," and I liked the guys. I also had to locate a replacement apartment, which takes time to search out. I looked at some real dumps but finally found a third-floor walk-up in an Old Victorian building. It was on a busy street but not far from the "L." It was only $185 and had two bedrooms, but I could take the living room for peace and quiet. When I picked her up at the airport she had a big black eye, so something had really happened to make her move. I loaned her money so she could get started, and we went to a used furniture store to furnish the apartment with the minimal needed to be a home. She was a really fast typist and got a job in a law firm, which enabled her to quickly pay me back.

I had summer break from school but not work. My sister had been raised on Jack's farm and would go to bed at nine p.m. and up to leave for work very early. I was just finishing up my last class at nine p.m. and got up early to get to the South Side office. We did not see each other that much except on weekends. Jonna, who I had traveled with in Europe until she disappeared, said she wanted to rent a room so we had three people to split the $185 per month rent. I had no idea what she was doing as I did not see her much either, but that was nothing new. The landlord sat in a bar around the comer that had a locked door. If you wanted to talk to him, a little window would open and you would ask for him. It reminded me of a speak-easy entrance.

Mother visited a few times, and one time mother, my sister and I went to a restaurant nearby as there was a commercial area. We sat down and were reading the menus. My mother suggested my sister try the chicken and she got up and threw a chair across the room and stormed out. I went after her and told her to get back in, but she said something and left. I thought this was going to be one dinner with the three of us together. I thought my sister had more maturity and she could have stated she was ordering something else but instead she had a hair trigger reaction. This was disappointing. What a screwed-up family. Mother was happy to see her younger girl and was nice. I had been through the ringer. Now I ignored this incident, as I did not want to be in the middle. I was just as opinionated as my sister but I did not feel chicken was worth creating a scene. I know she had years of her father filling her head with demeaning remarks about her birth mother. I was just sad that we could not seem to have a dinner together. One time I came home late and stepped on the living room carpet and it made "crunch" sound. I looked and here was a pile of dirt. I guess this was another way my sister dealt with things.

In the summer when it was really hot and no one had air conditioning people would open up the fire hydrants. Not a great thing to do, but it was a relief to get soaked in water. The beaches were a distance so this was easier. Chicago was hot and humid. The fall semester was interesting but required more work, so life was a blur. In the spring of my second year I took a leave from my Cook County job and found an internship at a rehabilitation hospital closer to our apartment; the work was light compared to being on the street. I enjoyed the work as it involved interviewing patients, giving short tests and making recommendations to the consultation meeting. The staff was small but professional and amicable. I still had classes and had to write a Master's Thesis by June. This involved research, interviews and doing statistical analysis.

I was engaged to marry a man who I thought would be a good husband, but he was in the communist group that I was leaving. I wanted to participate in Union activities but not be stuck in more meetings and restrictions on behavior. I had not had fun in college and I wanted to enjoy the music, dancing and being outdoors. I felt I had too many restrictions on my behavior with the church, the orphanage and working so hard. I broke it off and he quickly married someone else so I think he just wanted to get married and the woman was nice. There was another man in my psychology program who wanted to get married, but he had had a rough childhood and was not dealing with it well. I had not dealt with mine and I felt we would not be a good couple working on our issues together. Maybe we could have helped each other, but the truth was I wanted to leave Chicago and explore the West.

One time I drove my sister's car down to the "field" and had the rent money in the ashtray. It was a convertible and I did not know how to get the top up. So I saw all my clients and when I returned the rent money was still there. This gave me more faith in the neighborhood.

My sister worked with a woman who was selling her 1963 Chevy for $125, and I was interested. My mother and I had never had a car, so I was not familiar with the registration process. I sent in the paperwork to Springfield but did not know that with the rust from road salt the VIN tag had rusted off. I was going to the grocery store one day to buy food for a dinner party I was having and the Chicago police stopped me. I did not have plates, as each car had their own plates each time there was a change. They took me into the station and sat me down on a hard bench with a light hanging over my head. Was this being filmed? They interrogated me and I gave them what I knew. I told them the whole story and asked them to call my sister or mother. No one answered the phone and there were no answering machines then. My mother was not home. It was so frustrating, as who in their right mind would steal a rust bucket? Finally they gave up and I was free to buy some food. It turns out my sister was home but refused to answer, as it would be for me and not her. The dinner was a success despite my police detour.

Another thing I did was try to save an eighteen-year-old girl from working as a dancer in a mafia bar. The bar was a lower-level dive bar, with men who barely paid attention to the dancers, just their drinks. I got a job dancing at the same place and talked to her, but she said she was going to move on to a bigger bar that paid more. That meant getting deeper into the criminal pit. I was disappointed, but she had made up her mind. I decided to give dancing a try for extra income. The only thing I did not like was the bullet holes in the wall behind the dance stage. Since I was being paid $20 an hour to do something I liked to do anyway, I stayed until the owner asked me to go topless. So that was the end of my dancing career, but not dancing.

When my sister and I emptied the garbage we had to go together. One would carry the garbage and one would carry a baseball bat. When you opened the lid to the can, rats would jump out and the bat holder would swing to scare them. This was stressful enough, but we did not realize on the other side of the basement wall was torture equipment for taking photographs of children. I had noticed that the window of the photography shop never changed and the sun was fading the display. One day I was walking home from the "L" and there were five squad cars with lights on in front of our apartment. It turns out the fake photography studio was a front for taking pornographic photos of children in torture equipment. There were many Native American kids whose families needed the money. How sick do you have to be to do that work, or to buy the photographs? This was before the internet, and now it is even easier to watch all kinds of videos. There was an article in the *Chicago Tribune* with a photo of our building with the address in front. When my sister went to work she was teased about being taller than when she started. Now I watch for signs of fake businesses, but they could be online, too. I have spotted some.

The landlord said we had to move in a month. Not sure why, because we were good tenants and put up with the cockroaches and rats. I had thrown a party and about 100 people had shown up, but it ended shortly after midnight and people stayed to help clean up the leftover stuff. I was able to find an apartment close by that was on a quieter street, but there was an elementary school. This was important in that my 1963 Chevy was very hard to start in cold weather. I had ether spray to put in the carburetor, and I would try to crank it up without running the battery down. The kids thought it was funny to throw snowballs into the carburetor, which killed the spark. Even some gangs were not this mean. Jonna moved with us and shared the rent. As usual we did not see her much or she was sleeping. The move was more stress. My sister smoked cigarettes and with all the stress I was under and the second-hand smoke I began smoking, which was something I never thought I would do. She had reached her 21st birthday, so we had gone out to a few night places before and I had to doctor her birth certificate. We had gone to Fox Lake to see Ana Banana, a well-known stripper who put on a good show in the summer.

My sister had gotten engaged a while ago and was planning a wedding on the South Side in a Catholic church as her fiancé's family was all on the South Side. Meanwhile I was steeped in finishing my Master's thesis with the many questions and rewrites. It was finally done and I was able to graduate in June 1972. My graduation was nice in that my mother, sister and classmates were able to be there and they had a really good jazz band. It was a wonderful day and I was so relieved that I made it through the grueling schedule. No one took photos. Most of my money had gone to tuition, so I worked at Cook County a bit longer to get some money for traveling.

The wedding happened in May and my mother and my sister's father were there in the same room, which had not happened since 1951. Twenty-one years later. They did not speak to each other and her father insisted on leaving in the middle of the wedding reception, so my sister had to drive to the airport in her dress. My sister's mom did not come as she did not travel. So it was mainly my brother-in-law Ed's family and some friends. The bridesmaid and I made dresses out of light aqua fabric with white daises on it, and we had white wide-brim hats. My sister found a really beautiful dress and her husband was handsome in his tuxedo. So it turned out as a good end to a chance meeting. Now they are almost up to their fiftieth wedding anniversary and have four children and two grandchildren.

I, on the other hand, had avoided another MRS degree and was looking forward to hitting the open road heading west. I really liked Chicago with all its problems, complexity and culture. But it was also cement congestion and crime. I wanted to see wide-open spaces, mountains and wildlife. I wanted to breathe some fresh air and see if I wanted to live there.

One of my classmates had a girlfriend who I became friends with, and the classmate had been arrested for marijuana possession. I don't think he was a big user but he was annoying to me, as he made passes at me knowing Miriam was my friend. Her father was a judge and was outraged she picked such a guy to date and was really coming down on her hard. She spent some time with us and said she wanted to go out West with me. I was willing to go by myself, but I liked her. I had avoided my MRS degree and was looking forward to hitting the wide open road heading out West.

California was the happening place and I was a native Californian. I had lived here since I was four and had a lot of memories. Some were good, some not good. The law had changed for me becoming a licensed psychologist, so I wanted to see what else was out there. With Miriam accompanying me I felt more protected and would have someone to share the new experiences with, as I thought I could trust her.

1906. *Kalle Waisanen and Hilja Tauriainen wedding*

1921. *Hilja and Lillian (8) before losing father*

1921. *Aunt Ani and father Kalle after brain injury*

1928. *Ellen, Lillian and Elna after parents are gone*

1947. *Lillian caring for
Mary and Lois*

1949. *Lillian and Lois on
wedding day on Jack's farm*

1956. *Biking to the Evanston Beach*

1963. *Lillian and Lois
visiting Wisconsin*

1968. *Lois and Jonna leaving for Europe*

1969. *Lois in Paris (Paul's good camera)*

1982. *Lois and sister visiting San Francisco*

1989. *Lillian, Lois and Paula visit the Finnish Hanka Farm*

1990s. *Lois on top of Mt. Lyell on John Muir Trail*

1981. *Lillian visiting with Grands Jerry and Anja*

Visiting sister's family in Chicago

1991. *Lois kayaking in Glacier Bay, Alaska*

1996. *Christmas visit with cousin and kids*

2019. *Visiting cousins Lois and Lainey*

2005. *Lillian Shelton, 1914-2010*

CHAPTER 10

Trip up North

With my rusty 1963 Chevy Impala, which used to be white but now had more rust spots eating it up, I was ready to drive thousands of miles. I paid $125 for it and almost got arrested for stealing it. I had it checked out by a mechanic who said it probably needed a new radiator. Not knowing much about cars I thought I could just keep adding water and save some money. That was not a good choice. Gasoline was 25 cent per gallon and we were going far.

I decided to take my mother to the Upper Peninsula of Michigan, where she was born, as I might not come back from the West. I thought she needed to see the land of the "hell hole" and "snakes." I was curious what it would be like through her eyes. I had only been up there with Jay in high school. I was the only one who would take her. She begrudgingly said OK, but no motels as bad things happen there, no long drives but I was driving, and she wanted to find her Middle School friend Simi. She had no idea where she lived or her name after two marriages, but somehow we would find her.

We set off going straight north from Illinois to the Wisconsin border and it was getting to be five p.m. My mother said she wanted to stop near Green Bay, Wisconsin. I said that means we have to stay in a motel. She relented and said OK. I found an average motel; we had dinner, watched some TV and went to bed. However, at two a.m. I heard the hall door open and a man in a suit was walking toward our beds. I said "wrong room," and he immediately departed and I called the front desk who said they gave him the wrong key.

My mother went back to sleep, but in the morning she asked "Why are they bringing men into our room in the middle of the night?" Good question, as this had never happened before or for the rest of my life, but it had to happen while my fearful mother was with me.

We continued driving up north and the trees were getting thicker, the farms had more rocks from glaciers and we finally crossed the Michigan border. My car had been running smoothly, but after an hour-and-a-half it suddenly started to rumble, shake and finally came to an abrupt stop just as we entered a small town. Great, now what do I do? Is there AAA road service or a garage? We were in front of a small white wooden house, and the front door swung open and a middle-aged woman with a large cotton apron was staring at us. Then my mother exclaimed "Simi! I told you we would find her!"

I was totally shocked, as it seemed almost impossible that the car knew more than we did. My mother ran out of the car and the two long-lost classmates were hugging. We went into the house and she insisted we spend the night. My mother was relieved that there were no uninvited men here. They spoke for hours in the old Finnish they had grown up with. I felt comfortable with Simi, and my mother seemed totally relaxed seeing a classmate after many decades. We had a light supper and they came up with a plan to go to the farm my mother had grown up on in Arnheim. I was surprised she would want to go to the place where all the trauma and "evil snakes" had lived, but I wanted to see it.

The next day we had a breakfast and much coffee as we set out to find the farm. I put water into the radiator and hoped it would work. No one had lived at the farm since her brother, Arthur, had committed suicide there in 1938. We finally came to a spot in the road that both women agreed was where the farm was located. I turned into the dirt road but I could not get too far as the tall weeds had claimed most of the road. We got out of the car and the women decided that a break in the brush was where we should walk. We finally came to the remnants of the sauna bath with unpainted, jointed handmade logs in the Finnish style. Then up the hill we could see the house and made our journey into family and immigrant history. It had been a bright sunny day, but once we got into the house things started to change. I could see the wood-burning stove used for cooking, heat and drying things.

The steps to the sleeping loft were sagging so deeply we could not go upstairs. The house seemed small for parents and eight kids. There was one bedroom for the parents. All the boys and girls slept upstairs in a few beds, which meant there was little privacy. There was no furniture left, but there was a small trunk in the main room. I opened it and Arthur's Lutheran confirmation paper was inside with fancy embellishments on the sides. It was all in Finnish and it was reassuring that they had been participating in society. He was the last to live on the farm, and he left with a gunshot. No one took the certificate. It just sat in the trunk with the departed brother's spirit. I picked up the certificate. Suddenly the sky had turned dark. The wind really picked up and the house began creaking, groaning and swaying to the point we decided we had better leave before it caved in. I took the certificate, with no time to waste getting out. Once we ran out the door and were heading down the hill, the wind stopped, the sun came out and it was peaceful. It was surreal and no one spoke.

We visited some other people on the road who were in their generation. They all offered coffee, and I was pretty wired by the afternoon. The farmhouses had not been updated too much and you had a sense of what it might be like living there when my mother was growing up. The typical things were the large wood-burning kitchen stoves, simple furniture, a cellar to keep things through the winter and of course the sauna bath building, which was very important. After hours of Finnish and many heartfelt reunions, we took Simi back to her house and started toward Mass City, which is where Aunt Elna and Uncle Urho lived on a farm. It had been a larger town when the copper mines were operating, but now it has a blinking light at one intersection and a few businesses. This had been the location of the Mass City Co-op, one of many Co-ops that Finns started to share resources instead of each buying their own equipment, which they could not afford. As the youngest sibling, Elna was always upbeat and unlike my mother refused to talk about her childhood, while my mother dwelled on it. They exemplified two opposite extremes of coping styles. However, Aunt Elna, the youngest of the eight, was born when her father was taken away, age six when her mother was taken away, and as a happy baby that got the most attention. She had been spared much of the turmoil and had not gone through what the older children had experienced on that farm. Elna was under five feet tall but made up for it with her energy. I walked around their barn and outbuildings. It was a life from a past dairy farm. My mother and Elna were speaking in Finnish and were getting caught up. I was trying to soak up some of the history by viewing it closely. I went for an ATV drive with my cousin Harold on their 120-acre farm. He was visiting from Detroit, where he was an accountant. As a son he had worked hard on the dairy farm growing up and was not going to do that as an adult. His sister stayed in the house, but Elna had worked in the barn and the house. The sister Carole was living in southern Michigan with her husband and three children. I enjoyed seeing some of the 120 acres, where they had raised dairy cattle and rented out hay fields to other farmers. It was a peaceful, stable life.

On the way back we actually went to Jack's farm, as my mother had said there was a trunk with photos and other things from California in the house. She had brought it from California and left it when we fled the farm. Cousin Anna (Jack's fourth wife, and my mother's cousin) came out and was happy to see us and opened her arms for an embrace. She invited us inside, but my mother was not going to go that far on this return visit. We talked a bit and I asked if she had the trunk, and she looked surprised and said no. Later my sister said she had played with the contents but had no idea what happened to it. The same thing happened when my mother left behind a trunk with photos in Pasadena. The children played with it and it was probably tossed out as unattached history for them. I wanted one photo of my father, but it was not to be. I wish my mother had sent for the trunks but I guess she had enough problems. It was good to see Anna. She had been on Jack's farm for 21 years.

We had an important trip to see her birthplace, and I gained a better feeling for what life was like in the Upper Peninsula. Mother did not say this to me, but I think it was a successful trip seeing Simi, the family farm, Elna, Urho and Harold. I thought this might help update some of her old memories that were ruminating in her head. It was a like a totally different world that had been left behind as technology, employment and opportunity drained the area of the younger people. The history that remained was very important to the Finnish community and families. And I felt this was a very important trip for my mother to compare her memories with the recent visit, and important for me to spend some time with her that was fairly pleasant and not stressful. Our lives had been too busy working, studying and trying to survive. More importantly, I finally had a car that was able to get us to her birthplace. When we saw people in the lobby of her senior apartment building she was saying she had a wonderful time up North. So this was a success in making her happy for a while.

CHAPTER 11

Trip out West

After the trip to the Upper Peninsula of Michigan with my mother, I emptied my apartment packed one-half of the trunk in my 1963 Chevy Impala and my friend Miriam packed the other half. Miriam was a petite woman with curly brown hair, eyeglasses and a glowing smile. She always seemed to be happy. We were both unsure if we were going on a trip or moving out West. Her father was a judge, and he was very unhappy about her black boyfriend who had been busted for pot, and I was unhappy with her boyfriend as he made a pass at me. So she felt it was a good time to "get out of Dodge," and so did I. I seriously needed a break.

I was leaving all that I had known for 22 years my mother, my sister, all the moves, trials and Evanston which had been a good place to grow up despite everything. It gave me opportunity and a sense of purpose. My rusty 63 Chevy had a good V8 engine but I thought I could just fill the radiator up for 2,000 miles and it would be alright. The car mechanic warned me and I should have changed it. Gasoline was 25 cents a gallon, but we wanted to make sure we had enough money, so we had a couple ride with us to Denver, Colorado. Neither one of us had any outdoor experience but we had a tent and sleeping bags. I had bought a $1 backpack and wore bald tennis shoes. I had been on one camping trip with my sister and brother-in-law, but I stayed in the car with the doors locked. I was afraid of not having a locked door between me and the criminal who was trying to get us.

Having spent most of my money on tuition and was broke but that did not deter our enthusiasm for an adventure. We made it across the Mississippi River and found an Iowa diner with 5-cent Cokes and 50 cent hamburgers. The last time I had made this trip was when my mother arranged to have strangers transport me to an orphanage in Boone, Iowa. That was not fun, but this was a fun trip. This was different. I was choosing to look for a new life outside of Chicago. We found a campground and settled in for the night. I was terrified, as there were no deadbolts on the tent and it seemed fool hardy to trust that a stranger was not going to come and kill you. We heard noise, but cattle were wandering around rustling the grass. Finally, I was in a deep sleep when the couple woke us up at dawn exclaiming "It's raining!" I was not an outdoor person, but I thought that was what the tent was for and I was pretty upset with them. I was determined to get rid of this couple as soon as we could or at least in Denver. We drove through the prairie and climbed up toward Denver. I tried running and found out that high altitude took your breath away! We jumped in a cold lake and my lungs and diaphragm contracted and that took my breath away. I was learning new things every day.

Finally, the day came when we were able to drop off the "chicken littles," and we headed up toward Wyoming. On the way we picked up two students from the University of London who were hitchhiking across America. One was British and the other Iranian. They were clean, polite and had British accents, which helps. We came to a small town with a local rodeo so we decided to camp there. The rodeo was up close and personal, not the big ones in Chicago amphitheaters. We went to a bar afterward and the two Brits started imitating the bow-legged walk of the cowboys. I was shocked that they would be so oblivious, and quickly told them to stop as it might trigger a beating by beer-soaked cowboys. Now we knew our passengers had the maturity of ten-year-olds. They calmed down but I did not feel like babysitting much longer. On the way to Yellowstone we also picked up a young man in a long, white-fringed leather jacket, matching pants, cowboy hat and a guitar. He seemed ready to perform as he had no luggage.

I was not aware the bear situation had been going on for decades. The first tourists were wealthy people who expected to have nice accommodations, good food or had a private cabin that was grandfathered in when the Park was formed in 1872. The left-over good food was dumped into a huge pile for bears to eat while people sat on bleachers watching them for night time entertainment. Finally, biologists thought bears should be eating natural food and put an end to this practice. With the introduction of the automobile modem tourists would feed them out the car window and take pictures of Johnny feeding the bear! No one consulted the bears about this change from fast food to natural foods, or from a pile to a drive through feeders. The bears were hungry and were training their cubs to eat garbage from people's trash cans or cars.

In 1972, not knowing any of this history, we drove along and my overheating 63 Chevy, decided to pick a spot to stop right in front of grizzly bears. They slowly rambled toward my car and looking forward to food. Not one of the three men or Miriam would help me, so I got out of the car and popped the hood to see what I could do. The bears took note of my arrival, and slowly moved toward me and my terrified occupants. I got back into the car and we did this dance went on for a while. Finally, a Tennessee man in a Jeep stopped and put some water in my radiator. Thank you, kind man! We parted ways with the hitchhikers at the next stop. The fringed guitar player disappeared into the Visitor Center.

Then Miriam reminded me she had some family friends who had a grandfathered-in cabin on the west side of Yellowstone near a river. The cabin turned out to be a grand affair, and the mother had a few pounds of turquoise in her squash-blossom necklace. The two sons were close to our age but seemed very sheltered and younger. We were going to camp with them on the large property, as the "cabin" was somewhat stuffy after a semi-formal dinner. We talked to them and played a game of Clue. The cards were shuffled and we had picked out weapons, but then I said I know how it was done, who did it, which room and with what weapon. I was right. So we had to deal another game. Sometimes I just have visions of the future. The next day the boys took us to the nearby river, that was shallow and I was not sure fish could live in it. Miriam did her duty to say hello to family friends, and we left to do the usual Yellowstone Park sightseeing. Old Faithful, geothermal wonders and buffalo were all amazing to me. We camped in the Park. At a rushing stream we saw an American darter or snake bird that dives into rushing water to get food. I don't know how the small but sturdy bird could have the strength to withstand the rushing water.

We decided to head toward the Grand Tetons National Park, and there was a six-person limit. Young people were filling up the campsites whether they knew the people or not. There were many young people on the road looking for a better life outside of the traditional roles or just a summer trip. It was all so beautiful and I was falling in love with the outdoors and felt like I belonged there. I enjoyed sitting on rocks and felt nature had most of the things you need. Even though we did not know the people, we shared common values and concern for the environment. The next night Miriam and I went to an isolated lake and for some reason ended up stripping off our clothes and dancing along a log. It was free, innocent and playful. This was not Chicago; there a woman had to be very alert to her surroundings and a would-be attacker. I needed to play and let loose. We only did that one time, but it was worth it.

We reached Montana, and there was a sign for a ghost town that had been a part of semi-precious stone mining. We started out on a dirt road but then it petered out and it looked like you were supposed to follow a dry creek bed with rocks. My 63 Chevy was not built for this but I decided to do it anyway despite signs nailed to trees saying that "Trespassers will be shot on sight!" It was a rough trip and I don't know what we would have done if the car had gotten stuck, but finally we made it to a clearing. There were old buildings that were being repaired by the University of Montana Archeology Department. They were excavating the area for human remains, gem history and to create the ghost town. We just showed up a few years early. We were wondering where the person was who was going to shoot on sight, but we developed an impromptu play about living in a mining town with two characters to amuse ourselves. I liked Miriam's imagination; it was better than being a kid again. We felt watched but we finally went to sleep with the car doors locked. The next day we could see there was another road out of the town. I was very relieved, as I was not going to drive that rocky creek bed again. We bid farewell to gem history and proceeded on a dirt road toward Glacier National Park.

We went through Butte and Missoula before we made it to Glacier. We saw antelope jumping, had heard about the Jack- A- Lopes, which were half antelope and half jack rabbit. A young man was generous and took us up a steep incline in his Jeep to see Big Horn Sheep. We also went fly fishing for trout after we caught the grasshoppers for bait. We had fish for dinner. I was able to catch the fish but I don't think Miriam was into cleaning them. We stayed outside his cabin one night and he had put out a bathtub in the sun for us to bathe in when it was warm. I am sure he enjoyed some company and we enjoyed experiencing some of Montana living. We finally entered Glacier National Park, which was established in 1910 and bordered on Canada's Waterton Park. We stopped at a store and met two Blackfeet Natives while buying supplies. They told us about a backpacking trail across two mountain passes that sounded interesting. I had bought a $1 used canvas backpack from a friend who was going to bicycle from Chicago to California and wanted me to join him, but doing it by car was enough for me. Although I had just had my first camping experiences, I was totally drawn to being up in the mountain tops themselves. I had always climbed trees, radio towers and the mountain in Greece. To her credit, Miriam was into it, too. I had bald tennis shoes and we had canned food as we had no idea how to prepare for a backpack trip. We parked near the trail and started out on the trail the next morning and made it to the first camping area, which was all men. We did not realize that women were not doing this activity. To our surprise one of the Blackfeet native men came off the trail and asked if we were going to continue on the trip. We asked if he was going, and he said no, but we said we were continuing. So he left and we were wondering why he would expend so much energy to ask us our plans, but we were tired and went to sleep.

The next day the group of men went off in all different directions and we proceeded on the two-mountain pass trail. At times the trail was very thin, and near a 1,000-foot drop-off, which made me dizzy and I was afraid of falling off the edge. We saw there was a glacier and two men with pick axes, boots with crampons and ropes. We had no idea why they needed so much equipment. We just proceeded slowly across the glacier, me with my bald tennis shoes. I was used to snow and ice, so it did not seem that different to me, except for the steep slope which if you fell from, you probably could not stop careening down the glacier at a fast speed. We just kept on going. We finally reached dirt again and stopped to put some grapefruit powder on some clean snow as a refreshing treat, and were glad we made it across safely. Later I realized the men were probably on a training exercise and had more sense than we did. But historically people did not have all that equipment at their disposal, and they made it across.

In later afternoon we arrived at a high-altitude lake and our packs were getting heavy. We saw two men fishing and they asked us to join them for a fish dinner. We were surprised to get a fresh meal on the trail, and we opened some canned food. They were students from UC Berkeley and were experienced in backpacking the Sierra Nevada Range which is more granite and only black bears. They did mention that Glacier had grizzly bears, and Miriam was afraid and she and one man slept on top of a large rock nearby. I joined Kevin in a tent near the fire pit which was comforting while the fire lasted. I slept very soundly until I felt something on my foot that was warm and wet but there was a terrible smell. I could see the snout of a very large, smelly grizzly bear that seemed intent on my foot. Ken quietly slowly grabbed my arm and said "do not move." I was paralyzed with fear and my heart was pounding as though it was going to push its way out of my chest. The bear finally decided to leave and we took our first big breaths of relief.

Miriam and the other man had seen it happen and were wondering if we were going to make it through the event. The men had cleaned up the fish remains, but of course bears have 30 times the smelling ability of humans and fish is very appealing to them. But none near our tent, so the bear left. We waited to make sure the bear was gone and then preceded out of the tent to have a congratulatory "We are alive!" breakfast.

The four of us were continuing in the same direction over a mountain pass, so we welcomed the company in case the bear came back. We cautiously looked around every bend in the trail as though we had a better chance of survival. We trudged over one pass and camped in an area with mountain goats with kids. This was very thrilling to see them, but the problem was they move around all night and every time I heard a noise I thought it was the bear coming back. We made it over another pass and Kevin promoted eating at Sperry Lodge, which was one of the stone lodges built in 1910 by James and Louis Hill of the Northern Pacific Railway to promote tourism. You can ride a horse up, but of course we were doing it the hard way by hiking across two mountain passes. Kevin was from San Francisco and was used to good food and this gave us something to look forward to for lunch. We spent another night with an excellent view and then started hiking toward the lodge. We were able to clean up a bit, as you do get grubby on the trail with no bathroom facilities. The meal was very good food, especially to us first-time backpackers. Years later I was able to stay at the lodge for an overnight trip.

After this very special treat we started the steep descent down toward the road. The men were more experienced and faster, and they said they were going to move on ahead. They gave us their contact information in California, We slowly picked our way down the rocky steep trail with our knees complaining. We finally made it down to the road. All and all, we did fairly well, as we did not fitness train for the first-time backpacking trip. We were walking down the road toward the car. But after walking quite a while we were not finding it. When we saw the entrance trailhead we knew something was wrong. My 63 Chevy was stolen!! Who would steal that pile of junk? I was determined to make it to California and thought I will walk if I never get my car back.

We hiked to a ranger station to report the stolen car. We explained meeting the Blackfeet who told us about the trail, and them checking on us. It finally dawned on us they wanted to know if we would be away from the car for a few days! As Chicagoans, you would think we would be more suspicious, but we were not. The ranger said because the Blackfeet reservation was Federal we had to talk to the FBI. I was surprised there were agents there, but it turns out many criminals steal from national park to park across state lines. One man they were looking for was putting hat pins in people's pillows to stab them. Glad we missed him. Then there was the typical stealing of camera and equipment. This was a summertime job for some people.

Then we had the shock of finding out that the bear that had visited us in the high country had traveled to a ranger sleeping on the ground and severely mauled him! He was in surgery and was going to make it, but with a lot of physical damage. We felt terrible and relieved at the same time. That bear was on my foot and had decided to spare me and Kevin. They were able to kill the bear in two days.

I then realized this would make the papers, so I called my mother and she was very upset about the bear attack in Glacier. I said we were fine and not to worry. I did not tell her about our close call. I realize I had spent my life protecting her from worry, as she had her hands full just working. While this made me feel stronger it did not give me any sense of comfort or consolation.

They quickly found my 63 Chevy, which was towed to the FBI lot for processing. They had stolen sentimental jewelry and other items including Miriam's big camera. The FBI arranged a meeting with the tribal leader and we went along. He said he felt it was two men who were heroin addicts who had left the reservation a day ago. I was surprised that there were drugs on the reservation, as I thought drugs were an urban problem. Now Native Americans have the highest substance abuse rate, which is sad. So the FBI was able to complete their reports and keep that on file.

We were relieved to get our transportation back and decided to head toward Canada. My car had large rust holes from the extensive use of salt on Chicago roads, so a pack rat had decided to move into my trunk to start a family. At night Miriam slept in the front bench seat and I slept in the back seat as I was taller. The rat decided night was a good time to practice playing the seat springs. Boing, boing, boing! This was very disruptive to my sleep, so I wanted the rat out.

For some reason I cannot explain, Miriam wanted her camera back, and we found the two men on the reservation and we went there to ask for it back. I think we assumed the FBI was not going to do more. Foolishly we drove to their place and one man asked me to go for a walk, which I did. He threw me on the ground and was going to rape me. I cried and he acted surprised and said "You don't want to have sex?" I said no, trying to get up off my knees as quickly as possible so I could run if needed. I heard a radio show that said all the girls in a Southwest tribe were raped, so it was just a matter of if but a matter of when. That sounded so tragic to me to start your teenage years out with violence. But he responded to the tears and saying no. We slowly walked back to the house and I whispered in Miriam's ear that we needed to leave right away. We started driving north and I cannot explain why we did such a stupid thing as asking heroin addicts if they would return the stolen goods.

When we crossed the border and a Royal Mounted Police asked if we had anything, and I mentioned the rat. I thought maybe he could help us but instead I had to pull over and he threatened to have me arrested for "importing wildlife from the United States." I thought he was joking but he was not. Never tell a border patrol about harboring a rat. Animals cross the borders all the time for various reasons without papers.

Finally, he let us go. We did seek out a Canadian ranger at our campground who was able to trap and release the rat. But in the meantime we had given a ride to a tall Jewish man who was writing a book on trains including the Trans Canada train. He had a PhD but was not working until the fall. He had a stutter, but he was very pleasant in conversation.

Richard wanted to go backpacking, and after Glacier I was all excited about doing another trip, even though it would seem counter-intuitive after the bear incident. Miriam did not want to do that and said she wanted to go back again to the Blackfeet reservation and get her camera back! I couldn't believe it, as I was never going back to that place, and she knew about the rape attempt. Miriam was determined, so Richard and I went backpacking, which was a very different experience than in the United States. Canadian rangers did not seem to care where you went or if you had a permit. He lead the way to a mountain trail which gave a good view of the Canadian Rockies and we had the company of a herd of elk, and dark clouds of mosquitoes. We had to eat in the tent and basically could not leave unless it was urgent. From our perspective Richard could see that we were supposed to be on the next mountain over. That mountain was a lot nicer with water and probably mosquito free. But here we were so we might as well enjoy it.

The mosquitoes did not let up, so we had to talk in our tent till be went to sleep. The next morning we made a hasty descent back to the campground. Miriam returned in another day. We gave Richard a ride toward Vancouver, which was still 711 miles away, but he decided he needed to ride the rails and said he would meet us in Vancouver.

We stayed in some Canadian towns where people told us stories including the hazards of hanging out your laundry, as a moose could come along and drag the clothesline with their antlers. Canada seemed much slower paced and quieter than the United States and a sharp contrast to Chicago. We finally made it to Vancouver, which is surrounded by water and did a few things, but we wanted to be the outdoors. We met Richard, who said he would go with us into the United States for a short time. We made it across the border and then learned that Richard had visited a pediatrician he knew who had popular recreational drugs like LSD and marijuana. This was strange to me as the heroin addict I knew from Cook County Social Services said he got his heroin from his childhood pediatrician. Why would a pediatricians have drugs?

In Washington we visited a friend of my high-school classmate Marty His friend was married and had children. They did not tell us one child had hepatitis until we were leaving. We visited REI -Recreational Equipment, Inc., which displayed all the backpacking/camping equipment we were supposed to have when we crossed two mountain passes in Glacier. They had the most recent and expensive gear, mostly for men. For some reason Miriam decided to go on a trip in Oregon and said she would meet us later in Eugene. So Richard and I went to the ocean near Tillamook, where he dropped acid and proceeded to take all his clothes off. I did not mind but he stood out as a tall man with dark curly hair and beard. I just sat by the waves and enjoyed the ocean. However, as luck would have it a fire had broken out on the beach and the firemen thought we were involved. Richard did look a bit suspicious. He returned to where I was enjoying the ocean surf and put his clothes back on and convinced the firemen we were not into pyromania. When we went into the town of Tillamook for dinner where we got a lot of peering looks as the word had spread. Richard thought he knew someone in a cabin near the ocean, but no one was home. Richard went to the neighbor and asked where she was. He said she had left for a few days and would be back. Richard said it was late so we were spending the night there and he would tell him when we left. So we moved in. The small house was somewhat untidy so we began to clean it up and do the dishes, etc. I looked at the calendar to try to figure out the activities of the person who lived there and what she might be doing. It seemed to me she might be having a baby. I was glad we cleaned up the small house if she came back with a baby and we were happier to stay in a clean place. We left the next day and told the neighbor who waved goodbye.

We picked up Miriam, and Richard said he was going back to Canada to continue his book research, so we bid farewell and continued our journey down the Oregon and California coast. We visited the majestic Redwood Forest and saw the rocky California coast. Miriam did not know if she was going to stay or go back to Chicago, but she had a big family cushion in Chicago when the heat died down about her ex-boyfriend. She stayed in the San Francisco East Bay while I went down the coast to Monterrey. I had $200, and my rusty car, to my name.

I camped near a place with seals that insisted on barking all night and kept me up. The next night I had slept in a Church parking lot and did not know that it was Sunday morning. I had eyes peering at me while I was waking up, but I put my head back down until the service started. I was missing Miriam's company as we had had a long trip together and I was not used to being alone in a strange place. I had no idea where she had gone. Later I found her in a cult all dressed in white that could not talk to "outsiders." I was disappointed but it was her life.

I had not seen my cousin Leon since my mother and my trip to California in 1967. He had moved from Southern California to the Bay Area and said I could stay in an extra condo he had, as he and his wife were busy with her tennis career. He said California is a good place but people were transient. I took him up on his generous offer and stayed in the condo while I tried to figure things out. The condo had a view of the Bay Bridge and Golden Gate Bridge, but I was lonely. I wanted to stay in California and had $200 to my name and no leads for work. I had seen too much beauty on the trip and wanted to be closer to the outdoors. Chicago was a big dirty city with loose family connections. But here I had no one here but my traveling cousin.

I met a man who wanted to take me to the Napa Valley for wine tasting. Wine did not interest me but I thought this was a chance to see more of the area. We were driving toward the Napa Valley when I saw Napa State Hospital and I wanted to go in and see if I could get a job. There was a party going on and it turned out to be the retirement party for the Psychology Department Director. There had been some wine drinking involved and people were in a good mood. I asked the retiring man if there was a position for me, and he said there was one that only lasted nine months and I could apply. I got the information and went back to the car with a big smile on my face. To my surprise the job did come through, but it meant commuting from the East Bay to Napa five days a week, and I had to register my rusty car in California as a resident. The commute was not easy, as it was an El Niño year, which meant torrential rains and flooding.

To make matters worse, the CHP (California Highway Patrol) could not verify my rusted-off VIN tag and impounded the car in Napa. I told them the story and showed them the paperwork I had with me. I knew trying to communicate with the Illinois bureaucracy was going to be useless. Again, who would steal this car? I did find a commuting group, but they did not go every day. Finally the CHP gave up and let me register the car in California.

Despite these hardships, my work was interesting in that they were sorting the men who were criminally insane and being sent to Atascadero in Southern California from the mentally ill but not dangerous. It was fairly obvious who should go and who should stay. One man was an axe-murder and his objects were little boys. He was such a nice man, and when his family visited they were equally as nice. However, in his previous placement he was able to get an axe, escape, and kill another boy. He was going to stay here as he was not a threat to adults, but this was a real puzzle as to what was creating this big divide in his behavior. The project meant interviewing men and writing reports with my recommendations to my supervisor, who was a Psychologist with a PhD. He said my reports were good but too elaborate. He told me not to give pearls to swine. I was trying to please my employer but I remembered what he said.

The new Director was a psychiatrist who was easy to get along with and spent a lot on time with administrative things and writing a book. I was not allowed to work on the men's ward as the last doctor had been murdered by a patient. I was on the women's ward and ran a discharge group for women who unfortunately were caught in the time when Mental Health funding was being cut by Governor Reagan. If they were not in the hospital, where they were relatively safe, they would be on the street as there was not funding for community Mental Health services. That made them vulnerable and not receiving the help they needed. The movie "One Flew Over the Cuckoo's Nest" was popular and it made it look like mental hospitals were terrible places, but actually the patients who were stable enough could walk on the grounds or eat in the extra cafeteria. The street was dangerous and not treatment. This problem has not been really remedied since the 1970s. What is also important is services for children so they get help early and do not need them as much later on in life. Programs like Head start help to assess children's special needs early in their lives.

The Hospital had a budget for training and we had some excellent workshops such as Virginia Stair's family therapy using psychodrama and other speakers. This augmented my recent Master's training, as I did not have extra money for conferences or trainings.

I also worked with the Developmentally Delayed, as there were not community or school services for this group in the past. There was a work opportunity for those who were able to make coffins and it was a regular job assignment. A teenage patient hitchhiked out of the Hospital one day on his way back from making coffins, but he was located. One time we got a call from a pizza place in Napa that said a patient was dancing on one of their tables. A staff member was sent out to bring him back. When patients had freedom to walk around the grounds and unexpected freedom trips did happen.

I liked the staff and the Social Worker staff commuted on some days from Berkeley. During the intense rainy season there was a flu outbreak, and many nurses and Psych. Techs. had called in sick, so they had put the patients in the day room as it was less walking. I tried to help by getting clean sheets, but the pile was heavier than I thought, and I put my T10 vertebra out of place in my spine. I applied for Workman's Comp, but they said I was working out of class and it would get better. I had no medical insurance I went along with it, but my back still hurts off and on until this day. There was no union to understand my rights. All and all it was a good starting position. I was saving money. I needed to look for another position and a place to live.

CHAPTER 12

The East Bay

F inding a job at Napa State Hospital had been deceivingly easy, while meeting people, getting another position, graduate school and housing were not that easy. The long commute wore me out with flooding and time pressure. The Berkeley Social Workers that I liked were much older and were looking toward retirement, while I was twenty-five and just starting out in California. The education level was higher in the Bay Area, which was good, but it meant more competition.

Governor Reagan had cut the budget for Mental Health and I did not want to work for an agency with limited resources. I ended up doing some odd jobs and volunteered for the Berkeley Free Clinic Mental Health. One highlight was a Marine who came in and we were standing and talking in a room with pillows on the floor. He stripped all his clothes off and proceeded to throw me across the room onto the pillows. At that point I went out to indicate we needed some police presence. I was not hurt, but it pointed out that anything can happen with an unknown public.

The University of Illinois was behaviorist theory with rat mazes and research, which defiantly has its place in finding out more about human behavior. Roosevelt University was Freudian theory, which taught more about the history of psychiatry and psychology but also testing and real experience in an internship and writing the master's thesis. The West Coast was involved in Humanist theory, which emphasized treating the patient as a person with potential and using their abilities to achieve more balance and mental health. The Humanist Institute had a conference which I attended to learn more about this approach and what might interest me. Part of this was Gestalt Therapy, Play Therapy, Art Therapy and more individual and group techniques. I think there is a place for all types of theory and therapy to work together learning more about what actually helps people and their problems. Of course, there was medication for those who might benefit from that. I felt like I had moved to the right place but I needed work to pay my bills and find a place to live.

Meanwhile, my cousin traveled extensively and I rarely saw him, but his younger brother, who was 18, showed up from his home in Eagle Rock, California. We did things like hiking and photography together. He liked to fish, and the Pacific Ocean was a good place for that as well as streams. But he moved into another place to help his older brother with his many projects. I found it hard to meet people and I never saw people in the condo or even at the pool. It was a large complex with no people.

The job at the hospital ended in May and I had saved up money so I could find another place to live. My mother came to visit and even took an airplane, which was an amazing surprise. We were at the pool and I noticed she had no leg hair. It turns out neither did my sister, both 100% Finnish, I was 50% and I had it all. This is not a big deal but it points out how little we knew about each other. I took her to a restaurant and I ordered Brandy Alexanders after dinner even though we both did not drink. She swirled around in her chair pretending she was drunk and showed her sense of humor. She said she wanted to go to San Diego to see my cousin's younger sister, Aunt Ellen's youngest child. I agreed to do that, as it was a short flight from Oakland. We went to Mary's house and she was with her second husband and her son. The visit was fairly pleasant but I suggested that we go out to eat at a local restaurant. We were driving and my mother said "Take me to the airport!" I was shocked, but she insisted and was dropped off and we drove Mary and her family back to their place. I did not want to stay with them. I found a place in downtown San Diego that was cheap and there were many Navy sailors around. The window had a curtain that was blowing into the bare room and I had the urge to jump out of the window. I was deeply hurt by my mother just leaving without any notice. It brought back all the agony of abandonment and being taken to the orphanage with no notice. I calmed down and called Ali, the high school friend who had married and moved to New Mexico. The next day I boarded a Greyhound bus, which took time but was an inexpensive way to get to Albuquerque.

Ali had always said she wanted marry a cowboy, so she moved out West and did just that. I was amazed that she would jump into a marriage, as I was so cautious. The next day we went to Old Town and she said he was verbally abusive and she was thinking of a divorce. She was a sweet person but maybe too naive. I didn't think I could jump in and out of a marriage so easily. She had a good job so she would be OK. It was good seeing a familiar face and it made me feel more grounded after my mother's disappearance. Later Ali remarried and had two children with a nice man.

I decided to hitchhike back to the Bay Area and saw a woman on the road that was very attractive and was heading back to Malibu. We got a ride with a man in a RV with seven children who were very active. I think he thought we could calm them down, but they were swinging off the bars and jumping up and down. He had taken the children on a trip while his wife was having number eight and wanted some peace and quiet. I was amazed that he could handle all this activity He was going to the Grand Canyon, so we decided that might be good and were dropped off in a grove of trees as we did not have any camping gear. We both slept pretty well, but in the morning I woke up and she was doing a headstand as part of her morning yoga routine. We took a peek at the Grand Canyon and proceeded to get rides to Malibu where she could continue her lifestyle there. I went back out on busy Highway 101 and saw a man with a dog standing on the side of the road, and he was going to Oregon. He was a bit worn looking but seemed kind and the dog might be a plus. We were picked up by a Volkswagen VW van that already had people and luggage going up the Coast on Highway 1 near Big Sur. This was a definite hippy bus minus the marijuana. It was so crowded we had to lie on the luggage, but we could still see the beautiful California coast. We slept near the ocean, which was sandy, but the waves put me to sleep. One thing about moving so much as a young child: I was flexible.

We were lucky in getting rides through the San Jose area and the man dropped us both off near my cousin's condo. It was late in the day, so I did not want him out there in the dark so I asked him to stay in my cousin's upscale condo. I hardly even saw my cousin or his wife, so this seemed OK. He was able to sleep on the floor with his dog, but the next morning my cousin made an unexpected appearance. It did not look good, but they did not say anything. The man continued his trip to Oregon with his well-behaved dog. This was my last hitchhike, as there was a serial killer on the loose, the 1960s drugs had put a darker tinge on the Summer of Love and there was a gloomy recession. Things had changed, but I still believed this was a better place to live.

In workshops and the Gestalt group, I talked about some of my childhood experiences for the first time. It was very painful but it was a relief to open up a bit. It was a creative approach to resolving my past and I was going to working with people with similar issues.

In June, Kevin was going to Yosemite for a back pack trip, and I agreed to go along with him. I had bought some better backpacking equipment and he knew the Sierra Nevada Mountains. I was nervous about bears, as we had had that grizzly bear encounter in Glacier National Park, but he reassured me that black bears were really different. Being new to California I did not know in June there was still snow up in the higher elevations. The trail was a rushing white water of melting snow, and I had to cling to rocks on the left side and avoid being swept off the steep drop-off on the right side. I still had faith in his experience. The trail was steep and I was not used to the thin air at higher elevations. When we arrived at the permit-allowed camping area in Rancheria Falls, we saw a large group with about twenty backpacks lined up. Luckily they were leaving, but they told us that every single backpack had been broken into by a bear. That was not encouraging news, but we hung our food up after dinner and had the place almost to ourselves. In the middle of the night I heard a gentle noise but went back to sleep. In the morning we discovered the bear had gotten all our food. We did not want to return so soon and begged the few people in the area for food, and were able to get dried mashed potatoes and tea. This was generous of them, as backpackers are supposed to be self-sufficient. Kevin wanted to hike up to another lake, but I was too tired so I just enjoyed the scenery around Hetch Hetchy reservoir. The next night we had nothing for the bear to steal, so we were hungry but relaxed. Going back downhill was easier in that you were facing the rock you might have to grab.

I mentioned to Kevin I was looking for a place to stay and he said his older brother's fiancée was going to cooking school in France and her apartment was available. I tried living in Noe Valley in San Francisco, but found there was a lot of traffic and no yard with trees, plants and maybe a garden. The fog rolled in at night and it was cold and damp. One night a drunk man tried to break into the apartment and I told him to leave, but he would not leave. I called the police two times before they showed up and thought it was funny. After the Peeping Tom episode I did not think it was funny. I wanted a place with sunshine, plants and room to breathe.

The East Bay seemed like a better place to stay. Kevin said he was leaving his parents' house and was getting a place in the East Bay while studying at UC Berkeley Graduate School. He said I could join him. I did not know him really well, but we had things in common. He was even-tempered and smart. However, before we moved in together, he was transporting two marijuana plants and the police stopped him and saw the plants. He was charged with marijuana possession. His parents were very upset and wanted him to slay at home in San Francisco, which was quite a commute. They hired an attorney and the matter was resolved, but I did not know how. He rented a cabin behind a house that came with a cat. The cat had to have the window open, so this meant raccoons could come in and eat food. It was not ideal but it was a start. Next, he rented the lower half of the redwood house. I had to renew my car insurance, and the agents came out and almost denied my insurance because we were not married. The next thing that happened was that my rusty

'63 Chevy was stolen. Who would want to steal the rust bucket? It turned out it was two 12-year-old boys who could barely see over the large steering wheel. The police found it and it was returned to me for the fourth time in our life together.

I took a weekend EST course with Werner Erhard over one weekend. It was supposed to open you up to new possibilities. We were not to eat, take a bathroom break, wear a watch or talk. A man who had been an Army sergeant spoke to us for hours. I was tuning out but when they asked people to come onto the stage in a large auditorium, I volunteered. We were just supposed to stand there, but I was facing a huge crowd and I started to get weak-kneed and thought I might faint. This was a revelation to me that I needed to work on this shyness and uncover myself. In the Recovery Room we lay on the floor and a few people were having a mental breakdown, so I am not sure they anticipated that reaction. I went home and felt much lighter in that I usually use food as a pacifier and I had not eaten that much. It was a good feeling, but my old habits started creeping back in.

In the meantime I had found a therapy agency in San Francisco that was started by a psychiatrist who wanted to meet the needs of the client and it was run on group consensus. We moved to a bigger building and actually built the walls and decorated them ourselves on the second floor. The first floor was a large open area for people to sit and talk, and there was a methadone clinic run by medical staff. It was a path to getting a California license with a Master's degree. I had been asked to apply to a PhD program, but I had to write a biographical statement and we went to Kevin's parents' house as they had an office. But try as I may I could not write the statement. I was too overwhelmed by emotions and unresolved grief to write something glib. I did not want to spend years studying and writing a dissertation, so the license was a good solution to a career that gave me options.

I started working in an Agency in San Francisco and registered with the State of California for a license, which required 3,000 hours of individual and group therapy with clients and supervision hours. I mainly did individual hours with average adults with adjustment issues to more serious issues. I also did pregnancy counseling for those undecided about what to do, which included a wide range of women and couples. Roe v Wade had been passed, so there were more options to consider. Most people knew what they wanted to do; it was just a matter of airing their feelings. I also worked on the Hot Line, which could include suicide, crisis and just needing referrals. Eventually I co-ran a women's sexuality group for women who wanted to explore their sexuality. Men were still supposed to know what to do, but women needed to understand what they wanted and how to negotiate sexuality. It was very successful and many women felt more empowered with knowledge.

The Women's Health movement was part of women taking control of their own lives. I had good individual supervisors and it was a positive experience. One group supervisor had us come all the way to his Marin home and we were talking about our family of origin. I tried to present a clear picture of my chaotic life, but when I was finished the leader just said "An example of an inadequate mother and child." I was so astonished I left the room. I did not talk to him about it, and no one talked to me about the incident. I felt exposed and realized I had to come up with a sanitized version of my story, as I was being too honest and open.

The Gestalt group was good in that we could decide how we wanted to present and work on the issue. This could be a dialogue with the person you had an issue with or a part of yourself you wanted to explore or improve. I went over the "L" train incident where I was on the railroad tracks and my mother seemed to be dissociated. A woman hugged me as a stand-in for the mother I wanted, and it felt good. It takes time to heal a trauma, and it's good to have control on how you want to heal your wounds. This work was creative and gave people choices.

My sister and brother-in-law came to visit. They had been married in 1972 and they had their twin boys in 1976. My sister wanted me to come back to Chicago, as she did not think this was a good place for me. She was right in some sense: it was hard to make connections and people were on the move. But I was determined to make a go of it and wanted to stay. Plus the mountains were so beautiful and only hours away, as was the ocean and the desert landscapes.

One of the men in the agency had paired up with a doctor to do evaluations on the patients and they would do the billing. Since I had done this kind of work, I offered to do some of the evaluations and get paid for the reports. One night we went out to dinner in the city after work and too much wine. Later he drove me home, but I let him come inside. He was making moves on me and I was trying to be quiet as Kevin was sleeping. It got out of hand and Kevin came out at an awkward moment. This led to him moving out, which I understood. Later the man was under investigation about how he and his partner were billing the government. I was dragged in as a witness, which was embarrassing but I did not know what became of it. I just was more careful who I associated with in the future. He had proposed buying San Francisco real estate together which would have been a good investment but I declined as he was not trust worthy.

I advertised for a new roommate and a woman with long dark hair who worked in a pre-school showed up. She had an outgoing personality and was interested in the arts, so I accepted her. We were getting along fine but the landlady has seen that I read Eric Berne's book on Transactional Analysis and she did not approve. She said we had a month to move out. I did not know my rights and started looking for a new place. My roommate, Laney, said she was going on vacation to Mexico so she wouldn't be available to help in the search. I found my house in Berkeley with two bedrooms and $185 a month rent. There were five people on the waiting list, but somehow I got the house, which was located in downtown Berkeley; the other three houses were filled with PhD students. Laney returned from her trip and we lived together for a few years as I scraped by to get my license. Later she decided to move to Japan and stored her boxes in my darkroom. She was on the move, but I was trying to get settled. She had introduced me to a woman who was part of the women's artist community, which was important.

My next roommate was in Master's level Chinese studies at UC Berkeley and spoke Mandarin. I thought she was a responsible roommate, but she started hanging out with Rastafarians who smoked a lot of dope. I did not allow it in my house, but they could smoke other places. This was her undoing, as she was not able to do her studies and eventually became pregnant with someone's child and dropped out of school. I was always against drugs and drinking. It was depressing to see her fall into a deep hole; and she was my last roommate. Her friend was an English woman who also spoke fluent Chinese and was friends with one of the more sober men. He had come to Berkeley in a World War II duck that landed on the Berkeley marina. He was able to find house parts in the nearby city dump and make an airy home on the shore. The problem was the land was owned by the railroad, which asked him to leave and eventually used explosives to remove the rambling structure from their property. Before the homemade home was destroyed, I had photographed it and the photo appeared in a newspaper. They eventually moved to Hawaii. I gave up on roommates and never had one since, as I was making more money and could afford to live alone.

Meanwhile after years of working at the therapy agency, I was able to get enough hours to take the State of California exam. This meant hours of study and taking a course in Marin County on how to take the exam. Late at night I was driving home from the class crossing the Golden Gate Bridge and my 1964 Nash Rambler station wagon blew up and a tow truck appeared and dropped my disabled car and me on a dark off-road near the bridge. They were not concerned about me getting some help or my safety. I walked through the Presidio to a police station, but they were arresting two men and did not want to be bothered with me. I walked to Haight Ashbury, where a friend from Chicago lived, and he said he would help me to get my car towed. This seemed like an unfriendly place but at least someone was willing to help me out. After months of study and preparation I did take the exam and passed, which was great because not everyone had passed.

I had some private clients at Kevin's place, as it had a back room with a separate entrance. I saw some clients, but one night a man had a later appointment as he worked. He said his problem was stalking women and was thinking about rape, but his issue seemed to be anger with women in his life. We made some progress with his feelings and relationship, but I was uneasy being alone with him at night. This brought up the issue of whether I wanted to do private practice? The fees at that time were rather low and I wanted to buy a house. The client load could go up or down, and I wanted a steady income for the down payment and mortgage.

A discharge came from my right breast and went to the Free Clinic, as I still did not have medical insurance. They asked if I had a baby, which of course I did not, and suggested it might be cancer. I was 30 years old. So I was very upset and applied for government Medi-Cal. The nice man who waited on me was getting a law degree but he needed an income so was working as an eligibility worker in the meantime. The doctors were not sure about what was going on, but finally said they thought I was OK. I was too naive to ask for more investigation but took their word for it. This was probably a big mistake not to investigate with more medical advice.

All this led to the idea of working for Social Services, so I could save up a down payment for my house. I felt I was selling myself short, but I did not know what else to do. I started out in a lower position but people were very political, we had a baseball team and I enjoyed the work. I was the only woman so I became the manager and pitcher and we won most games. After playing baseball we would go out for cheap dinner and drinks at Bertola's. I started talking to a Mexican worker and we started dating. His family came from Mexico to do farm work but he and his siblings had college degrees. My social life was not good, and he was smart, but I did not realize when he drank to a certain point his personality flipped to very negative. One evening he pushed me down and my head hit the floor and a light bulb went off that this was love. It's perverted, but it had to do with my childhood. Its advantage to the perpetrator was they can say you fell and there are no marks. I was at his place one day and he had brought home case files, which was against the rules. He went out and I took the files and threw them in the nearby lake and left. The next day I felt guilty and rented a boat in the late afternoon and paddled across the lake to try to find the files. It was dark, the bottom was muddy and it was hopeless. This is one of the few times in my life I retaliated. After that he would show up at my house drunk and I filed five police reports on him for kicking in the front door, ripping the phone off the hook while I was trying to call the police, and once I was running down the street with him chasing me and a Marine saw this and apprehended him until the police got there. But the final straw was that I refused to let him spend the night and I heard my cat scream in the middle of the night but I went back to sleep. However, in the morning I found the dead cat and took it to the vet who said it was strangled. I felt I was next. After my cat was murdered, I brought myself to talk to a woman manager at work who asked HR to talk to him. Basically they said leave her alone or we will terminate your position. This worked, but in the meantime I had begun to drink more wine. Usually only on weekends, but this was a change. I was lonely and not sure I was doing the right thing working under my education level and was getting over this disruptive relationship. I did have some good experiences such as backpacking and meeting a women's art group where we shared our art.

One goal I had was to buy a house and have stability in my life. I had gone to "Get Rich Quick by Owning Real Estate" lectures given in hotel conference rooms. The men who wanted you to buy their courses said you too could have a great house, a fancy car and fancy women. The people who went were often immigrants, people of different races who like me were not going to inherit a family property or an inheritance. We were hungry and they knew it. What I got out of it was the upbeat "You can do it!" I did not have anyone supporting or encouraging me, so this was my support group. I also took real estate courses at night, as I knew very little about buying a home or home ownership. I did take the Real Estate exam but missed it by one point, but that was OK as my goal was knowledge, not being an agent. With this information I started looking, but was told I needed to barrow money to get a credit rating. I had never had a checkbook as I just paid cash like my mother. I bought a car on credit, and opened some store credit cards with my checking account. After saving for a few years they said I could buy a house worth $40,000, which meant something in a bad area that might require a gun and a pit bull. This was not OK for me to live in fear. One day I was walking by a California bungalow that had two units on a half-acre of land in Oakland. I asked about it, and the agent was a black man with a big yellow Cadillac convertible who said that it was being sold by an attorney. He did not tell me the reason the attorney had it was because the owners were in prison for selling drugs and gave it up as their payment. He did not tell me that there were drug users in the house as part of a notorious motorcycle gang. I proceeded to make an offer that was accepted, and then I found out I had to evict the people inside even though they were not tenants. The interest rate was 16% due to the recession and inflation. My mother was amazing in that she took a Greyhound bus all the way from Chicago with $5,000 cash around her neck under her clothes to help me with the down payment. I was so touched. She usually did not say directly that she loved me, but this was a sincere gesture of love. I took her to see the place before the unlawful residents had left. I wanted her to see what she was investing in besides me. She had to visit at my place in Berkeley, as the wheels of justice turn very slowly and she enjoyed my vegetable garden and fresh food. I made her fly back home instead of taking the long Greyhound bus ride.

The court date finally came and the judge approved the Sheriff's eviction. When the day came, the locksmith could not open the door so I told the Sheriffs to kick the door open, which they did. Once inside I saw motor oil on the carpet, holes and blood on the wall and broken windows. It gave me chills to think about what had happened there. I had taken a Woman in the Trades course on how to frame in windows and doors with basic carpentry skills. I worked till I fell asleep on the floor, and had a drill plugged into the wall in for protection. One night at two a.m. I was working outside and a man came by on a motorcycle and said he just got out of prison and did I want to go for a ride. I politely declined his offer and he drove off. A friend offered help from a man she knew, but he was arrested for accessory to murder. I worked very hard to get the house ready to rent and filled in the back storage shed with walls, windows and a door for tenants to use. To my surprise two friends wanted to rent the place and I could trust them to pay the rent. My plan to buy real estate took years and hard work, but I was starting to get somewhere.

CHAPTER 13

1985

In 1982, I had bought my first house and it was working out well, so I decided to turn my attention elsewhere. I had tried joining the IBEW and was going to become an electrician for better pay, but the men were not open to women being in the trade, so I backed off. The agency I worked for was very large and had many programs, so I moved up to a program just focusing on middle years to teens who had been removed from their parents. Most of the children were in foster care or relative placements. I saw a wide range of abuse issues as well as children who were doing fairly well. One girl was left by her mother in a motel and she was very depressed. I could identify with her feelings. So this was difficult but satisfying work. There was a program for teens leaving the foster care system that helped them make future plans before they graduated from high school or were emancipated. It was a good support program.

I had joined a speakers program that focused on self-improvement, social issues and some entertainment. A large committee created the four speakers one-night-a-week program. It was currently run by a professional speaker and a co-chair. We created the program and you were assigned or volunteered for one speaker a month. This meant you suggest a speaker, introduce your speaker on stage and complete an evaluation. It was stimulating, and the speakers were generally very good. I stayed on for a few years and eventually became a co-chair and also did a few speeches myself. I was comfortable on stage with a microphone, but was still an introvert. This was a progression from the Toastmasters experience in the 1970s where instead of trembling I was confident on stage.

I joined the Powderhound ski club as I liked to ski, but was not a dare devil racer I was cautious as I did not want an injury. We were a collection of good skiers to beginners. We had a meeting and one ski trip a month. Sometimes we went to out of state or to Canada, which was fun just to travel and skiers picked the terrain that they could manage as well as the racers. One trip to Sun Valley was my birthday and I was very pleased that they had a cake for me, as this did not happen too often in my lifetime. Sun Valley is a volcanic mountain and had steeper runs than California. We had many ski resorts hours away from the Bay Area, so we had plenty of places to go. It was easier when we could hire a bus and not worry about driving, but this became too expensive and we drove in cars. California snow can be good to cement in the spring. I enjoyed the people in this club and being on the snowy mountains.

One night I was at a party and a man came up to me as I was smoking a cigarette. It turned out he liked to backpack and we had similar jobs, we starting dating. At first I was very happy and things progressed to an engagement and making wedding plans. While we had similar incomes, he did not have much to show for it and had no bad habits. His father owned a car dealership, which gave him a good deal on a vehicle. Very slowly he was making suggestions on why we should do things his way as it was much better. While some were good ideas, some were trivial and did not matter to me. I felt a pressure to do things his way. We had planned a vacation in Hawaii before we set a wedding date so we went and had a good time. He lived in a small apartment not suitable for two and I wanted to sell the duplex, so I started looking for a place that would be mine but we could live in.

I had some connections in real estate and a commercial agent showed me three houses on one lot. It was located in a better neighborhood and as we stood in the driveway I liked the arts and craft look of the older homes. She said I could not look inside the buildings and had to make up my mind outside. I had heard of male brokers buying houses on a "drive-by," so I said "yes".

A friend of mine wanted to buy the first duplex so that was easy to sell. Even though I had been working for eight years and had a good credit rating, I had to get my fiancé and mother to co-sign the loan as I was a single woman. Once we closed escrow, they signed a quit-claim deed as I paid for everything. I never met the brokers selling the property and had to hire a locksmith to get inside one unit. There was one tenant in one half of the duplex who smoked a lot of pot, but with a notice he moved and I was able to clean up the place. Once inside I saw how charming they were with beam ceilings, built-ins and hardwood floors. They needed to be freshened up with a few more serious projects. Builders did a good job in the 1920s and 1930s. Randal, my fiancé, helped fix up the buildings but I did most of the hiring and work myself while working full time. I was still smoking and I drank more wine with the stress. I gained weight. I was also feeling like the noose was tightening with all his helpful suggestions. We talked but it was not helping much. I felt he would not have had the initiative to buy a house just supervise me buying three houses.

I had found two wedding dresses I liked and bridesmaid dresses, but my sister and Lainey canceled saying they had to work. Later Laney said she did not feel my fiancé treated me well, but never talked to me about it. I felt I was not working in a team, and I canceled the wedding two weeks before the wedding. It was a hard decision but I felt so ambivalent and conflicted about too many things. The wedding was fairly casual so it was not hard to cancel the contracts.

My mother and her friend Ethel from Pasadena where there, and they were both supportive, which was a nice surprise. Since my mother was in town we had gone over to Randall's for dinner and look at some slides he had taken. One was of me in Hawaii looking happy, slender and relaxed. Another one was of me looking very stressed and heavier, working on the houses. I was angry as it was obvious what he was saying was not as attractive heavier. I felt some guilt about the work he had done to help me get the units ready for renting. But recently I found a pile of receipts where I had paid him well for his work. I finally had called off the wedding and he said we would talk but we went our separate ways.

It was hard calling it off and I was so happy, then so unhappy and confused. I had tried to quit smoking, as I did not want smoke in the new house and succeeded in August 1985. The nicotine changes your metabolism and I turned to food as a replacement and gained more weight. I cut down on the wine but had not quit totally. My mother, her Pasadena friend and I went on a boat ride in the San Francisco Bay and I enjoyed some of their wisdom. Ethel was also a single mother when they became friends and they kept in touch all these years. Ethel said some of the things my ex had wanted were not a basis for a good marriage in her opinion. They left and I appreciated them being there and I know my mother enjoyed seeing an old friend.

All and all I loved the new living place with three units rented out, close to work and they were comfortable to live in. It took time but I did not regret my decision to buy it sight unseen. Through the years I did quite a bit of updating including sanding the oak plank floors, replacing floor heater parts, water heaters, painting most interiors and bolting the foundation for earthquakes. This came in handy in the 1989 quake, as it was a 7.2 and there was very little damage to the redwood buildings. The clay sewer pipes moved due to earthquakes, so I had to do upgrading of sewer lines, which was expensive. The three houses were not that much work, but things seemed to break just as I was leaving town and had to find repair people very quickly. My tenants were very congenial and tended to stay a long time.

I was working, land-lording and speaking and also became interested in the environmental movement after the Alaskan Exxon Valdez oil spill. I knew how important nature was for people and wildlife. Much of the building in the United States is done without consideration to the future. I did travel but we only had two to three weeks off, which I think is not enough to recuperate. Going to Mexico I could see Americans really partying to blow off steam. On a Mexican west coast cruise my roommate owned a restaurant, did modeling and she seriously hit the tequila. We went on a horseback ride and she got the

Mexican guides drunk nearing sunset. I pointed my horse toward the river we had to cross and the horse was happy to get back home. So was I.

Americans need more time off and there has to be a better system to keep productivity high, retain workers and still have time for relaxation, family and their community. Exhausted people do not make good decisions and sometimes they quit.

At work things were humming along and I thought maybe child abuse might end but the crack epidemic hit in the 1980s and there were many, many more cases. I don't know why it spread like wildfire, but it was very sad to see the waste of human potential and the impact on children. Some users were from high-risk homes but some were from stable homes. On the other side of society it was a time of fancy dining, clothes, and parties. There were well-off people who used cocaine at parties and did not seem to get addicted but it probably impacted some of them in negative ways.

Drinking good wine went with eating good food, but I was tapering off and quit by 1990.I did however, enjoy the music and dancing. Evanston was a dry town due the headquarters of the WCTU (Women's Christian Temperance Union) and had a religious presence. Having no bars meant less intoxicated people driving or wandering around. During Prohibition there were fewer health problems, accidents and domestic violence. But people thought it was a bad thing because some of the wealthier or younger people went to speakeasy run by the mob; but most of Americana stayed home, worked and had a mostly sober with a traditional lifestyle. I wanted a simple life and wanted to lose weight.

Women were trying to get the ERA (Equal Rights Amendment) passed so that women would be ensured of equal rights from the beginning of employment, education, domestic life and sexual harassment. It passed in 39 states, but that was not enough to pass. Although there are more opportunities there are still are many issues that need to be addressed. Since I worked in San Francisco for years, the Gay Rights movement became stronger and Havey Milk had rallies and read his poetry. I was very upset when Mayor Moscone and Councilman Milk were murdered. I dated a few women that were nice. I photographed the first gay rights parade, which was small compared to what it is today all over the country. There have been a lot of changes in people's attitudes since the 1950s.

The 1980s were a time of change for me giving up some things and thinking I was never going to get married or have children. But life was full of interesting challenges and adventures. I had artist friends who were single, never married and had no children. So it seemed somewhat normal to me. I know we were in a minority, but people have the right to live the way they want as long as they are not hurting anyone. I think they were devoted to their art or careers and were contributing things to society. It was a time of changes and challenges in the United States. Some of which we are still dealing with today. Things seem to move forward and backwards or stay the same.

CHAPTER 14

Ways to Grow

The Gestalt group was helpful for a few years, and I did try individual therapy but it did not seem to work for me. People would tell me what I already knew, or in one extreme example the woman moved her office five times and I had to find her new location after work in the dark. The last straw was when she said I was molested at the Boone orphanage, while the truth was they rarely paid attention to us, let alone touch us (except for the face slap). This was a big red flag, so I left. I had high hopes as she was the director of a children's therapy center and said she had knowledge of the effect of trauma at different developmental stages. The only good thing that came out of this was I made a chart of what happened to me at what age and it was useful for me to get a sense of what happened at stages in my life. I tried other people with no luck, or they were shocked by my story. Treating trauma is very different than treating other conditions.

I had dealt with other problems that interfered with my life, such as being phobic about crossing the Bay Bridge and driving on the freeway. I devised a program of desensitization by getting on the freeway and exiting at the next off ramp. I would try two exits and eventually I was able to cross the bridge and drive on the freeway, which was essential to living in California and working. I had tried biofeedback but my own programs seemed to help me the most but you have to be consistent and ask for help when you need it.

I enjoyed experimenting with different types of art. Previously in the mid-1970s, I had a darkroom in Berkeley so I could do my own photography, which was fun except for the chemicals. I decided to try a film-making class for women with a local film-maker. We were to come up with a short 8-mm film, decide the plot, script, costumes and produce it. The teacher had the cameras and was available for technical questions and support. I decided since I seemed to have underlying issues I would try to bring them out in the open. In Gestalt we could divide ourselves into parts and have dialogues with these parts. So I decided to divide myself into five easy parts and have a meeting with all of them at one table. Some are from childhood (**Child**, **Hiding** and **Tough**) and some from adulthood (**Responsible** and **Social**). They are not separate personalities but rather characteristics in a sub-type. Everyone has sides to themselves that vary in number, intensity and dominance. Some people assume they are the same person all the time, but we have different facets, abilities and needs that come out at different times. I had never made a movie so I tried to keep it as simple as possible. I used a round table in my living room so I could move the camera on a tri-pod around to each speaker, and each one had a costume. The main problem was that I was not an actress and it was too short a time period to get someone else involved. The parts were Responsible, Social, Tough, Child and finally Hiding. The dialogue begins:

Responsible: I brought you here tonight so you can introduce yourselves and express what you would like from the other parts and maybe plan an outing together so we can get to know each other better. I organize things, meet deadlines and make sure life is on track. When I am not here I like to read, study and learn new things, which takes peace and quiet. Tonight I will run the meeting, but I would like you all to participate to make this a success. Be honest but tactful with each other's feelings. I would like you to have equal time to express yourselves.

Social: While not well off, I grew up with people who had nice parties, social gatherings and I enjoyed being in tranquil places with interesting people. I like planning outings and would be happy to contribute that to our group here. I would like an upbeat gathering, dressing up a bit and I will provide the food and other party favors. I hope you are up for a fun time.

Tough: I like sports and outdoor things that require some muscle. I played baseball, swimming, hiking and anything that has some competition in it with good sportsmanship. What I would like to see is an outing where we were near some water and we could do something active together. I offer protection and do not take a lot of guff from people.

Child: You folks are older than I am, so I would like you to be more playful and not just sit around and eat. I like to play creative games where you have to use your imagination. I like swimming too, so maybe we can go to one of the lakes, throw a ball around or something like that. I like simple things that are not too complicated and experience the joy of being alive.

Hiding: I am not used to being around people, so this is harder for me. I like to quietly observe people in settings and maybe do some art work. You seem to be much more outgoing and confident than I am. I would like you to be gentle and considerate with me. I am OK with going to a small lake in the hills when it is not crowded with people.

Responsible: It sounds like we all have something to contribute to each other and are heading toward an outing on a quiet day at a local lake. We have food and some ideas about how we would like to spend our time together. Let's decide what works for all of us and make a plan together. (The trip is off camera and the next meeting is in a week or so after the outing.)

Follow-up meeting with the five parts:

Responsible: Well, I am glad to see everyone tonight after our outing at the local lake in the hills. Everyone contributed something and there was not a lot of conflict. We are different but we all have strengths and something to contribute. I got the permit for the table and sent out directions to the party so we would all be there on time. Let's take time to say what we liked about being together.

Social: I was pleased that people made an effort to wear sportswear and brought something to share. I did not want to be seen with ragamuffins. I appreciated Tough standing up to those people who were laughing at us for playing some easy games. They quieted down. And Child brought a ball to play with. I was surprised how nice it was to be together in one place.

Child: Yes, it was fun and I was not bored being with grown-ups. I jumped in the water because the ducks were nearby, but Tough came and pulled me out. I was OK and I appreciated him looking out for me. Social brought good food for us. Hiding bought the art materials so we could all do part of a mural. A group painting was something I had never done before. Responsible kept us on track so we found the right place and followed the rules.

Tough: I thought those people were out of line but they stopped teasing us. I just wanted everyone to feel safe and I don't like to take too much guff from people.

Hiding: Yes. I felt safe in the group and was not threatened by strangers in the park, even if their jokes were a little offensive. Social did a good job bringing food and some pretty plates and cutlery. I thought the mural would bring us together and let us express things that might not be easy in a group setting. I use art to express things in a safe way as well as enjoying it. Responsible is always there to make sure we are on track. Tough is there to keep us safe and walking was good and walking in nature was peaceful.

Summary: The point of this film or exercise was to emphasize parts of myself and how they were doing and interacting. It became clear that Hiding was the most impacted by all the trauma of the past, needs to come out of hiding and get support for healing the wounds. But she is already doing things that are helpful to her and that she enjoys. Later on I did workshops, writing and reading to help Hiding come out of hiding. Sometimes I read something that exactly describes my situation and a sign of growth. Writing is another outlet and there are many other ways to grow unique to the individual. Social can be a bit of a snob but she enjoys being with people and having fun. She has a good heart. Tough is strong but not that defensive, so he enjoys sports and being outdoors. Responsible had carried the burden of working hard and organizing everything to reach goals. She needs a break to relax, read, travel, not be in charge, or working all the time.

The benefits of doing this film were to clarify who I was as a person, I feel like there were no big conflicts just areas I need to work some areas and the film helped. I think people get in trouble when they are fighting themselves, or are avoiding honestly looking at themselves once in a while. I am not an actress and did not want to show this film to anyone. There are other exercises or projects I would show freely to the public and let them decide what they think, and give me feedback if they wished. Public speaking was another goal, as it clarifies your interests, builds confidence and more career opportunities. In the 1980s I started with the Toastmaster group as I was still quite fearful of public speaking. I accidentally joined the best group of people. They were a mix of interests, careers and abilities in speaking. The program has a progression of speaking skills you presented at meetings at your own pace. The speaking times were short, so it was not overwhelming, and there was also impromptu speaking for a shorter time so you learn how to think on your feet. There were regional meetings and contests. When I started I was shaking and had little confidence. But with deep breathing I got through it and there are private evaluation sheets so you get feedback. I really enjoyed the other speakers, and we would get together for special events. Some of the people had ideas I did not agree with, but the point was not argument but being able to express your ideas. I also attended storytelling contests, which were amazingly good. I did go to bigger meetings and volunteered for an impromptu speech and spoke on something I knew nothing about and it worked. I got used to using a microphone and standing in front of big groups. This program is free and has a well-designed progression of challenges.

In the 1980s I also joined a committee that put on a program with four speakers on four stages on one night. A church volunteered the spaces as a community service and we donated money. You could take a speaker assignment or come up with your own ideas and discuss it at the meeting. Most of the speakers focused on human growth but some were on other topics of interests. There were two large rooms and two smaller rooms, so the topic and speaker could match the room size. Some were professional speakers who wanted to try out a topic on an audience, while some speakers were not professional but just had an interesting story. It was a very interesting and stimulating program. I did some speeches in the smaller rooms. A few times there were bands like Red Hot Chili Peppers, and one night there was a large crowd of about a thousand people with a well-known speaker whose life had been the subject of a movie.

After getting experience, I became the co-chair with a man who was a professional speaker. If he was not there I could handle running things or a meeting and the committee members were very responsible and did their introductions, handling the speaker and getting the evaluations back to the committee. Only one night I had a speaker who was so nervous I did not know if he would make it, but he calmed down. We charged a nominal fee and the speakers were paid according to the room size. I did start a satellite program in another community, but it did not last too long. It takes a committed group and we all worked full time. It was a growth experience for me and something I would like to see in other communities. Today people give speeches on TV or Podcasts, and the internet, which reaches a wider audience. This can be positive or negative.

What little family I had was divided. After 1985 I went back to Evanston about once a year to check on my mother and see my sister and her family. The twin boys were born in 1976, a niece in 1980 and a nephew in 1982. I made simple quilts for all of them. I had photos of my mother and sister with twins and niece at about 1 year old, but something happened after my niece was born between my mother and sister. My mother went to the niece's christening on the South Side of Chicago with the father's family. Something happened and my sister would not let my mother visit and told her kids that their grand-mother was dead. I asked my mother what happened and she had no idea as my sister was drinking at the christening but otherwise OK. My sister refused to talk and would get quite angry. Her husband tried to ask her in front of me, but it was the same angry response. My mother had been nice to her as she did not raise her and missed out on her growing up years. Aunt Elna would see her, but did not convey much. My sister's stepmom was my mother's first cousin so my sister grew up with the "other side" of the Waisanen family and had cousins to play with growing up. True, my mother left my sister with her father when she could not take care of her and had ten dollars to her name. Her father could provide for his daughter and was always on the farm. But I am sure my mother's actions were frowned upon in the 1950s. My sister cut off our relationship for years. Later I would visit my sister and then my mother. My mother would ask how they were, and I tried to say only the good parts so she would not worry. Visiting the "family" was a split between the Evanston suburb and the South Side of Chicago. I did not get further involved. My mother sent cards and money to her, which were put in the trash. Eventually my sister and I did visit. Before my mother died she said she wanted me to have a relationship with my sister, so I tried. The ironic thing was that I worked with families that had murder, molesting, jail, drugs and fights. Sometimes they were able to forgive and work it out, but not my family for some unspoken reason. This was a disappointment to me, but bearable as I had never had a family and some things are best left alone.

My relationship with my mother was strained in that when she called the conversations would always go back to her childhood and her sufferings. I could not get her off of that topic, so I avoided her or would cut the conversation short. I was tired to communicate with her but did not have much patience for this talk. So this left me with no family to speak of, and I knew when my choice to not marry would make my life outside the bounds of the average person and more solitary.

I continued going to the outdoors whenever I could get away from work. I would backpack the Sierra Nevada Mountain range. My longest trip was from Tuolumne Meadows to Mammoth Lakes, which is 28 miles, 5,700-foot ascent and 2,700-foot descent. The climb over Mt Lyle is 2,000 feet in 2, miles but the snow on top was refreshing. The whole trip is beautiful and worth doing.

I wanted to do the whole John Muir Trail, but it was 211 miles, strenuous and required food drop-offs unless you had an outfit carry food on mules. I did not feel like I could do it and it is one of my disappointments in life. I did, however, do a horse trip from Sequoia National Park to Kersarge Pass on the west side of the mountain range. While the horse did the walking and the guide and cowboys did the cooking, it was still strenuous as I was not used to sliding down steep, slick granite rocks looking over the horse's head into a steep drop off. I was amazed the horses were willing to do this. The cowboys let the horses run free at night in the meadow so I would camp in the trees for protection with the bears. The other people camped in the middle of the meadow and a man nearly got his head crushed. The Sierra Club brought beer but did not drink much, so the cowboys were able to help out. The leader was a thin middle-aged woman who would sleep on the canvas-covered pile of food, and if a bear came she would slap them in the face. She said that she drove cattle across the mountains by herself. I was feeling a bit wimpy, but I enjoyed the trip very much as I did not think I could backpack across the mountains. I did want to do every of the many passes on the Eastern Side of the Sierras but did not make it. I did shorter trips in Desolation Wilderness, Trinity Alps, Lassen Volcanic Park, the Coastal range and Colorado, Alaska, and New Mexico. Being out in the wilderness gave such peace and connection to nature. Eventually we had to have water purifiers, bear canisters and be careful of breathing in tainted dust, but it was always a pleasure to be in the mountains. I got my pack down to 20 pounds, which allowed me to go faster. When I was off the trail I we would go to Hot Creek, which was a geothermal feature in a river with fish on the colder side. You could go closer to the hot bubbling water or go back to the cooler water. There were regulars who went later in August and early September as many of the tourists had left. This trip was an annual outing and I would camp in the high desert with a man from Arizona who came every year. It was very different than camping in a camp-ground. You had a sense of being in a wide-open space with coyotes! I found out people had been partying there in the 1960s and I am sure people used this site for many years back in history as a refreshing change from the trail. Later it was closed due to geothermal unrest. On weekends I would hike in the Tilden Park hills, and when preparing for a backpack trip I would put two-liter soda bottles full of water in a day pack and go up and down steep hills. Otherwise I would go to a gym after work to have a break from the stress. I enjoyed the aerobics and step classes. It would clear my mind so I could enjoy my time off of work. Diane, a friend of mine, taught a class on Women as Serious Artists and Using Personal Symbolism in your art work. They were interesting to learn about all the great women artists in the world and to deepen my connection to my own symbolism. Painting or any art form is a relaxing respite from life.

In 1986 I was on Bancroft Way and saw some tables with Finnish goods on them. I found out that there was a conference called Finnfest associated with them. This included meetings, lectures, food, dancing and a Tori or marketplace to buy goods. It was a cultural connection to my heritage. I knew Finns had started the Co-op grocery stores in Berkeley, as they had Co-ops wherever they lived to share goods and bring down prices by membership. After that I went to many Finnfests, and it really makes a connection to my family history, my mother and learning about another country. Being a part of another country and culture gives you a different perspective on being an American. Changing your perspective is growth.

I was heading into the 1990s with a fulfilled life but also some holes left in my history, such as what did my father look like? Could I form a close relationship with a man? Did I want to stay in the Bay Area? When can I retire and have a more relaxed life? What else did I want to accomplish or be in my life? I was pretty content but it was a non-traditional life-style that has advantages and some disadvantages. But making the effort to grow as a person is important.

CHAPTER 15

Hitting the Wall

It was 1991 and I had been working at the agency for 14 years and was trying to decide if I could make it on my own in private practice or stick with the agency that offered many different programs. I was eligible for retirement in six years, but that does not mean I could live on the pension and I would be too young for Social Security. I had a small private practice and had some night hours for working people. I had a good idea of what kinds of presenting problems I wanted to work with and the ones I did not, but not having the support of an agency and working alone was a drawback. I had taken a private workshop on promoting a private practice but there were many pitfalls including working alone, renting a space, setting fees and having regular clients when the point was for clients to get better and leave therapy. The more successful you were, the less work you had to do.

I had reversed the effects of the 1980s by quitting smoking, drinking and losing some weight as I replaced nicotine with food. But emotionally and mentally I had been through a lot with buying the houses and maybe my last chance to get married. I was doing well financially and had a safety net, but I was very security oriented. I had moved to another position that was an improvement but had a high case load. These were children where it was unlikely they would be going home to a relative, so we were looking for a stable long-term home or adoption. It was demanding, as some of the children had lasting effects from abuse, neglect and seeing too much. My job was to assess these needs and what would be the best situation for them to have a better life. This also involved writing recommendations to the court on the child's behalf. The process involved interviewing everyone involved, finding resources and of course evaluating how the child was adjusting in many aspects of their life. It brought up old issues for me and visual flashbacks, but this helped in that I understood what they were going through. There were demands from the court, emergencies, and dealing with a large agency and my department needed revision of the process that had been inefficient. Childhood only lasts so long, so the best intervention was needed. Due to the uptick in cases I was feeling exhausted. The stress I was experiencing was called "hitting the wall," or serious burnout. Americans used to work six to seven days a week but now we have the five-day week. Some have overtime but most only have a few weeks' vacation and not everyone takes this time off. My agency had flex days, which helped give me three days off in a row, but there was no let-up on the workload.

Since I had been backpacking since 1972 I decided to go to Alaska for one month with leave without pay, vacation time and Alaska prices. This was expensive but to me a necessary intervention to more serious physical and mental exhaustion I was feeling.

The tent, special clothes and utensils were not making my pack too heavy. Outdoor gear had become lighter since my first trip in Montana in 1972. I spent time reading about where to go and how to avoid grizzly attacks, which resulted in my own varied but safer itinerary. Leaving in later August I avoided mosquitoes, but made a netted hat just in case. A previous tenant who moved to Anchorage said I could stay with her. She had taken her pick-up truck, cat, found a teaching position and bought a house. I admired her spirit and self-reliance.

The milk-plane ticket meant the plane stopped in many places. In Ketchikan the plane had no coffee but had plenty of champagne, so they told me to get off the plane, go to a bar and order some coffee. The men in there were rough and I heard about last night's fights. I noticed that people came to the plane to hug the crew, as it was way to see friends. This was very different than the Bay Area. I finally made it to Juneau, the capital, where I was going on a kayak adventure trip in Glacier Bay with an outfitter. I had seen photos of beautiful turquoise icebergs and wanted to see them up close. We had to bring polypropylene, wool and waterproof layers as the ice water could result in hypothermia. The rest of your gear had to fit into a wet bag. I had never been in a kayak before, but thought this was a good place to start. We flew in a small float plane to a remote location after flying across beautiful glaciers to a shore.

All the kayaks that were double kleppers which were lined up on the shore. The group was 12 people and seemed friendly. I was paired with a man from New York City who knew nothing about being in the wilderness. We had to put skirts on around the klepper opening, and he wanted to stand up to do this, which was a big no-no. I decided to get him situated and then get in myself. We were told to paddle eight miles, which seemed like a long way for my first trip, but the water was calm. The tide changed 33 feet each day, so the guide would pick a camping spot that eliminated drowning. Our first night was McCarthy Mountain, where a friend had told me about a grizzly attack that killed a man who was trying to take photos of the bear. The photos helped ID the bear and they shot it in two days, but it made me nervous to sleep there.

The food was OK but the guide was not a cook and his helper seemed very young. The next day we went closer to a calving glacier, and it was breathtaking to see the force of tons of ice falling in the water. It also meant the glaciers were melting, but the colors were fantastic blues. There was no way to bathe and you did not want to take your clothes off in the cold. But I had rented a sleeping bag that remained warm if it got wet, which came in handy. We headed toward the John Muir glacier, which he had seen during his 1879 Alaska trip. The glacier had retreated thousands of feet since his trip. This made me sad, as we were losing the ice to global warming. We hiked up to the overlook of the glacier and the NYC man went out toward the edge, which is soft loose soil, but luckily he did not fall off the edge. A fall would have meant a rescue or recovery. The guide had warned us about an ocean storm was headed our way, and by the time we climbed down to the campsite the wind was so strong and we had to double up in tents so we would not be blown away. The tents were old and started to shred with gaping holes, so the rain could freely enter our shelter. We were served a very simple beans-and-meat dinner in our tents and we were in grizzly country. The guide said not to worry as he had a ship-to-shore radio if we needed one. The reality was the radio did not work. We were in the waterlogged sleeping bags that kept us warm. But the body heat made it seem warm and moldy. The kitchen was being destroyed by the wind. Again the guide tried the radio, but with no luck. He said he did not worry as there were ships around, somewhere.

The next day we saw the shredded tents and the scattered remains of the kitchen. But we did get some beans for breakfast. We later heard about a Danish couple that was out in the ocean in this storm and had been rescued by experienced Alaskan kayakers. They were so lucky to be alive. We paddled back toward Juneau while seeing many Arctic birds that were summering in Glacier Bay and seals that were feeding on fish. We saw one whale, but it was distant. I was really dreaming of a shower after peeling off the stinky wet clothes that we needed to survive. The fourth day we paddled back, and while we were waiting for the float planes to pick us up we had time to take photos of the turquoise ice stranded on the beach. The absolute first thing I did in my hotel was take the best shower of my lifetime. The group met at a hot tub place and we had dinner. I really enjoyed my first kayak trip. It was intense at times, but a good start.

The next day I went to Mendenhall Glacier, and not being used to the wet slippery rocks, I fell on my right elbow, but luckily it was not broken. There was no bus so I hitchhiked back into town. I liked Juneau, as it was the government capital and had some nice amenities, but it was landlocked so seemed like an odd choice for a capital. I then flew to Anchorage with a stop in Sitka, where I knew a Finnish woman named Lois who did tours but I only had time for a walk around town before the plane took off again. I had brought a backpack and suitcase not knowing if I would be able to backpack, and found Kathy's new house. She said I could stay in the basement, which was below ground in permafrost. She was happy in Anchorage, as she did cross-country skiing near town with moose and other animals. She said teaching was good, but sometimes there was a bear on the playground and they had to delay recess for the children. I left my suitcase there and took my backpack on the train to Denali National Park. We passed through forests with utility posts with old glass resistors on them. People still could flag down the train when they emerged from the woods to get to civilization. We did pick up some people one time. When the train got to Denali Park, I was planning on staying in the Backpack campground that was near the Main Lodge, as I thought it would be safer. Later I found out that a grizzly had killed a moose on the front steps of the lodge. We had to store our food in a thick steel storeroom, so the bears could not get in. I was nervous but was able to sleep in my nylon tent. The woman next to me worked at Prudhoe Bay for British Petroleum (BP), which gives their employees generous leave time so they do not go crazy. I was glad to have someone nearby for safety. In the morning I caught the bus through the park, as cars are not allowed. It was wonderful as the animals were used to the bus and went about their normal business. There were bears, cubs, foxes, birds and at the end of the route, caribou. The vistas are vast and it expands your world. We got off at the end of the road to see the 20,308-foot Mount Denali, which people climb. As we boarded the bus, a caribou faced the bus about 20 feet away and started to charge it, but diverted at the last second. It seemed to me it was saying this is my place and leave us alone. At dinner I spoke with the BP woman about her geology work in the oil fields. She was given a month off and was paid well but was deciding how long she would stay there.

I took the train to Fairbanks and rented a car to drive to Chena Hot Springs. The permafrost road melts so the road is like a roller coaster with its constant up-and-down pattern. In the winter there are many Japanese tourists who come for the northern lights. It is a shorter trip for them. But now Chena was quiet and I soaked in the hot tub and decided not to stay there. I picked up a Japanese hitch hiker who was afraid of my driving on the roller coaster road, but he was polite and did not say so. Today melting permafrost is a threatening

Alaska in many ways. In Fairbanks I was able to go to a museum restaurant and shop a bit before sleeping in a bed. I did notice that there were furriers that were full of fox, mink, and other fur coats for people who wanted them. More recently we have high-tech fabrics that are much better at protecting from us from wet and cold. But nylon is not as big for a display of wealth.

The next day I flew back to Anchorage and stayed a night at Kathy's before heading east. Kathy was working and enjoyed her privacy. My cousin Jim, who retired from the U.S. Army liked to travel and wanted to come up spend some time with me. He flew to Elmendorf Air Force Base and I was to pick him up there to drive east. But first he wanted to see the Russian jet come in. We headed east and found King Mountain, which was his family name. I wanted to call my mother to let her know I was OK per her request. We found a bar with a pay phone, and when I walked in all the men looked like they lived on the bar stools. I found the phone and after the call I left as soon as possible. We camped there for the night. We went by Palmer, which grows very large vegetables, and I managed to find a cantaloupe for breakfast. We walked on the Matanuska glacier and had breakfast. Going east we made it to Lake Louise, which had some homes, fishing and a few restaurants with bars. I was making dinner and opened a can of tuna and poured the oil on the ground. What a big mistake with grizzly bears having a nose 30 times stronger than ours. I did not tell Jim and hoped we were OK. We went to the only restaurant, and the man said there was grizzly activity in the area among the stunted but real blueberry bushes. We made it OK, and I drove Jim back to the road to Anchorage, as he had to get back. It was nice of him to come out and keep me company for a while.

I finally made it down a long bumpy road toward the town of McCarthy with a beautiful view of the 150 Wrangell-St. Elias Mountains. It was getting darker, which was about ten p.m. The Kennecott River was raging whitewater and there was a steel cable which you could pull yourself or have people pull you across sitting in a large wire basket. I was not strong or brave enough to do that, and there was no one there. I slept in my car and prepared for the next day. In the morning there were people who were willing to pull me across the wide raging river, as this was the only way to the town of McCarthy. I looked at the few shops and there were notes explaining why the people were not there at the moment. It seemed so trusting and friendly. I decided to walk to the Kennecott Mine for lunch. When I finally arrived, I was told there had been grizzly bears on the road but I had not seen them. I had lunch and I learned that the copper mine was important for World War I and ran from 1911 to 1938, with 300 miners and a small town. My family was copper miners, so it was interesting to me to see another area, but this was really isolated from supplies. The scenery was breathtaking and there was a backpack trip where a small plane would drop you off and you walk back, but I was too insecure to do this alone. This time I took the shuttle bus back to town and of course there were no bears in sight.

I was able to get a pull across the river in a wire basket looking down at the torrential waves of the fast-flowing river. There were rafting trips down the Kennecott River, but it was raging and I thought the kayak trip was enough for now. I retraced the bumpy dirt road going South toward Valdez. It was slow going and I could not make the miles to Valdez so I stopped at the top of Blueberry Mountain, as Finns are fond of blueberries. I ate dinner and was going to sleep in the car when the wind starting picking up so strong that I had to get into the front seat with a seatbelt in case the car was going to roll over. I had noticed the snow sticks on the side of the road were about 20 feet high, which means the area gets a lot of snow and bad weather. I managed to get some sleep but the car was rocking quite a bit.

The next day I made it to Valdez and inquired about the ferry to Whittier, and bought a ticket. I looked around, as it was a working town but was on the ocean. I found a good a place for dinner and it turned out they had a good band and I was asked to stay, so I did. We danced and drank and by midnight it was dark. It was now three a.m. and I had not found a place to stay. A nice man said he worked for a big company with barracks and we could sneak in to get some sleep. He had to work at six a.m. but I could stay. By the time I woke up he was gone. Alaskans work and play hard during the summer, as in the winter they might be stuck inside or go down to the lower forty-eight. I snuck into the men's shower as a man was leaving, and managed to get out without anyone else seeing me. I did not want to get the nice man in trouble. I usually don't stay out so late or drink that much beer, but it was fun with nice people. However, I was not feeling too good. I got on the auto ferry boat to Whittier and we went by the Columbia Glacier, which made me feel more hopeful about the future of the planet.

We finally made it to Whittier, which had a very long tunnel made in World War II to bring military supplies to the troops to defend the Northwest coast. But before we got to the tunnel I had to figure how to get my car onto the train. There were flatbed cars with ramps but I did not know if I was supposed to park the car and get into the passenger train or stay with the car. There was no one to ask, and no one seemed to care what you did. I just drove the car on the flatbed and put on the parking brake and stayed. Alaska was so different than California, where the rules are stated clearly and you must abide by them. We finally got into the very long totally dark tunnel and I had the radio on to keep me company. Elvis Presley came on and his voice seemed to resonate through the tunnel in a larger-than-life performance. I was in a giant cavern with Elvis. Finally we came to a break in the tunnel and saw a beautiful lake with mountains. At Portage there was a man to help me back off the flatbed train. I guess this is harder to do. I found a motel with a large bear on the sign, so I had to stay there. The owner was in the bar, and I rented a small room with a TV and a bath down the hall. I ate dinner there. However, I noticed later on that people kept coming and in and out of a smaller building in the back, which to me meant they were buying drugs. I was nervous but if stayed in my room I should be alright, and I was. Drug users usually sleep late in the morning. I noticed as I was leaving that there was a lingerie place next door so maybe there was more going on here, but it was an inexpensive night.

I took a right toward Homer to camp near the Kenai River and visit Soldotna where I ate and bought a carving on a moose antler. The next morning

I was leaning over the trunk while I packed my belongings. The keys slipped out of my pocket just as I was slamming the trunk shut. The timing could not have been worse. This was bad news, as there was no one in the campground so I walked down the road toward a building I had seen driving in. It turned out to be a rafting company that let me call AAA for help. They said it would take about nine hours to get there and I would have to pay extra. I gave them the rafting company address. I then inquired about a rafting trip, and they had one in an hour for three hours down the river. The river was famous for fishing and there were fishermen lined up along its banks with guides helping them. The water was a deep, almost turquoise blue with red fish appearing on the surface. It was a magical sight. We stopped for lunch, which I appreciated as I had no food. The river flowed but was gentle and it was a wonderful day. When I returned there was a few more hours left, but they let me sit in the waiting area. The driver finally made it down and was able to open the trunk and charged $100, which did not seem like much as he came from Anchorage. I felt the whole experience was worth it to go on the rafting trip.

Driving down the highway on the Kenai Peninsula the radio reported that there was a fishing derby that was ending that day, which was good because the crowds would be leaving. They also said that there was a shoot-out up on the ridge near Seward with a man in a cabin and a Sheriff's helicopter. What was I getting myself into? Finally the man surrendered and cars started pouring out of Seward, as the derby had also ended. Then I heard the winner of the derby was an eight-year-old girl! She caught the biggest fish, and in Alaska that can be a big fish. All those big fish hunters must be as surprised as I was. Her father had provided the boat and equipment, but it was a big thrill for her.

Seward had a beautiful bay with mountains that were only 6,000 feet high but they started right at the water, which made them more dramatic. I went to a restaurant bar and sat down next an old bearded man who was eating a steak dinner and offered a bite. For some reason I took it and a man walked in and started talking to the bartender. He assumed I was with the old man. Later he talked to me and said he was moving to California and where was I from? I told him I was going on a tender boat as I knew the owner, but he gave me his phone number so we could talk in a few days.

The owner of the boat and his lady friend were very welcoming to their big house. My friend in California had made arrangements for me to meet his brother and go on a tender boat which collects the fish from the other boats in Prince William Sound. We went out to the boat the next day. I had to climb straight down a 30-foot steel ladder and I was scared and the man from the boat was disgusted. I shut up and started descending to a very nice boat with nice accommodations, kitchen and working decks. The crew did not want a woman on their boat, so I made myself as scarce as possible. They all ate beef and they could not look at salmon for dinner. They had an inspector on board who looked at the fish and could tell if it was one they could catch. He identified some that came from Canada, which was a mystery to me. I slept well and the next day some guys asked me if I wanted to go on a small boat to look at some traps. I said sure. We went on land and I saw river otter tracks but no animals. Then we went out into the ocean at a fast speed and the boat was flying over the waves. I learned that we were going to check some illegal halibut traps and there was a state airplane flying overhead. Would this be a problem? Halibut is tightly regulated as it has been over fished, and I think most fish have been over fished. The tender boat we were on could hold 250,000 pounds of salmon, which I thought was outrageous. There was nothing in the trap so we headed back to the tender boat. After dinner they said it was their last outing of the season and they wanted to party, which I totally understood but did not know what it meant. But at 3 a.m. in the morning they woke me up and said they had found a ship that was willing to take me back to Seward. I had to get up now and jump ship. I was half-asleep but got my things together and walked out on deck, where a very large ship was waiting nearby our ship. It moved very slowly closer until they said it was close enough. They held my hands on both sides as I balanced on the railing and they would tell me when to jump. The boats moved slowly together and apart and I knew if I fell between them I would be crushed. They knew this too, but were holding on to me and focusing as were the guys on the other ship in silence. Finally they said "Jump," which I did and landed in the arms of the other crew. They threw my stuff over the railing and bid me farewell. I was then escorted to a cabin that was decorated with posters of scantily clad women, which did not make me comfortable but I slept very soundly.

In the morning I discovered that this was an even bigger ship and it was full. I felt really bad for the fish and did not like the size of the commercial fishing industry. The crew had good food and were friendly. During the day they checked their crab pots and we were escorted by a large pod of dolphins leaping so high I was amazed. It was a sight I have never seen before or since. When we got near the port of Seward they found out the fish-processing plant was full and they could not take a large boat. The fish are refrigerated but I know some of the fish were going to be wasted. They asked me if I wanted to go out to sea with them and do more fishing! The guys were nice, but I did not want to see more fish being trapped and I did not know them. I asked if they could drop me off at the port, which they did. The owner of the tender ship was expecting me and I was to stay at his girlfriend Linda's house, as she was planning on climbing Mount Marathon the next day. Mount Marathon is an extinct volcanic mountain that is only 3,500 feet high but it is very steep, and is the location of an infamous annual Fourth of July race that includes elite athletes. They had to separate the men from the woman, as the men would push the women aside to win the race, which of course was very dangerous.

I called Trace, the man I had met, and said I was going to climb Mount Marathon the next day and he was shocked and warned me not to do it. I told him it was a leisurely climb, not the competitive race. The next day while we were climbing he was out there with binoculars watching us climb. Going up was slippery, as the rocks are wet from the constant sea fog and I had to hold onto the branches on the side of the narrow trail to pull myself up. You had to be careful not to slip and slide down the mountain. This was slow climbing, but I was confident. When we got near the top, Linda decided that we had done enough and we should do the steep descent on the other side. This was easier, as it was a shoot of loose rocks and you just had to dig your heels into the rocks and let gravity pull you down the mountain. Racers usually do two miles per hour up and twelve miles per hour down! But if you fall into the rocks, you might need a hospital. During the race they had ambulances waiting, but today we were not hurt. The last challenge was a steep sheer wall that required digging your boots into small toe-holds. This was unnerving to me, but I managed to get down on firm ground. Linda was going to do the race next year, so this was good practice for her and a once-in-a-lifetime adventure for me. I appreciated the couple offering me two unique experiences of going on the fishing boat and climbing Mt. Marathon. They were nice people and I wished them well in their life together and their business.

On a later trip I met an 18-year-old in Seward who said he made $85,000 a year on summer boats. Trace and I went to Homer to get to know each other, and he was planning on attending college in the Bay Area to get another Bachelor's degree in Environmental Science. I was involved in environmental issues so I was interested in spending more time with him and offered him a place at my house until he got settled. Trace was easy-going, had a sense of humor and was a hard worker. I bid farewell and he planned to come to the Bay Area in October.

There was a hunting and fishing camp on Kodiak Island that just opened up and the rates were less. I drove back to Anchorage and I was able to catch a plane. My objective again was to see bears in their natural habitat, as there was talk about developing Kodiak. I had been told not to fly if there was bad weather, as 22 people had already died from plane crashes that summer. It was a sunny day and I was the only woman and non-hunter in the group in the airport. The pilot was very unhappy about having a woman sit next to him in the cockpit, but the rest of the plane was full of cargo to be dropped off in remote places. The pilot would not talk to me so I just enjoyed flying over the 75 percent of Kodiak that is mountainous, a wildlife preserve or Native land. We were getting close to a bay and I thought maybe this was my stop, but we suddenly took a nose dive into the ocean! I did not realize the plane had no floats on it but it could float! The water was washing over the windshield but I kept quiet. As we headed toward land, the plane was gently lifted up on an underwater ramp to a dock above water. Then a man with a duffle bag appeared and was so happy to see us. He had to sit in back with the cargo, as there was no other seat. He had just closed down the fish-canning plant and was headed back home to a desert in Arizona. The engineer said he got paid good money to start up the plant, keep it running and then close it down at the end of the fish-processing season. It was just lonely with a lot of fish and people who did not always speak English. We went down another ramp into the water and we were able to take off again.

The next landing was on gravel run way in a deserted area with no buildings or people in sight. He landed the plane, threw my stuff and cargo on the ground, and took off. What a charmer. I was expecting someone to greet me, but there was no one. Then I saw a native man in a small motorboat that had come to pick up the cargo. I said I was there for the bear/fish camp, and he was surprised as he said no one had told him I was coming! I could have been out there all alone, but we made the connection. They were a new business and the communication was not worked out. We took the boat loaded down with supplies eight miles into the interior of Kodiak. He and his business partner had made four small brand-new cabins with an outhouse. Uphill there was a bigger building with living quarters for the man, his wife and new baby. This was also the dining room for the guests. I think I was one of the first guests at the hunting/fishing camp. The dinner was good and mainly salmon at every meal. I happen to like salmon so I did not mind. The wife was Japanese and had been working at a fishing cannery where she met her husband who was involved in this business venture. Their baby was quite young.

The next morning we climbed into the small boat and headed farther upstream rise in the land. The tide was going out so fish were trapped on the land which attracted grizzly bears, seals and sea gulls. It was quite something to see these three species of animals hustling for fish and not paying attention to which animal was next to them. I took photos and we watched them for quite some time. This was a lot easier than tracking bears in the wild. However, when we were going to return to the boat, we realized there were a mother grizzly bear and two cubs between us and the boat. There was a cliff behind us, so we were trapped. The mother bear stood firm, staring at us and was not going to move. We tried to avoid eye contact, because that is seen as a challenge. The man took out his 44 magnum and held it straight up in the air while he proceeded to talk to the bear in a soft, comforting tone for 45 minutes. At first the bear seemed intent on moving in on us, but eventually the bear began to relaxed a bit. The man was shaking and I was standing behind him trying to be relaxed. The two cubs were playing and not interested in the drama. Finally she decided we were not a threat and moved toward the fish. We took deep breathes and cautiously moved toward the boat to take off as soon as possible. Grizzly bears can be unpredictable. I paid quite a bit for a bear experience in the wild but he said his wife would be very unhappy if she knew about this as they just had a baby. He asked if it was OK if we just went fishing for the rest of my time. This was not my intent, but I felt I had seen the bears doing something very natural and agreed to go fishing. That night after dinner I was not confident enough to walk around the water front after our encounter and went to bed early.

The next day the man left to pick up a father and son and I went kayaking upstream and saw some shell mounds from native encampments and the entrance to Munsey's Bear Camp for hunters. When I returned we all had lunch and left to go fly fishing on a river for Dolly Varden char. When we arrived there were smashed fish parts all over the area as the bears had a party the night before and they were sleeping in the bushes above us, so we did not talk. Let sleeping bears lie. I enjoy fly fishing as it is active and you are not just standing there with a rod. We did not catch anything but it fun to see the remains of the bear party. We returned to the camp for our salmon dinner and I did not see the father and son but it was nice to know there were people nearby. The next morning we headed out toward the ocean and loaded into a bigger boat that had plenty of room for the four of us. I liked being out in the ocean as it was big and there were no other boats. We each had our ocean rods and the father caught a fairly large salmon and the son caught a salmon and the guide said it was from Canada and we were supposed to catch American fish. Who knew as there was no accent? Then I caught a ling cod and with its very big mouth was trying to bite me and the guide smashed it in the head. The father and son caught more two more fish as did the guide and we eventually made our way back to camp. I asked if I could have my photo taken with the large salmon and promised to say it was his fish.

The next day I was transported back to the gravel runway and the return pilot was friendly and pointed out high lights of the Kodiak mountains and sites on the way back to town. Kodiak has a mix of Alaskan native, American and international residents. There was a small history museum about fishing and Native traditions. I learned that Natives owned their own parcels of land can sell it to developers who take people out hunting. Some have permits and some pay large fees to hunt without permits. I am not sure how much of this happens but the wilderness is still fairly intact with a large bear population. Any land, air, wildlife and human beings can be altered, destroyed or saved in incremental steps. I really enjoyed my time in Kodiak and felt I experienced something that was very special. The people I met were living a life that had stopped in time and were surrounded by wilderness.

This was the end of my month in Alaska and I had covered a lot of territory, seen great natural beauty and enjoyed many bear sightings. I met a man that was going to join me. I felt he was a free spirit working up here and then trying to improve his life. The trip had lifted a great weight off my soul.

There was also another side to Alaska as there was some drinking and drugs in some subcultures as well as escapee from the lower 48 states. But there was also a real pioneer spirit and idea of helping your fellow neighbor out so they would survive and help you. It also challenged you to be a bolder person and figure things out on your own. Why did I not have the courage to open my wings and fly? Would I be disappointed if I stayed until retirement? I had taken many risks to get where I had gotten. I knew I was not a lightweight, but how much was I limiting myself? These were very important decisions to think about when I returned to work. This trip had been worth all the money it took to get through all the places and adventures I had experienced. When I returned, some people asked me if I had been on a cruise? I don't think so. Sitting on a boat watching the world go by while eating a lot of food was not for me. I needed to be on the ground with the land, people and animals.

Trace flew down in October just as the 1981 Oakland fire had burned 3,000 homes above my house. He was wondering if he had made a mistake. He found work building custom race cars for wanna-be's with money. He enrolled in night school for classes he needed for his new degree. He was enterprising and busy, so I had my house to myself; but I said we needed to go out on Saturday night, which we did. We got along fine on a day-to-day basis.

One incident was pivotal in my final decision. A friend of mine was a single parent of a young adult son who was very promising but somehow he ended up going to East Oakland, buying drugs and was shot and killed. The funeral was a very difficult one and the mother was sobbing. I was emotionally drained and exhausted when I got home, and I had to lie down. Trace had made dinner, bought flowers and was expecting the evening to be a good time. I was resting and could barely eat but eventually did. He got angry and was expecting praise for his efforts. We were not on the same page, and he did not want to talk about it, and I felt I couldn't count on him to understand. I guess I could have explained it all. He was a parent, so I thought he would understand a son being murdered.

This was the first time I had lived with a man besides the brief time with Kevin. Trace was a hard worker, I thought his race car work was creative and he was pursuing his goal. I admired him starting out on a new path in his 50s. I was in my 40s and trying to decide if I was staying at work or starting out on a new path. He had been married, divorced and had an adult child. The backdrop for all this was his military service where he was on a ship in the Mediterranean that was bombed by Israelis but it was not acknowledged due to political pressure. People were killed and the incident was swept under the carpet, so to speak. He was suffering from PTSD and getting help, but it was a slow process. We had both been through a lot, and he was trying to get help, but he was immobilized by depression at times.

We went out once a week and it was fun to have a built-in partner for a change. I can see one advantage of marriage being you knew who you were spending time with. We went to Cabo San Lucas on a trip, which was good. Again something happened that made me uncomfortable. We were paddling kayaks out to Los Arcos. I fell off the simple kayak and he was athletic but would not help me get back on top. A Mexican man came out on his Jet ski and was able to get me back on the kayak. Back on shore I was slammed by a big wave, I did face plant and the wave forced sand down into my stomach. He was not sympathetic and wanted to get a margarita. Where was he at? I don't need to be babied, but I did think he was not concerned at all. I was upset, had two margaritas and got sick. He went off to the hotel bar.

His high school reunion was coming up and he bought expensive cowboy boots to show he had made it. We flew down to Dallas and met his sister, who was nice but smoked cigarettes in an AC car. The three of us drove west and stopped at a small town with a large metal smoking gun as a Bar-B-Que place. People would hang out at the river to cool off. A unique place to me was a Dinosaur Park that had real footprints from the large creatures. We stopped to have lunch at a Lubby's cafeteria and I enjoyed the peach cobbler. We finally made it to San Angelo in West Texas, where he grew up. The main industry was sheep ranching and wool.

We went to the High School Reunion and there were about 200 people who were very outgoing and talkative. I thought it was friendlier than the Bay Area, where it was harder to talk to strangers. But this was a reunion of people who had grown up together and were catching up. He introduced me to a woman and implied they had a relationship but she got angry. It gave me an idea how he grew up, meeting his sister, seeing Texas. We had dinner with a couple around their pool and they made a racist joke to shock a Californian. I mostly enjoyed the trip but it was not a place I would want to live in.

One important night we went to Reno, as I was going to Idaho to fish and he had to return to work. We had a lovely dinner, he proposed and I accepted. We went out so I was really tired and we had a misunderstanding and he stormed out of the room. The next day he would not talk about it. But when I returned from my trip, I did want to talk about it and all he would say was "I guess I shouldn't have done that." Done what? Proposed, or stormed out of the room? He would never answer. It seemed simple to me to clear it up so we understood each other, but that was not going to happen. I was not able to live with this much ambiguity so things were waning. It was harder this time to give up and back out of the relationship.

I think part of my problem besides a lack of trust was not being familiar with how men think. I was looking for what I needed in order to have a really good relationship for both people. I never had a father to observe or see how they deal with women and communication. I know feelings were harder for them. I think women have put up with too much control. I thought being a Fatherless Daughter that maybe I was putting up with anyone or anything. We both continued our busy schedules and going out on weekends. He was getting his credits for his degree and thinking of transferring to a four-year university in Northern California. I was definitely not moving up there as my life was in the Bay Area. Living together was fairly easy and I learned some things about myself in the process. But the time was running out for our relationship.

In 1994 I decided to return to Alaska for a shorter trip and Trace wanted to come with me. I was reluctant but gave in. We went to Denali, and it was getting colder, but we went on a glacier rafting trip where we wore three layers of clothing including an orange Mustang Survival suit over wool and polypropylene clothes. The ice was beautiful but of course very cold and when we went to our tent it was snowing. I said we were finding a motel, which we did with a hot shower that felt really good. We went to Seward and he saw some of his friends and we had dinner with the couple we met before. He had friends that had sled dogs and we went on a land ride as the dogs have to keep the dogs is shape for the winter. It was fun to see them run so fast. He had to get back to work and school so I drove him to the airport. I think he was making an effort, but maybe too late.

I continued the trip as I had rented a cabin in the Kenai River area from the State of Alaska. Before I left a woman had been killed by a bear in her kitchen at Lake Louise so I was a little nervous. I had to walk six miles to the cabin that had four people in it thinking they could stay there. I had to invite them to leave but before they left they took me on a rowboat trip around the lake. I really enjoyed the three nights and two days there as I had the Jack London fantasy of being on a bigger adventure. However, there were no shutters to close. The wind would howl at night as the lake was a glacial cresset. The cabin was tied down with cables so it would not blow away. The next day I rowed around the lake and the flying graylings were following along. I was amazed they could fly so far out of the water and they followed the boat. A helicopter landed on the lake and two men were fishing and then they took off. I had the whole lake, cabin and area to myself with a few bears. I wrote a bit and did some sketches, but just enjoyed the peace and quiet. I knew with no communication it was a bit of a risk, but it was worth it. I hiked the six miles back and drove back to Anchorage for my next adventure. I felt I had a bit of Jack London's spirit, and one of my dreams had been realized in a fairly safe manner. I knew the wilderness could be harsh.

After that I flew to Katmai National Park with reservations to stay in a cabin as this was one of the best places for large bear viewing. We flew to King Salmon to get on a float plane that clearly landed in water. We were greeted by rangers who explained the bear policies to us. You were not supposed to get closer than 50 feet from a grizzly bear etc. They had centralized the food storage that kept the food smells in a fortified place. From the dining room window in the morning you could see the bears walking toward the river to do their day's fishing. At night the stuffed bears returned to the peninsula, where they slept. I called it the Bear Commute. During the night sometimes they would use the end of the cabin logs for dental floss and you could hear a gnawing sound. During the day, if you wanted to go to a viewing stand on the other side of the river, you had to cross a pontoon bridge that had many bears on either side in the water. This was definitely not a place to fall into the water. They could elect to come out of the water, but they might miss a fish. There were piles of fish roe that had been deposited by overfed bears.

The famous Brooks River Falls had many bears trying to catch salmon as they leaped upstream to spawn. Many professional photographers were there with giant lenses and the patience to get a good shot. It was fascinating how the bears would organize themselves in terms of seniority and the females and cubs had to stay away from the males. If the female bear wanted to eat, she would have to quickly make a move in the water and get back to her cubs, so they would not be attached or killed. I was thrilled to be close to them but their life was a struggle at times.

A dentist on vacation was nice enough to make a videotape of my trip. He had been there before. My cabin had been empty, but a woman showed up who was OK, but she ordered early morning coffee to be delivered to our door. She slept through it while I was awakened every morning. I mentioned this, but she would not stop the order.

There was really no place to go if you were not catch-and-release fishing, which I know fish can die from the hook injury. One night the three of us went to a Forest Ranger office for a lecture. At night there were a few people drinking beer and talking in the dining lodge. I enjoyed the company. The resort said I could take a kayak out on the lake, but some of the bears liked to go under the water, catch a salmon and pop up in unexpected places. This made me nervous as I would rather watch from the shore or the viewing stand. It was a wonderful experience to witness the bear's daily routine.

They offered a day trip to the Valley of the 10,000 Smokes. We drove part of the way and then hiked up to the volcanic part. It was very dark, dried lava that was very sharp, and you had to be careful not to shred your boots on the edges. It was a totally different environment than the calm river and lake. When I returned I saw a path of bear paws that had existed for hundreds of years. This was an incredible place to view bears living their lives without disturbing their routines. I felt like I had been in bear paradise with bears up to 1,500 pounds that had an unlimited supply of salmon and little interference from humans. I wonder if humans would ever realize how important it is to save this paradise. This was a great once-in-a-lifetime experience and I was glad I made the effort to get here. I could not paint some of the vistas as they were too beautiful. I did so many great trips as I was not sure I would be able to repeat the experience in my lifetime.

After all the adventures, I had to go back to work. It was 1994 and I was 47 years old and was thinking about retirement, even though that was not going to happen for a while. Trace was getting ready to go to Humboldt to finish his degree. He worked hard so I knew he would do well. If you focus on your goals there is a good chance you will get there or somewhere else that is meaningful. It had been good to live with someone for the first time and can see the advantage of being together before a big commitment. Ideally, people should be married to live together but that may not always work. It gave me a different perspective on relationships and my role in them. We had shared parts of Alaska together and I had had wonderful adventures alone. At this point in my life I wanted to find out more about some of my issues and find out more about my family, as I did not have much information.

CHAPTER 16

Post-Alaska

Returning from Alaska after 1994, a friend had picked me up at the airport and he was interested in my backpacking trips as we had done trips in the Sierras. The trips in the Sierra were easier to negotiate with the good weather, rough granite stone, beautiful vistas, shorter routes and no grizzly bears. You need a permit to control the amount of people in popular areas, and it gives the rangers an idea about usage and emergency contact if you don't come out. But Alaska has huge wide-open spaces that expand your mind and view of the world. It was disappointing to return to an urban environment, but this is where I lived. It had tighter spaces, more people, crime and traffic congestion. When we climbed the stairs to my small house we sat for a while to give the highlights of my trip before he left.

My mother had come to visit while I was gone, as it was a vacation for her that was safe in my house and inexpensive. I thought she had gone to a rescue mission in San Francisco, which is odd but not for her. It meant Bible study and praising Jesus. I was telling him, now I have to deal with my mother. His mother was dead so I did not dwell on it.

After he left I was sitting there and I heard footsteps coming from the basement stairs. I was very startled and was ready to call the police, when my mother's face appeared from behind the door. She had been hiding in the basement while we talked! My heart settled down and she acted like this was normal. We talked a bit and I looked at the room she was sleeping in, and it was all torn up. I asked her what happened and she did not have an answer. The bed was something I made and put a futon on it, so it was not substantial, but other people had slept on it with no trouble. I had to rest and get ready to go back to work. We went to sleep after I pulled her bed back together. The next day I made sure there was some food and the cat was OK. She then announced she was going back to the rescue mission where she could help out. She liked helping the down and out. I said OK, and drove her back to San Francisco. When I returned I was relieved as going back to work was going to be hard with all the back logged work, emergencies, and getting caught up on other changes in my cases. I had thought about her taking one of the one-bedroom units in the duplex, but I realized that while she was able to negotiate the steep hill to the store, she had to cross a very busy street where people routinely drove fast. Also, since she could not drive to other places, she would have to rely on me to take her places including medical care, church, shopping and company. I was not sure I could do this with my workload. She could be very nice but then she could pull an eccentric act or talk about her childhood. That was very stressful for me. The neighborhood was very ethnically diverse, but no one really talked to their neighbors so I would not call it friendly. She was not social but I did not want to be her only social contact. The truth is that she liked her building in Evanston despite people starting to die due to old age and health issues. But she still liked the tree-lined streets and her central location. She had saved most of her rapid moving for my childhood.

Another time she came out to visit, my sister was visiting too, and she threatened to leave rather than talk to her mother for the same unknown reason. I did have one dinner with them together on my patio, but it was not easy conversation. My sister's husband said he was going to divorce her if she did not stop drinking, so she came out to my place to dry out. I took her to the mountains and mother stayed at my house while we were gone. My sister slept much of the time, but I took her Yosemite, the Eastern Sierras and South Lake Tahoe. My mother then went back to the mission, and when my sister was leaving I picked up mother on a comer in downtown San Francisco as we drove to the airport. There was silence, but mother tried to talk to her, but then said, "Well at least I did not have to go to an orphanage." What? How could she say such a thing when I was forced into an orphanage in Boone! My sister was oblivious but I would have really laid into mother if we were not on a five-lane freeway with heavy traffic and my sister being there. I was so angry. We dropped off my sister and went back to the East Bay. Soon my mother left too, as I was not going to allow her to go back to the mission. It was in a dangerous area and it was too risky. So both were gone and I could look at my life.

Work was good, as I saw children were developing and happier when placed in good homes. We followed the child for at least a year to make sure things were going smoothly with the family. I decided to join the Alameda County Child Abuse Training Committee, which put on monthly trainings for professionals and offered CEUs toward their license renewal. It was a low-fee locally based program that helped, as going to a conference was expensive and time-consuming. In a year one could accumulate quite a few hours. Similar to the other speakers program, we would discuss the program and select speakers for the lineup, which were only 12 per year. There was a Child Abuse Council coordinator who would come to our meetings, have Board meetings and receive funding to pay the speakers and other events. March was Child Abuse Awareness month, and there were ads about paying attention and reporting incidents. It was hard for some relatives to report abuse in the family, and there are mandated reporters like doctors, schools and other organizations. Usually only the worse offenses would be adjudicated into the system, but it was worth having a record of incidences that could become dangerous or deadly. The Bay Area had many good speakers due to the many educational institutions and organizations, so it was a worthwhile endeavor.

I also decided to run Supervision groups for workers getting their required hours towards their state license. These usually met once a week for a given period of time, and then there was a break. I would prepare a topic and have one person present a case. The younger workers had energy and were just out of their Master's graduation, so they were getting their hours for licensure. The Alaska trip had given me an expansion of myself identity as a person who was capable and enjoying life. Was I selling myself short if I stayed to retirement? Maybe I was, but it seemed like my life was full enough and I enjoyed the work but, not the workload. The effort it would take to start a new independent work situation was daunting and I might not succeed. I am a person who needs security, so it seemed like the best choice was to stay until retirement.

Other things that happened in 1996 were that I went up to the foothills where my cousin Leon lived and bought a small house with a studio next door. It had a lot of trees and was close to town. I rented both units, so it was not a financial burden for me. I just had to fix it up a bit.

In 1995 I came out of work one day very tired but I saw a familiar face of a man who was standing near his car and I realized it was Jay, my high school boyfriend. He invited me to dinner, and just like that I accepted. It was like we were back in the old days, but of course we were not. We went to a place on the Berkeley marina and had a nice dinner with wine he had ordered. I was not drinking much wine, but I went along with it. He said he had hired a private eye to track me down. He had moved from Georgia, where he had married his first wife, had a son and then divorced. He had not seen her since but he had an invitation to work in Louisiana and start his own law office so he accepted. He did not mention his second marriage or daughter, and I did not want to talk about my love life. He was also the National Chair of the United States Veterans Association and had flown to Viet Nam with John McCain and other representatives.

I told him I was looking for my father, who was a decorated veteran in World War II, and he said he would look for any records he could find. I was so excited to see him I drank too much wine, and when he was leaving he kissed me. Later I thought it was not great to wine and dine me but I went along with it. He called my place the next day, and Trace answered and said he did not appreciate him letting me drive with so much wine. Trace was right and it felt good to have someone stand up for me. I was not sure of Jay's motives or why I went along with it. I was vulnerable to someone I had loved dearly. It was great and unreal. I wrote a letter to him at his DC office, reminding him about looking for my father's records if he could find them. I had trouble getting any information. I did not hear from him until 2011.

Art had always been a consistent interest of mine. UC Berkeley had a Post-Master's program in Art Therapy. There was a two-year program at UC Berkeley that was Post-Masters and gave a certificate. The classes were on weekends or some nights, but they were so interesting that I enjoyed them as well as the students and staff. One class on Family Therapy required that we write a paper about our family, which is something I could have used a long time ago. My family lacked grandparents, a father, sisters and brothers, aunts and uncles, cousins or any in laws. I started to think about it and I rarely saw my mother, mainly on Sundays. What would I write about? I was totally blank.

It was more comfortable for me to see it as a research project and send out questionnaires to the relatives I knew of or had an address to see if I had any family. I had met people in the 1989 reunion where no one really talked to me or my mother. Most of the relatives were on the "other side," or that of my Great Aunt and Uncle. Because everyone on my mother's side left the UP farm and were scattered all over the United States to survive and had little contact. Some of the living relatives did respond and I appreciated that, but many did not. I had gone to Finnfests and took a DNA test, which resulted in finding the one paternal cousin in Illinois, and she wrote about her father's life.

I felt I could not write an overview with only a few responses, as it would not be comprehensive. Most of these people were on the "other side," that of the great aunt and uncle, but most of these people I never met and thought they looked down on my mother and me because of the poverty and my mother leaving her younger daughter to be cared for by her father. I felt she did the right thing, but that was not popular in the 1950s. I had no real idea.

Instead, I wrote about what it was like to grow up without a family and an absent single mother. I did make a family tree from what I knew and at least tried to get names. On my mother's side, I put their occupation, health or any outstanding category. On the "other side "of the family there were a lot of PhDs, medical personnel, nurses, dentist and people who lived a simple life near the family farms. The instructor was nice and gave me an A− and said that I had been through a lot and she thought I was dyslexic. After rereading the paper, which was very hard to write, I agreed with her. Something was up with my writing that I could not see while writing the paper. This exercise was unsettling to me, as I felt stripped naked and alone. But it also spurred me on to start looking for family. Can I ever find a photo of my father? Can I find out about the Shelton's and where they immigrated from in Europe? Can I find out more about my mother's family instead of all the horror stories she told me? What about the large family in Finland?

In 1998 we graduated from the program, and then they announced that they were not an approved program by the American Art Therapy Association, and we would have to complete 3,000 more hours working in a specifically art therapy location to get a license. When we signed up, they said our license and their certificate was all that was needed. We were all seasoned professionals, so this was not the worst news, as we could continue doing what we were doing and incorporate art therapy if we wanted to. But it did seem somewhat shady. I was glad I did the program as I learned a lot and the classes were well done and interesting. It did spur me on to look for more information about my father and other family members. My questionnaire opened the door to meeting some of the relatives on the "other side" and going to Finland.

Lainey knew a man who worked in a warehouse by day but he did genealogy at night. So I sent him what I knew and he went to work. He was able to get documentation on my father's first wife and their divorce papers. It looks like she was using him for military benefits while she raised her four children after her husband died. For a second I thought I had four sisters and brothers and was very excited, but it was not to be.

The genealogist found a relative who was related to my Jewish side in Cincinnati, Ohio, home of the reform Jewish movement. They were fairly well off and into baseball. A woman had photos, which she sent me of my great-grandparents and great-great-grandmother. This was a breakthrough, but she was a young mother and did not have time to connect with me. My paternal great-grandmother was 13 years old when she married, so probably an orphan; had three boys and sadly died at age 21. Then the great-grandfather was able to remarry and had other children. He died in a "poor house" with family living all around him. I found a step cousin but they knew nothing about the Shelton's. Then the man decided he did not have time to continue, but he really helped me move forward. I was filling out a family tree and getting a better sense of my paternal history.

Later on when I moved to the foothills I joined the genealogical society and a volunteer took my DNA information and I was able to move much further along with the Shelton side, which went back to the 1700s in Virginia. The maternal side of the paternal side was even more interesting, and it showed a range of people who were not just poor farmers but had a range of talents. However, my father's branch did seem to be on the unlucky side of things.

The woman was able to trace my ancestry to a famous country and western singer who I have not met, but did fly to Oklahoma City to hear his concert. His branch also included a notorious woman who was called the Black Widow in that she killed her father and four husbands and seemingly got away with it. But there was no contact with living souls. So where did that leave me?

I had two great experiences in Alaska and had opened up my feeling of confidence and enjoying life. I had some family experiences that were somewhat stressful in that I did not have a unified family. I did research to look for more family, and got information but no contacts. I took a certificate course in Art Therapy that was very interesting but also disappointing. I bought a house in the foothills to have a place for retirement. However, I sold it and bought another one in 1999, as it was bigger and closer to my cousins. I had been in and out of a live-in relationship that was good but not good enough. Now I was ready for retirement but still had some time to go. I was reflecting on why my life was the way it was and could I make it different.

CHAPTER 17

Fatherless Daughter and Never Married

Making progress toward my future life felt good, but I wanted to look at being a fatherless daughter and a never married woman. In the past they were "old maids" or "spinsters". I had never had a father, so it was not something I missed, except in the 1950s I knew it was not the normal way to live. My mother had worked as a Rosie the Riveter, but those jobs dried up when the men came back from war. She jumped in and out of three marriages before we ended up in Evanston, Illinois, which was a suburb of Chicago. Kids would ask "what does your father do?" as the social status were tied to his work and income. I avoided answering those questions. On TV I saw families where the father, mother and children all got along and only had minor problems. I knew we were poor, but there were families with fathers that were also poor. We never had a car, as men drove cars and some of those were pedophiles trying to pick me up. I never asked about my father, and in sixth grade Josephine, said he was dead, but I did not believe her. I think when I was older and my medical records were fifty percent blank I wondered what he died of or did during life. Later my mother said he had struck her while she was pregnant with me and she filed for divorce. That seemed like a good choice, as growing up with fighting would be not have been good. I later found out that my father had lost a brother and mother before thirty three years old. My father was beaten if he did not want to work as hard on the farm. He was a Golden Glove boxer, served in World War II in the Military police in Germany and was decorated with a Bronze Star. He had a temper, so I believe my mother was hit. He was probably alone and trying to find love like my mother without much experience of feeling loved.

When I babysat I did not always like the way husbands treated their wives, and in high school they had a Daddy Daughter Dinner Dance, which of course I could not attend. My first boyfriend was very kind and we did very nice things together, but we finally separated. It gave me a model of what I would like in a partner. The other side was how to deal with advances and boys that were not very nice, and I did not want to be an unwed mother. I never felt I needed a man as I was trying to make it myself. But the truth was men made more money, were promoted more quickly and there are very considerate men if you can find them.

The other important part was that my mother was "men negative" as she felt her father had "killed" her mother by having too many babies when she was ill. I did not take murder literally, but I was aware that having too many babies had killed many women and the father would marry another woman to take her place. She told me horror stories about what men did, and they did frighten me. How do you tell when a man is not what he seems?

I did not know how to negotiate relationships very well. On the internet was a statement that fatherless daughters were likely to drop out of school, have early pregnancy, use drugs and live in poverty. This seemed very dire to me, but it's not easy finding your way as an unprotected girl living with a mostly absent single mother. Gloria Vanderbilt in the 2016 video "Nothing Left Unsaid" with her son Anderson Cooper said that "a fatherless daughter feels like everything is possible but never feels safe." I think that sums up my vulnerable feelings, and I chose safety rather than trusting a man. I wanted to get married sometime, but I did not want to be defined by a man.

After six proposals, saying yes, really trying and then backing out, I was getting the idea that I was afraid of marriage. I did want to have children but I did not want to be a single mother like my mother. We had lived in marginal places with lower rents but things got more expensive. I was 48 with my last back-out and I don't regret any of those decisions, as I had achieved many of my goals and was fairly content with my life.

I started a group for never-married women that went on for years. Most of us were in our forties or fifties. I started out with focusing on topics but they wanted it to be more of a support group. We were all educated, had our own homes and were looking for a partner, but we had busy lives. Marriage was not the goal, as it was more building self-esteem and how to make our lives better. Three eventually did get married: one married at age 40 and had four children by age 46! Another woman married an outdoor, travel person and they honeymooned in Patagonia. The third one married a man she was friends with but finally agreed to marry. The other three of us were career women. I was living with Trace, but that ended. It was a good group, but did not go deep enough for me. I like going deeper as it was my life's work to figure things out for myself and other people.

As stated before, my family lacked grandparents, father, siblings, aunts and uncles and cousins. My mother was my whole family, so the important person in my life who shared a repetitious grim scenario about her family. Later in life I found out a little bit more about her family by traveling to Finland and meeting some cousins. Finnish history was one of being exploited by Sweden for 600 years; then Russia, which was negating their culture opportunities for education and advancing themselves and their children. This created poverty, famine, minimal education and a sense of being less than as a person or a society. Finland was able to get their independence in 1917 and slowly prospered, but it was a huge struggle to make that progress. There were social, political and intergenerational struggles that impacted the average citizen. As a result, Finnish children were encouraged to be independent and contribute to the family at an early age. Men and women shared the work, had more equality and democracy was important for all.

There is the idea of intergenerational trauma that can be passed down by events or even DNA. But more specifically, I found out my great-grandfather in Finland was a circuit judge who was not home much and the family suffered.

His wife froze to death, and my grandmother and great aunt became servants on a larger farm when they were young teens. The great aunt married one of the famer's sons and they immigrated to Northern Michigan at the end of the 19th century. My grandfather and great uncle also became miners. The great uncle, Otto, died at age 31 in a mine in Montana. My grandmother immigrated when she was 18 and married the remaining son. So, two brothers married two sisters mainly out of convenience and speaking only Finnish. My mother said it was not a good marriage and she was her mother's emotional support as well as a hard worker. Her parents were dead by 1928 due to illness injury and illness. My grandmother was in an inescapable situation, and my mother did not have much of a childhood and her strong attachment to her mother might have been a defense against her bitterness. Children can only handle so many problems that are above their developmental stage. My mother asked her mother why they could not leave, and the reply was they had no money or place to go. My mother was trying to rescue her. It seems like three generations of women in tough situations that led to their death and children that had to fend for themselves. How much nurturing did they get?

This is the immigrant story in many cases, and people react differently to such impoverishment. My mother's reaction was to drop out of school and try to parent three younger siblings. Orphans were not treated well and she was humiliated by neighbors and insensitive boys. She turned to religion, which helped give some hope. When she left at age 20 during the Great Depression, she was determined to move to get work and a better life. She was successful in working and she vowed she would never get married or have children, as she had too many hardships in her early years. I think she was sincere in her intention, but after the war she was unemployed and lonely. There were many post-war marriages that were very short, and I was the product of the second marriage. She got divorced before I was born. I give my mother credit for moving around to get better jobs and saving up money to stay home with me for the first two years. However, toward my birth, as mentioned there was a lot of stress, death and demands on her time. She was described as very distraught. I think her intentions were good but the situation was not ideal. Her marriage to my father seemed to be two needy, neglected children trying to make positive connection without much guidance.

Since I grew up with a single mother who was my entire family, I wanted to look at that primary relationship and how it impacted my later relationships. In the 1950s, John Bowlby, an English psychiatrist, did research on the baby's attachment to the mother (or caregiver). The basic research design was that the baby was with the mother and a stranger comes into the room. The mother leaves, and when the mother returns they observed their reunion. There was extensive research and it resulted in categories of attachment. Below is a simple review of attachment styles, but of course there are variations in circumstances that influence the quality of the attachment. The basic styles that Bowlby introduced were as follows: **Secure attachment** is one where the mother is consistent, the baby feels content and there is not much disruption in the bonding process. They can share feelings and the baby seeks support when needed. **Insecure attachment** is caused by inconsistent or lapses in nurturing, which makes the baby unsure about what will happen when it expresses needs. One form of insecure attachment is an **ambivalent attachment**, in which the care is not consistent and the child has mixed feelings about being close or distant from the mother and they might withdraw. In **Anxious attachment**, the child feels anxious about being near the mother and is watchful and not relaxed. Fear of abandonment, insecurity, not feeling valued spoken to or cuddled. The child might be detached from relationships or clingy. **Anxious-Ambivalent attachment** is a combination of both styles. It's hard to get close but needing closeness. Later, the **Disorganized Attachment** was introduced by Mary Ainsworth, but this is a more extreme disruption of the child's relationship with the mother and the mother's behavior might be undermining a sense of safety and connection. The child might exhibit more extreme acting out or withdrawn behaviors that are disruptive to bonding. Negative influences such as substance abuse, mental illness, depression, chaotic environment, neglect or abuse can cause short- or long-term problems in the child's care and development. Other people might also be involved in the child's care. With a great improvement in the bonding relationship there can be repair, but there maybe be some residual effects from the previous disruptions.

Bowlby said the critical time was between ages two and five years, which set the tone of the child's development. There have been more expansions of his theory, but he was the pioneer. If the infant is experiencing ambivalence and anxiety, it makes him/her more vulnerable to insecurity, low self-esteem, problems in educational development, social problems and ability to make connections as an adult. I feel infancy is an important time, especially if there are major events during this vulnerable time. This is a brief overview, and the reader might benefit from reading more about attachment theory and it's impact on relationships if interested. The internet provides much information on attachment theory.

It seemed like three generations of my mother's family issues created insecurity, loss and disruption of the family. My mother lost out on security, nurturing and education. She had too much responsibility too early. She was very ambivalent about marriage and children. She said if she had a boy, she would give him up for adoption, which might explain the couple who was ready to adopt me and picked out a name. However, I was a girl or she changed her mind. I do give her a lot of credit for giving me a good start living on her savings. However, I feel she was ambivalent about caring for a child and knowing how to raise one. She had good intentions but had bad circumstances.

My mother decided to leave California and went to the Upper Peninsula, where she had grown up. However, she probably had no intention of staying there. She impulsively married a man with a farm and had a baby. She wanted the baby but felt she could not stay there, did not have funds and the father was able to provide a stable life. This sacrifice haunted her. I felt maybe I was next. Life was not going as planned and we left the farm when I was four. It was years of instability and struggle to keep a roof over our head and she was depressed. As a result I found myself in very insecure places and alone at age five. She said we were on an adventure, which I went along with for a while, but then I was frightened, barely functioning and withdrawn. This did not give her much satisfaction in being a parent. It was a depletion loop. Living conditions got better, but also there were traumas that disrupted my sense of safety and even being wanted. The most traumatic thing was being abruptly transported by strangers to an orphanage. If I had been told that it was temporary, I would have been more relaxed. I feel that damaged my bond with her and I felt on my own in the world, but I was not going to make foolish choices and be at risk.

I had no control over her, but I did over myself and my behavior. When I returned from the orphanage I was part of her life but I was looking for my own life and future. I detached to protect myself. She did not know how to bond with me and I wanted her to realize what she had done by sending me off with strangers, but that was not going to happen. Then she detached by not being home at night and we were distant. I feel she was depressed and maybe was hiding for her own good or to protect me. I don't know. I feel if she had an opportunity for more education, she would have done better in life, as she was smart. This happens more in single-parent families with few resources. We actually could qualify for Welfare for Aid to Dependent Children, but she was determined not to be on Welfare. The advantage would have been she would have been home more, but I respect her desire to support us by working. This is a short summary, but I think this had a big impact on my ability or willingness to form marriage relationships. My relationship with Jay was a welcome relief to be with someone I wanted to be with, but I was too young. I had to act a role of being more mature than I was, and I was still trying to figure out who I was as a person. But it met a big need to have good company with someone I cared for and who was good to me. It helped me, but he was not my parent and there was some confusion.

I think my attachment to my mother was Anxious-Ambivalent, and this had a big impact on me being able to form a secure relationship with a man. I had no father, for better or worse, to use as a role model for men. A frightening father would have been worse. Some research has shown that children who had fear of abandonment or fear of engulfment were less likely to marry. That is, they were literally or emotionally abandoned or felt they were engulfed by the needs of the parent. My mother used to say "we" feel or think something when I had my own feelings and opinions. I felt that I was a person with valid needs and goals, and deserved to be respected. I had limits, and it was hard to express my needs or affection. Some men were a threat to my safety, and other men were not available to talk or experience things on a deeper level. I really needed depth. I wanted to give love, share a life and be flexible with someone I could trust. I put most of my efforts in helping people and other causes. There were many people I enjoyed talking to on a short-term basis but not as a long-term relationship. I don't regret very many of my choices that I made in life.

Long story short, my trust level was not very good, and I was afraid of being dragged down and away from my goals. I was afraid of being humiliated and demeaned. To me this explains why I would accept the marriage proposal until the fear set in, took over and I would back out. Some were just practical reasons such as location or non-negotiable differences. I did not want to work hard for a goal and lose it. I did not want to be a single mother, as I knew what struggles and hardships my mother had while working full time. I guess I did not see a lot of positives in marriage. With a fifty percent divorce rate, I felt the odds were not very good.

I have seen women pursue the man who they felt was good for them. I am not sure I had the self-confidence to do that. How do you know how they are really are without spending years with them? Life is unpredictable, but I finally had stability and I did not want more uncertainty.

In my many years of working with children in very hard situations, I saw cases that were worse than mine, but there was someone or family that was helping them early on. The family was trying to work together to support each other. Of course, there were absent parents, death, violence, and drug abuse that could not be worked out for anyone's safety let alone a vulnerable child. There needs to be more alternative care that is positive for children.

The positives in my life were that my mother had no bad habits, always paid the rent/bills even though she made very little, read a lot of books, was steadfast in her religious participation, had a sense of humor about the absurdity of life and people, had good saving habits, was a good cook when she was home, and came through on big items to help me but not in daily interactions. We were lucky to have a local affordable health care system. Some of her qualities helped me through life to overcome some of the rough spots. She was a strong, complicated woman who I was attached to in a stressed, cautious manner. She would say I was the best thing that happened to her and I was a wonderful child. She might be thinking this, but it did not come through in actions toward me. This resulted in my needing proof or much reassurance that what the person was saying was true. Actions spoke much louder than words. Maybe I needed more actions than people were used to give living together full time.

Being alone can give peace and quiet. People can be enjoyable and interesting, but the opposite can also be true. I feel it all worked out and in today's world people are looking at alternative life-styles. There was nothing wrong with the traditional family structure if it allows people to become productive citizens who might be different from their parents. A two-parent family is ideal if it is a positive arrangement for all concerned. Society can fill in some of the gaps with child care, early education, basic health care for all, providing reasonable-paying jobs for men and women on all social levels and a willingness for the society to support the welfare of most of its citizens. It is up to the person to make the most of their opportunities for their own benefit and that of their community and the larger society. Prevention is important in avoiding life-threatening illness, but the surrounding environment has to be healthy. The importance of positive communication, parenting and sex education can be taught in schools. This being said, my mother was much disciplined in her daily health practices and she still got breast cancer, malignant melanoma, and Alzheimer's disease, but she lived to be 96 years old. Good mental health can be taught, as much of life is your attitude, self-esteem and goals in life. The role of the family, schools and government has always been debated and still is being debated.

CHAPTER 18

Retirement

From 2000 to 2003 I had treatments for my shoulder and most were ineffective. One professional tore my rotator cuff but denied it, I finally found a surgery who could repair the damage and the main problem which had left my left as useless. While I was waiting for my shoulder to heal, I was trying to get rid of all the belongings in my 1,200 square-foot basement that was quite full. I had clothes from different parts of my life, wedding dresses, camping gear and tools and supplies for the houses. I hired an East Coast woman who did not seem to have any pressure in her life about working. She could lift things and had a methodical, careful and supportive style. Her initial test was a cabinet full of plastic storage containers and other carry-out food containers. I was so busy I just threw them in there in case I needed them. She asked if she could remove them, and I said "Sure." She was relieved that I was not a hoarder but just a busy person. The basement was harder in that I had dreams associated with some of the clothes and items that could help me have a better life. While I was deliberating, she added taste and quality into the mix as she had grown up in a different class. Buy a quality item, not the many inexpensive items in my procession.

A used wedding dress store was happy to pay me for the unused dresses. It began getting easier to let go of things as we worked in my spare time. As much as we unearthed, there seemed to be more. While this was going on, I wanted to complete the house projects that I had no time for while going to work. I tiled the large cement bench on the patio; scraped, sanded and painted an exterior flaking wall. I had a new roof put on and touched up the trim. I was not sure if I wanted to sell the buildings when I moved, but I needed them to be in good shape. I worked on the landscaping a bit and put salmon-pink geraniums all over as they were free and easy to grow. The front of the property needed some attention for curb appeal.

Meanwhile, back at work full time I was getting tired of doing adoption home studies but I liked the hopeful couples (gay and straight) and the positive effect on children's lives when placed in good stable homes. The paperwork was exhausting, and I was burning out. I got my work done but it was not easy. Finally, in February 2004, I was able to set a date for retirement at 27 years. My licensing supervision group of fairly new employees could not believe I had been there that long, as they intended to get their hours and look for more comfortable jobs. It made me wonder if was a generational thing (they were born in the late 1970s), or was it the demand of a big agency in an inner-city location too rough for them? I know the police department would hire new recruits, train them but after two years they would look for an easier area. as the demands of that job were hard as the clients had more serious problems. One worker who was presenting in the morning worked till two a.m. the night before which showed fortitude. When I started we were young and idealistic; what were their expectations? Maybe I lived during a more interesting but stressful time.

Rosalind, who had been a friend early on in our careers, helped organize the luncheon at El Torino's on the Marina near the office. She had put out art materials on a table for workers to make collages and insert old photos. There were very amusing and creative pieces. We had a speakers table in front and I was getting teary eyed. It was well attended, and that meant a lot to me. Happy Trails was the theme, as I was moving to the foothills. I don't understand people who just leave without some ceremony, as work is a big part of people's lives. I understand people move around more and do not expect to get a retirement. How will they make it?

I carried a box of things from my desk, but gave away many things like my large poster of mountains and a lake, which got my attention during stressful times. My energy was very high, like a cork popping out of a campaign bottle. I don't understand people who have no idea what to do, as I had a long list of things I could not wait to get started as I had many ideas.

Instead of getting ready to move I wanted to do some trips that I had been a priority. My first trip was to go to the Smokey Mountains in Tennessee on a timeshare as it felt safe. There was a serial killer on I-40, I flew in late and drove east and got off at a sign that said motel and food. The "motel" turned out to be a steep circular, dirt driveway with a red phone on a yellow table under a hanging light. The sign said "Please call for the front desk." I called, but no one answered. I walked around to the back past a Rolls Royce limousine and saw a man pacing back and forth on a cell phone near two cabins and a hot tub. He saw me, and without stopping his conversation he waved his hand for me to get out of there. I quickly left and assumed it was prostitution, escort service or drugs in the country.

I did find Rose's Family Restaurant, which had a table where the family were eating and had two tables for guests. I ordered chicken and vegetables for five dollars and it was good. I got back on I-40 and decided I would go to a place with brand-name motels near Clarksville. Welcome to the country! The next day I found the resort in Sevierville, and the people were very friendly. The concierge could get tickets to singing theaters with family members age four years old, and then stair-step to the parents. They groups were very talented and dressed for Sunday church with old-time songs. I went to a Dolly wood's horse competition, but Dolly Parton was not there. I saw a Chinese acrobatic show and I wondered what they thought about Tennessee. I hiked to the tallest mountain but that day was the end of hurricane Arlene. I was one of the few people hiking up to the top with an inadequate rain poncho and I was soaking wet. The Cherokee museum was very interesting as was just being by the pool for a while, as this was a nice relaxing break in my new life. Nashville provided the new Grand Old Opry, which was not as homey. I went to the State records department to see if I could find any Sheltons, and I did find the census record of my great-grandfather after he remarried but no other information. Not liking the city I went to a government hotel on a lake that was quiet and peaceful. That was a nice send-off for my first post-retirement trip. I felt at home there, and later I learned that my relatives had lived there awhile.

When I returned, I made reservations to go to the Vince Shute Wildlife Preserve north of Minneapolis, which had 90 black bears on 360 acres of fenceless land. The Sierra Club leader was a gentle woman who had never led a trip before. We had a camping area, a cook and we were making a kiosk in the parking lot for tourists to learn more about the bears while they waited for the bus that took them to the observation deck. We made bird houses that were strung in the trees near the deck. I liked the people and met a woman from Pennsylvania who wanted to raft down the Colorado River and I really wanted to do that trip. When we parked near the observation deck, we had to put a pail of bear poop near every tire as the adolescent bears would chew on the tires. This was not a good place for a flat tire. It worked. The sub-adults left our tires alone.

Near the last day they asked for a volunteer to help feed the 90 bears in the camp. My hand shot up and I was selected. We had bright-colored safety vests and went to a food-storage building. We saw a bear trying to break into a trailer and the leader yelled at "Trouble," whose name was appropriate. The bear backed off. Most of the bears understood the rules and there was little trouble. We had to pass an area for 600-pound males who each had their own dish evenly spaced out so there was less competition for food. They were a bit intimidating. Once inside there were many five-gallon buckets with different kinds of dried food. We filled our own five-gallon buckets with healthy food and then I accompanied a guide toward the females and cub area. The females had little huts made out of natural branches to hang out and feed their cubs. One mother had four cubs, which meant she was very healthy. I was allowed to feed one bear by myself by pouring food in its bowl. Sometimes we would see a bear and the guide would say to stay back, as that bear had an attitude.

There were cubs climbing a trees, which is their day care, while the mother was off doing things. They do not come down until the mother gives the signal, which could take hours. I was able to take many close-up photographs, which were thrilling. The BBC network had a robotic rock that moved silently among the bears as they were making a film for the British audience. When we were done, we went up on the observation deck to see a photography class that was taking photos of volunteer bear models. There was a path right near their tripods and a new bear was coming in as it wanted its photo taken. It was all very peaceful and cooperative, as black bears are related to dogs and adapt to human beings much easier than grizzlies or polar bears. This was being in paradise for me. The founder of the preserve, Vince Schultz, was a lumberjack who was tired of the bears breaking into their cabins while they were working. They had been shooting the bears, but decided to try a more peaceful approach and feed them. This worked and the bears coexisted with the men; in fact, two of them would sit at Vince's feet after work. Obviously feeding wild bears is not a normal or recommended practice these bears were used to being fed. The American Black Bear Association took over the property to protect the bears invite biology students to study and to educate the public on living with bears, which brings in donations for bear food. Karen and I decided I should come to Pennsylvania and then make plans for the Colorado River Trip. I drove to the Upper Peninsula of Michigan to visit my Aunt Elna and Cousin Harold. It was a drive but closer than Chicago. I enjoyed seeing them. This was a very unique trip and it made me very happy to see so many contented bears in one place.

There were more trips, and I did not allow enough time to finish emptying my house for the May move. I was in a big crunch and the woman who had been helping me had moved back to New York. I had decided to rent the place out, as I was not sure I was cut out for small-town life and the tenant was moving in fairly soon. I put an ad on Craigslist for five-dollar sofas that were in good shape, and those went in two days. The movers came to take all the big stuff but the little stuff adds up. Duncan, a friend, helped me by taking a pick-up truck load up two days before the deadline. One of my cats decided to hide in the house and we could not find her. He was getting grumpy, so we left with him driving the truckload and me driving with my car full with the one cooperative cat. We ate pizza and spent the night at my new house in the woods with boxes scattered all over, and I think I found blankets for sleeping. The next day I thanked Duncan and I drove all the way back down to find the hiding cat. Rosalind came over to help me look, and we left food and water out while we went out to dinner. The Bay Area rush hour traffic is horrendous. We came back and the cat relented and we were able to get her into the carrier, which I placed on the passenger seat. While driving she turned around and sprayed me really good to show me her displeasure about the move. Six-hundred miles in two days and I was ready to donate her.

The moving was so stressful I got shingles and hives. There were new things in country living, such as the propane tank, well testing, and getting used to the completely black nights with no other homes in sight. I could hear bears or deer walking by at night but could not see them. The mountain lions are quiet but the coyotes howl and the foxes can yip. I was not afraid of the animals as much as the people, as I had always lived in urban settings. One night the cats were laying on the bed and coyotes starting howling and their little bodies were so stiff I tried to massage them to relax. I knew that there were animals that would like to eat my little buddies. The cats were only allowed outside when I was home or I locked them up. I knew people who had lost cats, dogs, goats and chickens and that were not protected. However, dogs are the biggest killer of livestock, and wild animals and cats are the biggest killer of wild birds.

One night a man came up my front stairs at ten-thirty p.m. and through the front window asked if this was the Bible study. I said no and he left. He returned in a short while and asked if he could use my phone as he ran out of gas. I said I would make a call for him, which I did and it seemed legitimate. He disappeared into the darkness and I had no idea where he was, but he never came back. A woman had her house burned down by a carpet cleaner, so I was on alert.

My cousins lived nearby, but they seemed busy all the time and had two wonderful children. There were 14 relatives around and it felt like I hit the family Jackpot. They would have holiday gatherings, dinners or Taco Night down the road. Leon and his wife Nancy stayed and their kids went to college, but most of them moved away or died, but it was a positive change in my life to have family around in a beautiful place. It meant a great deal to me.

I was working on cosmetic repairs such as the kitchen wallpaper, which had pink and blue rocking horses. I just painted over it. The layout was good, with two bedrooms and a bathroom were at one end of the house and my large master suite at the other end, so guests could get up early and I could sleep in. Early on there was an outdoor fire with helicopters overhead, and they closed my access road. I had already bought ten gallons of house paint to replace the Pepto-pink color. I was locked in for three days, so I painted the whole one-story house gray with white trim. Later Marty did the high eves when he came to visit. I was not upset about the fire then, but more recently this has become a bigger problem as global warming progresses.

The darkness and quiet became very soothing. Karen, the woman I had met at the Bear Camp, came out and we went to Yosemite on our way to the rafting trip down the Colorado River. We met the group in Flagstaff, and when we were greeted at the front desk they asked us for our emergency contact. What happened on the last trip? After an orientation meeting we were driven to Lee's Ferry and started our 246-mile journey down the Colorado River. The leader was a young woman with two men and they were good cooks, guides and made us feel safe, but the water was very cold and gritty. We each had a pad that we could put anywhere on the dirt to sleep on, and I asked Karen where she wanted to camp. She avoided me, so I put my pallet away from the crowd. The start time was five-thirty a.m., and people went to bed at nine p.m. on the pad. The next day I tried to talk to Karen, but she just ignored me for the rest of the trip. I am a night person and was lucky to meet a lone Australian man who liked to stay up late, talk and sometimes we would hang out with the crew until they kicked us out. The crowd was a cross-section of

America from Fifth Avenue NYC to rural Mississippi. I really enjoyed going through the layers of stone and geologic time. When we went through big rapids we were swamped by big waves in a safe situation, but it was an intense one-time adventure. Toward the end we went to freshwater waterfalls and could "shower" with clothes on. At a rest stop, the guides were asked what happened to the people on the last trip, and they said they were still in ICU recovering! The food was excellent and I was very glad to have seen one of the wonders of the United States.

The Australian man was going to take a bus to explore Arizona, as he was afraid to drive in the United States. At the end of the trip, Karen expected me to drive her to Las Vegas airport from Flagstaff, but I said I was driving toward California. She said she did not want people to think we were gay. That was the last thing I would expect to hear from her. The couple she had hung out with drove her to Phoenix and I never saw her again. The trip was wonderful, but you never know what people are really like, but meeting her lead me to the Colorado River.

The early mornings really wore me out, so the first stop was a motel near Needles. All the dirty clothes were piled into the laundry facilities and I ate at a cowboy bar with good grub. I had a deep sleep and the next day found a campsite at Mt. Whitney. I enjoyed the scenic drive home through Mammoth Lakes, Hot Creek, Mono Lake and Lake Tahoe.

Before I moved to the foothills I had been on a ski trip in Kamloops, Canada and I met a woman who lived in the town I was moving to. She said there was a sports club that had been going for years and join it when I arrived. This was a big improvement over the Bay Area. I also joined the Sierra Club, which I had joined in 1983 but was not active except for a few trips in various mountain ranges. This group had meetings, speakers and some causes they supported including the Lodge Clair Tappaan near skiing and hiking. I eventually got involved in putting on the speakers and the 25th anniversary gala with the group founders.

There were the Democrats, who were a small enough group to get to know people, support local candidates, and one time I went to the California convention as a delegate. In a smaller rural area there are more immediate issues that impact most of the citizens that need to be addressed, and it's beneficial to have input from people on both sides of issues.

Drought and fire are bigger issues than ever before as everyone needs water. There are people with other needs such as internet for education or their business, medical care and other types of jobs. It's a balancing act to meet the most important needs for the most people under current conditions.

Creating art had been an ongoing source of enjoyment all of my life, and I have done art on my own for many years. In a smaller place it was hard to find an art community. There was one good gallery but another place opened up that had studios for rent and shows. I was in shows, organized one and sold some paintings, but my main interest was enjoyment and meaning. There was a lot of entertainment in the area with plays, shows and music. I thing I hit the jackpot in moving here. The community was very special, but I did not meet a special someone. Some did and divorced, and some stayed together and my life seems to stay the same.

In 2005 I got a phone call that the police had picked up my mother for wandering the streets in the dark without a coat on. I had made many trips to Evanston over the years, trying to keep her in her apartment, but she was declining and this was the last straw. During one visit in an extreme Chicago heat wave, I had to convince her to go to motel with air conditioning. However. the next day she demanded I take her to her top floor apartment with no AC. Nine hundred seniors died but she refused to use the AC that was later put in for safety. I had been through her turning against me and siding with a drug addict who took most of her savings and Meals on Wheels food. I had taken her to the hospital when she thought she was having a heart attack, but it was the wrong hospital so the billing was a nightmare. I was not surprised, as working with me was not one of her fortes. I had hired agencies to try to make sure she was doing alright. I had been flying out to Chicago for many years and now it was time for full-time care.

I visited many homes in California that took Medicare and found one 30 miles away. The flight from Chicago to California was actually pleasant, except she wanted to get off at Salt Lake City at 34,000 feet in the air. The facility was large, but the staff had regular meetings and was available for questions. She was doing better, as she was not given unnecessary medication and she had good food. As Christmas came, I had a little celebration for us, but it was meaningless to her and it was usually not a good event. She did respond to seeing me and I took her out to lunch at a restaurant that would accommodate her wheelchair. They were very nice about the fact that she tended to spread food all over the floor and never said anything. I took her to a beauty shop and then she started bobbing her head to the beat of the overhead music! She had never said dance was OK, but now that she forgot it was not OK she was enjoying it! There was a huge fire that surrounded the nursing home, which was on top of a hill. The roads were closed and I watched the evening news, which had a TV news helicopter flying in the smoke. The smoke cleared just in time for me to see her place was isolated but safe! After three days I could drive down there, and I asked her about the fire, and she asked "What fire?"

Sometimes she would say things like I wish I was up in the sky on that cloud. Does that mean heaven? She always wanted to be in heaven with her mother who died in 1928, or 76 years before.

Her health was good despite her memory, and she was easy-going person. Where was this person all these years? I have two theories about this: 1. Her early bad memories were erased from her brain and now the good memories and cheerful personality could emerge. 2. She was a controlling person and a bully to me, but living in the nursing home she had to go by their rules, so she gave up the control. Whatever it was, it made my life a whole lot easier taking care of her affairs and visiting her. My childhood was dominated by her childhood, and I wish this peaceful person had emerged a lot earlier in my life. I think people who have a lot on their plate use control of their children to make them feel better, as they do not feel in control of their lives. Children can't be the cure-all, as they also have needs as separate human beings.

Retirement was moving along and was a good time until December 26, 2007 when I had another mammogram that was viewed by a good radiologist. In 2002 in Berkeley they said there was "something" in the right breast and repeated the exam but said it was OK. From 2002 to 2007, I had false negative mammograms for cancer. They missed it until the local radiologist said he wanted to do a biopsy, something that should have been done six years earlier. When he put the needle in blood, was squirting all over, and he said "not a good sign." The holidays had mostly been bad for me, but this was a real low. After that there were many tests and the news kept on getting worse and worse, and it came to Stage 3 breast cancer, aggressive type. This started a year-long treatment of chemotherapy, surgery, radiation and recovery. I went for a second opinion, but staying local was better. The year 2008 was pretty much one long medical appointment. Laney flew in from Hong Kong, where she was working, which I appreciated, but she would not sit with me on my first chemotherapy appointment. I appreciated her flying all the way here but I was really tired. Later she sent a card with two women hugging, which meant a lot to me. The saving grace was an RN who had a support group of women with breast cancer at her home after working all day. The women there were going through all the treatments and were a wealth of information as well as support. I was alone in my dark house, and during chemo was not eating more than a cracker a day. This was not good for me, but no one asked how my food was so I did not say anything. My cousins took me to chemo, as it was winter and the roads were slippery with ice and snow, and they also took me to a 6 a.m. surgery. I had three days of morphine and rest before I had to go home. I hired a woman to help me, but she made things worse. It was easier to do things myself. One symptom of neglect is having a hard time depending on other people, especially when they make things worse. When I lost my hair, Marty showed up and took me to the beauty shop to get my head shaved. He even took photos of my Mohawk, which was very nice of him. My cousins were a support by providing a family atmosphere that I had never had before, and I enjoyed their company. By the time I got through radiation I finally had some hair with gray curls, It took a year get my energy back. I was told I had a 75% chance of living ten years, which sounded good to me. I did not want to spend my I retirement this way, but I was not in control and had to learn to be more relaxed.

Some enterprising local people had started the Altar show, which allowed people to make their own altars to loved ones, ideas, political and personal events. It was wonderful to see the creativity of people of all ages. I did altars for ten years, which included my mother, Aunt Ani, Emily Carr an artist, protecting bears (two times), family imbalances, egg collages and more. Friends came up from the Bay Area to see it and celebrate that my treatment was over except for five years of follow-up medication. The Altar show had a lot of meaning to people in the community. Faced with a somewhat bright but less certain future, I had to decide how I wanted to spend my time. I decided to not be on boards or running things, as I had done quite a bit of that in my life and wanted to spend time painting and traveling.

Living in the woods was too much work dealing with trees and snow. I wanted to move into town where I was closer to medical treatments, socializing, and conveniences. I loved the peace and quiet, but it was isolating. This meant work to sell this property and buy an in-town property.

In 2006 I had finally sold my property in the Bay Area, as a woman said if the ten-year bond market shifts, sell your place. I did not know what this meant but I followed her advice and avoided the recession. I had a choice of paying taxes on the profit or reinvesting into other properties, which I did. With George W. at the helm, we went into a big recession, which meant high-risks loans caused many people to lose their housing. It meant I had to hold onto the properties or lose a lot. Al Gore lost, so we were not beginning to address global warming, which could have saved much loss of life, property and livelihoods.

While I could manage to care for the properties, I hired a property manager so I did not have to think about it. They just take a percentage of the rent. Finally being tired of waiting, I sold a house in 2013, another in 2014 and bought a house in town. I sold my house in the woods in 2016 to finally move myself to a much more convenient location.

After 2008, I was still able to backpack on the John Muir Trail in the Sierras, but now was not able to go as far or as fast. I just enjoyed being at high elevation and seeing the beauty of nature. One night the large full moon was over a high lake and the stars were piercing the sky with little lights. The stillness and great beauty was a tonic to my soul. My longest trip was 37 miles from Yosemite to Mammoth Lakes over one mountain pass. When I had started backpacking in 1972, it was mostly men, but things had changed. On one trip I met a young woman backpacking alone but was being surrounded by four men. They left but she came over to me and asked if she could camp near me, and I said sure. It turns out she was doing the whole 211-mile John Muir Trail, which requires a lot of stamina and also planning food drops, as you cannot carry that much food even if you have a mule. It goes from Yosemite to Mt. Whitney. In the morning she was wearing sandals, which are unusual on a very rocky trail, but I bet she made it to the end. I met another woman with just a tarp that you attach to a tree. I had a tube tent I made that you tie to trees, but it had netting at either end for bugs. My backpack was down to 20-pounds so I would not suffer. But then, many Americans do not leave their cars that much on vacation. I mainly wanted to enjoy nature or maybe do a drawing or painting.

I traveled on most of the major continents but also in the United States, as I was very curious to see how people lived, learned about their history and kept current on issues. I tried to understand. It did not have to be a fancy place for me to be entertained. Usually I met someone who was really interesting and it spurred me on to find out more about the history of the area. I enjoy artistic expression. I would seek out local art and history museums. In some places it is only traditional art and very little personal art. If you go to enough places you begin to see the pattern of the country. There were some places I was not comfortable in and would not return, but at least I learned something. Growing up and working in places with extreme poverty, I understood what was going on, but did not necessarily want to be exposed to crime. Sometimes I did like a comfortable place just to rest, relax and reflect.

In 2011 my best and worst trip was going to the Heritage Festival in New Orleans. I was so enthused that I bought tickets for both weekends, as I had a place to stay for one week and could add on extra days in the beginning just to explore. I knew Jay worked in the area so I contacted him and asked him if he had time for dinner. We had not seen each other since 1996, and now it was 2011. We met at an old established restaurant and had an intense four-hour conversation about everything we had not talked about such as our breakup and what had happened to us. How we felt about our lives, and a great deal of emotional sharing. I brought some photos of his family, his college graduation and a few of us looking young and awkward. It turns out his first wife had destroyed all his photos so he really appreciated having some. I had fish that tasted a bit off but I thought maybe it was the sauce. I apologized for my awkward ending. He said he misrepresented himself as an FBI informant and felt bad. We both forgave each other which was important and sometimes never happens in relationships. We talked about mutual friends and other details of our lives we had not mentioned before which included the good and the down times. Four hours later we finally noticed that the full restaurant was empty and they were cleaning up for closing and we'd better leave. We took a taxi and I was dropped off first and I just put my hand on his as we did not speak. We met the next day and he showed me some of the sites. I then found out about his twenty-five-year marriage, his daughters struggles and his eighteen-month-old granddaughter. It was fine and we shared another dinner which was very different than the previous night.

The next day the Heritage Festival started and he did not want to go and had work to do, so I went alone. I enjoyed some music but I started feeling really sick and was not able to hold down water. I was very woozy and dehydrated. I felt

I had to leave at five thirty. I wanted a taxi to my hotel to rest, hydrate and maybe get medical attention. I asked a policeman where the taxis were and he wanted to see my ID, which was out of state. He then handcuffed me and had me sit on a thin metal folding chair. People walked by and stared, but how could I explain this or ask for help? The officer slouched in a chair and looked stoned, which scared me. I kept silent but did give him an angry look. A squad car came to transport me to a police station. I had no idea where I was except it was a totally African American area and station. They took my belongings, including my flip phone. I sat there in pain with only a metal cell toilet for emergencies. I told the nurse I was a cancer patient but did not know I had food poisoning until later. I think all the years of being threatened when I was sick made me silent, and I was totally weak and exhausted. It took hours to get the fingerprints, photo and charges, as no one was talking to me. There was a large barred area with men laying on benches or the floor. Some police were robotically watching a TV show and did not seem to have anything to do. There were three teenage girls who had driven without a license. They asked me what I was in for, and I replied "trying to get a taxi," and the girls left. At ten-thirty p.m., I finally got the paperwork, and there were totally false allegations of being drunk, disorderly and resisting arrest. I don't drink, was silent and cooperative so these were totally false charges but no one cared. I could not call Jay as he was out of the area and I did not have his number. Finally before midnight they were going to transfer me to another jail and I objected. They said I could pay $750 and they would let me out on bail. The ATM machine was conveniently placed where we were standing. They gave me my purse back and I asked where I could get a taxi. They were hostile and ordered me out on the street at midnight. The heavy metal door slammed shut and I saw some lights a few blocks up the street. I was in the dark and tripped over a raised sidewalk due to old tree roots and fell in the grass but was unharmed. Prostitutes were lined up on a curb of a busy street near a rundown motel. They tried to get a taxi on their cell phones, but Saturday was an extra heavy drinking night. I saw a taxi and waved it down and thanked the ladies for trying to help me. The driver was an Arab man who was yelling at someone in

Arabic. He had the phone in one hand and was wildly gesturing with the other hand. It seemed like an accident waiting to happen which would be a perfect ending to a terrible nightmare. Pulling up to my hotel, I looked into my wallet which now had no money! Luckily the driver took a credit card. I was grateful to be in my hotel room with a bathroom and slept until the phone rang at eight a.m. It was Jay and he asked how my night was. Not too good, and I explained I had a court hearing on Monday. He generously cleared his calendar and went to court with me.

The judge had not bothered to show up, but Jay spoke with the District attorney and reached a nolo contender agreement. Some of the men in orange jumpsuits smiled at me as I guess they were in the same jail. They would not give the bail back even the form said I would get it back when I showed up for court. I was free to leave. We went back to the jail and got my pocket money back but not my camera. I later found out some police steal from the evidence room, I took Jay out to lunch as he had to get back to work. I then contacted the Times Picayune, but did not realize they would write an entertaining article. Some of the feedback to the article was sympathy, another victim of the police but some said I was tarnishing tourism.

I filed complaints with the police review board, FBI, Governor, Mayor but it was like a feather in the wind. I felt really powerless. Arrests happen all the time and are a big money-maker, especially with out-of-state people who pay the money to get home. I guessed that the police, attorneys and even judges made milions from this practice and the corruption was pervasive. I found two other victims of the same policeman, who was a narcotics detective so he was able to get to the "goods." I think I was a victim because I was alone and sick. The total cost was $1,000 and Jay was working pro bono. I had traveled to so many foreign countries and had food poisoning, but was never arrested. I was so lucky to have Jay to help me. I had wanted to impress him on how well I was doing, and this was not part of the plan. He said he had a case of a businessman who was drinking in the French Quarter and was arrested when Katrina was bearing down on New Orleans. The businessman was put in Angola, a notorious prison. His relatives did not know where he was and it took Jay a month to find him. I guess it could have been worse. It was good to really talk to Jay and it meant a lot to me. We were able to cover topics we had not been able to approach when we were younger and I gave him some family photos.

I sold my festival tickets and was alone in New Orleans. I was frightened by the sight of a police officer, so I decided to spend two days in the Bayou with alligators on boats. I visited a French Plantation run only by women as Napoleonic code was different than English common law. The most competent child ran the property versus the oldest son. It was safer to be with alligators than stoned, crooked cops.

In Jackson Square I met a fortune teller who said I had been to court, etc. After the reading she told me that locals were more often victimized and drunk tourists, but there were exceptions. The next year the FBI investigated the police department year and 500 officers decided to retire or resign. The sad thing is false arrests happen to people all over the world for political and monetary gain, or political suppression of freedom of speech.

Every place I went had some high point I will never forget, but now I was more cautious in my surroundings. I did some tours as the tour company makes the reservations, provides safety and transportation and you just follow along. Japan is fairly safe and the countryside is beautiful. At night I took an independent food tour that went to at least five different places I would have never found. I was pleased to figure out the Tokyo subway system to get to the tour and back to the New Otani Hotel. Many people feel safe going on their own, but my eight-month Europe trip and New Orleans was enough. In Hong Kong Laney and I took a ferry to Landau Island to do some hiking on beautiful trails and a ceremony to the dead. In Hong Kong I was able to see a Finnish film at their festival, and took the metro to make the nine a.m. start time. It was mostly Chinese speakers but they laughed at all the right places with the English subtitles. That was reassuring that humor can be universal. Now Hong Kong is struggling to keep democracy and many are leaving. People's fate changes over time and people have had to migrate all throughout history, but it seems like there are more refugees or maybe just more media coverage.

Meanwhile while writing this book, I was not feeling much attachment to my mother and was wondering if I ever did. I think I must have had a bond. Time can change things so people are closer or father away. I signed up for two workshops on Attachment, which I had studied working with children, but this was personal. The Los Angeles Expressive Arts workshops on Zoom allowed me to attend and stay at home. One presenter was not helpful to me but the other one had a carefully designed program that built as the day went on to writing a love letter to my mother which is as follows:

Dear Mother- Although I signed my letters "Love Lois" we never said those words to each other. I wanted to take time to put my deepest sentiments in writing. Maybe because you were an orphan you did not get as much love and did not know how to show it to me, but I think there was love there. While the abuse, neglect and cruelty dominated my feelings knew I appreciated many things you did for me. You were a very hard Worker and kept on looking for better work. You succeeded in getting a job that you liked even if you were not home to see me too much. I appreciated you providing a roof over my head even if we moved a lot. But I really appreciated you leaving Jack's farm as life would have been very sad for you and me. You were smart to pick Evanston which made our lives much better. You had the vision and you were right. You enjoyed clean living and figured things out. You were creative and made new solutions to problems instead of accepting the obvious choices. You taught me how to be more creative in my own life. You did not believe in yourself but you had many characteristics such as a keen sense of humor about people's foibles and petty solutions to life. You were strong and can speak your mind even if others did not agree with you. You were not a person who showed affection or concern about me but you helped out in the most important things such as braces, college tuition, and helping with the down payment with my first house. You and your friend Ethel were kind when I called the wedding off. I wrote a poem about us leaving the UP with your fast determination and courage. Holding my hands as we moved through the snow and silent dark trees watching us escape. You were strong and determined to escape your bad memories and find a better life. It was painful but you made your choice. This kind of courage has been a model for me to take risks all though my life. You had 'sisu' and were able to show how strong women can be. I am proud of you and wanted to say I love you from the bottom of my heart. Lois

I felt an outpouring of love and appreciation toward my mother that had been buried for quite a few years. I was amazed at the depth of the feeling about her strengths and strong presence. This workshop did what no individual therapist or person had been able to bring out in me. There are the rational and emotional defense mechanisms intermingling, and every person has their own style of coping and survival. I know I couldn't feel all the emotions I had when I was younger. It was too overwhelming. I don't feel just because someone is your parent they are a good person and some children don't care about their birth parents. Sometimes it is better to separate than become violent or emotionally damaged.

While my mother was still alive, there were moments of silence when we looked at each other and there was a great deal of warmth shared between us. I don't think she had been able to express warmth in a way that was understandable to her or me. Before she died, my mother said some amazing things considering her advanced Alzheimer's disease. She apologized for not having an inheritance for me, she said she was not a good mother and wanted me to have a relationship with my sister. While this was decades too late, it meant something to me. My mother died in 2010 when I was on a trip to see Aunt Elna and my sister. My mother said she was dying but she did not look sick when I left. I was at my Aunt's house when I got a call from the pet sitter that my cat was dying and then one from the nursing home saying my mother was dying. I drove down toward Chicago, but I felt was I was not going to make it back while she was alive. I did not make it. I was at the Chicago Art Institute and said the Lord's Prayer and went to a Blues Festival in the rain, which seemed appropriate for the day of her death. I tried to make her last years safe and comfortable. I moved her closer so I could visit more often, and we shared some positive moments together. I wrote an obituary and held a memorial at my home attended by my cousins and some friends. I appreciated their company. Later Lainey, a cousin and I did a grave site burial at the shared tombstone. I wanted to commemorate her death as many relatives just disappeared and they deserved more recognition for their time on earth. It took me decades to find out my grandparents were given to a University for science and were in a "Potter's grave" and I recently got the first photo of my father 43 years after his death. I feel people could write a summary of their lives for posterity, history and a retrospective viewpoint.

The next years I traveled, supported candidates, causes and painted with shows and sold some. Art was for enjoyment and exploring some themes. Generally, I was having a very good life. I had one remaining rental house that had not regained the pre-recession value but in 2019, I thought it was time. My tenants bought a house and I started fixing the rental for sale. I had a pain in my rib but the doctor did not know what it was and I had plenty of work to do. As luck would have it, there was months of torrential rains and I needed to replace a large deck and a septic system. Outside work was delayed, but we could do indoor work. I hired many people, as workers tend to specialize. I had a general worker who was a big help, but he kept looking at me and I was exhausted. He saw something but did not want to express it.

Then at one point my voice disappeared to a thin whisper and local doctors gave me antibiotics. I then consulted an ENT doctor who said my vocal cords were paralyzed and he could do a surgery. He ordered tests that indicated it was cancer. The surgery was successful, and I could talk. Two weeks later I had an oncology surgery that verified it was the same cancer that had advanced to stage four. I returned to the local cancer center with a very different perspective than the first go-around. I had 12 years between cancers which is a good amount of time but this was very disappointing news. The rain continued and we were only able to get heavy equipment out to the site on a Sunday two days before the close of escrow and the last house was sold! This was a big relief to end my 32-year real-estate career in time to put my total attention to the medical problem and just enjoying life. However, this time the cancer attacked my ribs and spine and I was in a lot of pain, and it seemed so bizarre to me to be eaten alive. I had a hard time adjusting to the condition but also that I had an ambiguous expiration date. But slowly the medicines worked which allowed more activities. I was able to live a somewhat normal life, except I had to be very careful how I moved as I might cause more spinal fractures. I gave up skiing and hiking but was still walking and dancing.

I had made final arrangements for my mother and me, so things were pretty well taken care of for my final rest. It makes you realized how much time you wasted and how many young people rush into death in so many careless ways. Cancer treatment takes up a lot of time, as there are many appointments. You get a close look at the health care system and how computers are becoming more imbedded in-patient care. There are new treatments, but they are very expensive, which leads to $180,000 a year for one medication and steep co-pays. Charity helps some people with co-pays and the government covers many things. Public health is a good way to screen and educate people about preventable diseases and other countries provide these services. My cynical self thinks that Baby Boomers were exposed to many chemicals when we were younger and one company advertised better living through chemistry. Some insect pests were gone, crops were bigger, our hair was shiny, our clothes did not wrinkle and smelled good, offices were modern and construction and home improvement products made our lives easier, but at what cost? Women are getting breast cancer at a younger age, however there are new but expensive treatments. Research continues and is promising to help cure widespread diseases such as cancer and ever-evolving viral infections encouraged by global warming.

While I was enjoying life and will do so as long as I can, I have lived a long enough life to feel like I have accomplished my goals, was fortunate to be born when I was, had a mother who was strong in trying to forge a better life for herself. She was not able to go beyond certain obstacles which is also true for me and many other people. But I continue to enjoy simple things, being curious and happy about everyday events, and some people that make my life much more interesting. My life was not traditional but it had purpose and meaning.